WOOLLEN MANUFACTURING IN YORKSHIRE

THE MEMORANDUM BOOKS OF JOHN BREARLEY CLOTH FRIZZER AT WAKEFIELD

1758–1762

THE YORKSHIRE
ARCHAEOLOGICAL SOCIETY
FOUNDED 1863 *INCORPORATED* 1893

RECORD SERIES
VOLUME CLV
FOR THE YEARS 1999 AND 2001

WOOLLEN MANUFACTURING IN YORKSHIRE

THE MEMORANDUM BOOKS OF JOHN BREARLEY CLOTH FRIZZER AT WAKEFIELD 1758–1762

EDITED BY

JOHN SMAIL

YORKSHIRE ARCHAEOLOGICAL SOCIETY

THE BOYDELL PRESS

2001

First published 2001

A publication of the Yorkshire Archaeological Society
in association with The Boydell Press
an imprint of Boydell & Brewer Ltd
PO Box 9, Woodbridge, Suffolk IP12 3DF, UK
and of Boydell & Brewer Inc.
PO Box 41026, Rochester, NY 14604–4126, USA
website: http://www.boydell.co.uk

ISBN 0 902122 88 6
A catalogue record for this book is available
from the British Library

This publication is printed on acid-free paper

Typeset by Joshua Associates Ltd, Oxford
Printed in Great Britain by
St Edmundsbury Press Ltd, Bury St Edmunds, Suffolk

Contents

Illustrations

Acknowledgements

I wish to thank Mr W. J. Connor and the other members of staff at the West Yorkshire Archive Service in Sheepscar, Leeds, for their assistance and encouragement in making this volume possible. I also wish to thank Sylvia Thomas and more recently Chris Webb who in their capacity as editors of this Record Series have helped make this book possible, and these thanks also should include the anonymous reader who made helpful suggestions on bibliography and terms. Finally, I would like to thank the University of North Carolina at Charlotte and the Pasold Research Fund for supporting the research which has allowed this work to be published.

Introduction

In the West Yorkshire Archive Service at Sheepscar in Leeds is an item identified as Accession 1444 which consists of the two memorandum books which John Brearley of Wakefield filled with his jottings between 1758 and 1762. According to the correspondence on this accession, the books were deposited with the Leeds archive on 6 May 1968 by P. R. Simpson Esq. of Bishopstoke, Hampshire. In his letter, the donor noted that they had been handed down in his family but beyond that there is no more specific information about their provenance.

The books themselves are leather-bound octavo volumes, one of which has been significantly repaired. Both are filled from front to back cover with bits of information which caught John Brearley's fancy. All of the entries are short: none are longer than a page, and most are only a few lines long. Each entry is distinguished from the rest by a horizontal line, and all entries begin and end on one side of a folio. The entries are made with a variety of different inks and pens, and in places even the handwriting seems to change. However, the consistency in the orthography and in the tone of the entries suggests that only one author was at work.

The entries themselves cover a wide range of topics. With the exception of the reports of two near drowning in the Calder, none of them has the character of news, either local or national. There are also only a few scattered accounts, all of which are located in the second volume. The majority of entries relate to Brearley's occupation as a frizzing miller and more generally to the Yorkshire cloth trade, but many other subjects are also represented, from geography to religion, and cooking to science. Only rarely do the entries refer to other entries on the same page let alone elsewhere in the book, and there is only a rough chronological order to the small proportion of entries that are dated. Indeed, it is difficult to tell the two volumes apart simply on the basis of the entries found in each. Given this and the degree of repetition of ideas, it is safe to assume that Brearley used these books simply to note down ideas which he came across, when he came across them, rather than as a more systematic repository of information.

JOHN BREARLEY OF WAKEFIELD

Although we get a wonderful sense of his world from the books which he left, very little information has survived in other sources about John Brearley of Wakefield. While he never says so directly, it is clear from the memorandum books that Brearley was brought up in Rochdale. Whether he came to Wakefield with his parents, as an apprentice, as a single adult or with his family is unknown, but he was probably in the town in 1758, the date of the earliest entry in the book, and was certainly there in September of 1759, living at Bridgend, when his son John was baptized. Two more sons and two daughters followed, the last baptized in June 1766.[1] No entry for his death or that of his wife was found in the Wakefield parish registers, so we do not know when or if he left the town.[2]

[1] The other children were: Robert, 28 July 1761; Benjamin, 25 Aug. 1762; Betty, 30 Dec. 1764; and Jane, 24 June 1766. There are only two other Brearley baptisms in the Wakefield registers: Charles the son of a Benjamin Brearley was baptized in 1768, and Joseph the son of Edward Brearley was baptized in October 1757.

[2] Given the scope of the search, I did not pursue this question in registers other than Wakefield.

Brearley presumably served some sort of apprenticeship in the woollen textile trade, for he wrote these books while he was working as a frizzing miller and possibly also as a cloth dresser. Brearley's trade involved putting a short and curly nap on a piece of cloth. This was accomplished by running the piece through a water-powered mill which dragged the fabric across a frizzing board onto which sand had been glued. A few accounts suggest that Brearley may also, at one time, have worked as a cloth dresser. From information in the book, it would appear that Brearley's standard of living was that of a skilled artisan. When he began work as a frizzer at Sir Lyonel Pilkington's complex of mills on the Calder at Wakefield (as well as a frizzing mill, there were fulling and corn mills there) Brearley was paid £2 8s per month, just under £30 per year. However it is not clear if he received anything in addition to his wage from the clothiers and merchants whose cloth he frizzed, nor if he ever made any money at the myriad of schemes he jotted down in the books. Given his wage, one assumes that he rented his house; no mention is made of a house coming with the job, but the family may well have got a little extra from a garden or a cow.

Quite a bit of Brearley's personality comes through in the books despite the relative absence of personal information. He was clearly an energetic and excited person, always eager for the new bits of information he noted down. He was also very optimistic, for he recorded innumerable schemes for making easy money, though one is obliged to observe that if his commercial ventures had the same chance of success as his perpetual motion machine, the optimism may not have been well placed. He was also, however, of necessity careful. Several entries warn of the dangers of spending too long in the alehouse, both because of the cost and because one's loosened tongue might reveal crucial commercial secrets. These generic admonitions were clearly meant personally, for one entry is a vow to himself 'never to drink to exces nor ett to excess nor call att James Scofilds'.[3] He was also quite cynical about friendship, noting that people were not likely to do much for you unless they could expect to benefit from it, and reminding the world and himself of the need to keep receipts when paying debts, lest sharp people try and collect again.[4]

This cynicism extended into other matters. Rather conventionally, Brearley assumed all women were willing to play the whore to get what they wanted. His take on organized religion was similar. Given his hostility to Methodists and Presbyterians, one assumes Brearley was an Anglican, but he was not a devout one. He was sure most ministers were utter hypocrites, and the best reason he gave for attending church was that it gave one an honest public image. Brearley was also quite certain that those with money, authority, and influence were likely to get their way in the world. At the same time, it should be noted, Brearley never openly challenged his social superiors, and he certainly wished to retain the traditional authority of the man within his family.

THE YORKSHIRE TEXTILE INDUSTRY CA 1760

Since so much of Brearley' s attention was taken with the workings of the Yorkshire wool textile industry some space must be given to describing it as Brearley must have experienced it. To readers familiar with the history of this vibrant industry, there is nothing revolutionary in Brearley's account that would alter the accepted wisdom

[3] Vol. 1 f. 207r.

[4] Vol. 2 f. 106r. Brearley's attitudes about ale and about honesty in the world of commerce are consistent with the argument Margaret Hunt has advanced about the cultural outlook of the eighteenth-century middling sort: *The Middling Sort* (Berkeley: University of California Press, 1996).

about the state of the wool textile industry in Yorkshire around the middle of the century.[5]

A grasp of the industry must begin with the distinction between its three main products, woollen cloth, worsted cloth, and goods made using a combination of woollen and worsted yarn. The manufacturing processes for these three kinds of cloth differ significantly.

Woollen cloth – principally broadcloths and kerseys – was made from short-stapled wool. After being cleaned, the wool was carded using paddles fixed with small hooks which crossed and intertwined the individual fibres. The yarn spun from the prepared rovings or cardings got its strength from the interlocking of the short fibres, but the yarn used for warp (the lengthways threads in the cloth) were usually spun harder (that is with more twist) than the weft because it needed to be stronger. In Yorkshire, woollen yarn was woven on both broad and narrow looms. The former was usually between a yard and a half and two yards wide, the latter usually about a yard. In addition to the kind of wool used, woollen cloth was distinctive because of the way in which it was finished. When a woollen cloth came off the loom it was not usable, for the yarn used made the cloth very loose and flimsy; thus all woollen cloth had to be fulled after weaving in order to complete the production process. Fulling, always done in a mill using water or horse power, involved beating the cloth with heavy hammers and water in order to felt the short fibres in the yarn into a single continuous fabric. Although the degree of fulling could vary, the result, in most cases, was a cloth in which the original threads were not visible. After fulling, most woollen cloth was put through a complex finishing process in which the nap of the cloth was alternately raised by brushing it with teasels and then shorn smooth. Subsequent finishing processes might then be done, of which the most common was frizzing.

Worsted cloth – principally shalloons, callimancos, camblets, and everlastings – was, in contrast, made from a long-stapled wool. This wool was prepared by combing rather than carding, a process which produced long strands of fibre all in parallel with each other. (The by-product of combing, the short fibres in the fleece, was called noiles and was sold to the makers of woollen cloth.) Combed wool was spun into yarn which was much finer than woollen yarn and was proportionally stronger. The finished cloth, which again might be made on a broad or narrow loom, did not require finishing; indeed it was not suitable for either fulling or dressing. However, some kinds of worsted goods went through other finishing processes, many of which involved using glues and/or heat to put a glaze on the fabric.

Finally, the many varieties of mixed cloth – principally serges, bays, swanskins, and ells – were made using worsted yarn for the warp and woollen for the weft, the former providing strength, the latter bulk. Some of these goods were fulled and some were not depending upon the finish which was desired.

[5] The traditional accounts are Herbert Heaton, *The Yorkshire Woollen and Worsted Industry* (Oxford: Clarendon Press, 1920); Ephraim Lipson, *The History of the Woollen and Worsted Industries* (London: F. Cass & Co., 1965); W. B. Crump, *The Leeds Woollen Industry: 1780–1820*, Thorseby Society Record Series, vol. 32, 1931; and W. B. Crump, *History of the Huddersfield Woollen Industry* (Huddersfield, 1935). More recent analyses include the following works: Pat Hudson, *The Genesis of Industrial Capital* (Cambridge: Cambridge University Press, 1986); Pat Hudson, 'From Manor to Mill', in P. Hudson, M. Berg, and M. Sonenscher, eds., *Manufacture in Town and Country before the Factory* (Cambridge: Cambridge University Press, 1983) 124–46; and 'Proto-industrialization: the Case of the West Riding Wool Textile Industry in the 18th and Early 19th Centuries', *History Workshop*, 12 (1981) 34–61; D. T. Jenkins and Kenneth G. Ponting, *The British wool textile industry, 1770–1914* (Aldershot: Scolar Press, 1987); D. T. Jenkins, *The West Riding wool textile industry, 1770–1835: a study of Fixed Capital Formation* (Edington: Pasold Research Fund, 1975).

It is important to note that each of these main types of cloth was produced in many different grades depending upon the quality of the raw materials and workmanship. For example, the best woollen cloth used at least some imported Spanish wool mixed with domestic wool taken from the best parts of the fleece. It was carefully combed and spun, and after fulling it would have been raised and cropped many times over to produce a perfectly smooth, even nap. Coarser cloth (including most of the goods which were frizzed on mills like Brearley's), was made following essentially the same process but with cheaper materials. In the case of worsted cloth, an important variable in production (besides the initial quality of the yarn) was the pattern in which the cloth was woven. In addition to a simple over-and-under weave, cloth could be woven with a twill or even with complex patterns yielding simple geometric or floral shapes. Finally, colour was an important variable. Different kinds of effects could be achieved by dyeing the wool, the yarn, or the finished piece, and of course the quality of the dyes used could vary enormously.

Within the West Riding, the manufacture of different kinds of cloth was, to a large degree, geographically segregated. The production of woollen cloth, especially woollen broadcloth, was concentrated in the region around Leeds (and to a lesser extent Wakefield). Narrow woollen cloth was by this period made largely in the region around Huddersfield since the neighbourhood around Halifax, formerly dominant in narrow woollens, was, along with Bradford, increasingly given over to the manufacture of worsted stuffs and mixed cloth. Over the Pennines, in Lancashire, both woollen and mixed goods such as bays were produced.

The various kinds of cloth made in the different parts of the West Riding also tended to be produced under different systems of production. Woollen cloth, particularly broad woollens, was typically made by master clothiers working in an essentially artisanal mode of production. These individuals were usually householders of some substance, but they employed relatively small workforces who (with the important exception of spinners) would have worked alongside their master in the workshop. As Brearley's memorandums indicate, a few producers in and around Leeds and Wakefield were beginning to expand beyond the confines of this artisanal system, but these manufacturing concerns were untypical. The narrow woollen cloth made further up in the Pennines foothills was also produced by artisanal households, but there is a sense that these producers were, on average, less well off than their counterparts further down the valleys. In the worsted districts, however, cloth was increasingly being produced by small manufacturers who were running at times extensive putting-out operations.

The finishing and marketing of the cloth made in Yorkshire was concentrated in Leeds, Wakefield, Halifax, and then Huddersfield in that order. The first two were home to quite substantial merchants who had by this time come to dominate the trade in their region's products – whether abroad, to London, or, via travellers, in domestic markets throughout Britain. However, while the wealthiest merchants were found in these two cities, those in Halifax and Huddersfield should not be overlooked. Many in Halifax in particular were capable of dealing directly with overseas customers even before the opening of the Calder Navigation undermined the advantages that firms in Leeds and Wakefield enjoyed in terms of transport. Many of the dyers and cloth dressers in all four of these centres were also operating on a relatively substantial scale by the middle of the century. In most instances, masters in these finishing trades worked as subcontractors, taking in goods which a merchant firm had purchased, and performing work on the pieces as directed.

The complexity of the production and marketing systems in the region makes it unwise to imagine that any single group enjoyed control over the industry. Merchants clearly employed the largest amounts of capital of anyone in the trade but, because of the continued autonomy of the region's cloth halls and of the domestic clothiers the halls served, there was no sense in which this capital allowed merchants to dominate the region's trade. Most merchants in the region focussed their energies on marketing, rarely becoming involved directly in production. The interactions and interdependencies between merchant and finishing firms in the region's towns introduces a further layer of complication. As Brearley's entries show, merchants in Leeds and Wakefield often depended wholly upon dressers or millers in Huddersfield for their purchases in that market, giving such firms a relatively large degree of autonomy. It is also worth noting that a successful career as a dyer or dresser often served as a springboard for the next generation's entry into the ranks of the merchant elite.[6]

However, if, on the whole, Brearley's memorandums confirm our conventional understanding of the trade, a close reading of the text provides a degree of depth missing from conventional accounts and, as I have argued elsewhere, it situates the trade just at the moment when the crucial developments leading to industrialization took place.[7]

One way in which Brearley's volume illuminates the conventional account is by its direct comparison between the various branches of the industry in Yorkshire and the woollen broadcloth trade of the West Country (Gloucestershire, Wiltshire, and Somerset). Students of the two regions have long noted that the production systems were quite different, for clothiers in the West of England were substantial capitalists employing relatively large workforces, while those in the West Riding operated on a much smaller scale. This difference is confirmed in Brearley's comments. However, while he confirms that in general the West Country produced cloth of a higher quality than Yorkshire did, Brearley clearly shows that the product lines of the two regions were much closer to one another than is usually thought. Cheap goods made in the West Country competed with the more expensive of Yorkshire's products to an extent that makes a simple two-sector model unworkable. Indeed, the fact that he (and by implication his contemporaries) paid such close attention to the West Country industry suggests the reality of this competition.

More importantly, I think that Brearley's memorandum books give us a sense of why the wool textile industry, and particularly the Yorkshire wool textile industry, was so vibrant during this period. What we have in his detailed accounts of the day-to-day experiences of clothiers and journeymen, dressers and dyers, millers and merchants is a sense of the impact that the market was having upon the trade in these crucial decades. Fashion, for example, was clearly already a formidable force in the region's trade despite its reputation for serving the low end of the market. A generation before Brearley's time, clothiers in Yorkshire made cheap woollen and worsted textiles of a very generic sort. By the 1760s, colour, weave, pattern, and finish were becoming important selling points. His own trade, that of frizzing miller, was part of this trend. He notes that in 1728 there were only 2 frizzing mills in the county, both operated by horse, whereas by 1758 there were 46 in all.[8] Frizzing was popular because it was a way of making relatively coarse goods look nice. The same could be said for the somewhat deceitful practices, outlined at length in the books, used by

[6] See R. G. Wilson, *Gentlemen Merchants* (Manchester: Manchester University Press, 1971).

[7] John Smail, *Merchants, Markets, and Manufacture: the English Wool Textile Industry in the Eighteenth Century* (Houndsmills: Macmillan, 1999). I first encountered Brearley's book while doing the research for this book, and his information figures largely in the argument advanced in the latter part of the book concerning the origins of the industrial revolution in the trade.

[8] Vol. 1, ff. 39v and 38r.

millers and clothiers in the region to improve the finished look of their pieces without using more expensive materials or more labour. (To an extent it was such practices that gave Yorkshire cloth such a bad reputation and at the same time made it compete with the West Country's offerings.) Chalk, porridge, flour, soap, glue, flocks, cow and goat hair were among the substances which might be added to a piece to enhance its appearance relative to its price, a relationship which was increasingly important.

The books also note the extent to which the influence of the market was affecting the way in which the West Riding's cloth was being made and sold. Clothiers, for example, had to be very much aware of the factors affecting the saleability of the cloth they made, noting the colour combinations which were in fashion at particular times of the year. They also had to be cognizant of the many different markets to which Yorkshire cloth was sent. Consumers abroad (in Holland, Russia, Spain, Portugal, and the American colonies) and those at home (Scottish crofters, northern farm workers, the members of polite urban society, even soldiers) all required particular kinds of cloth in particular colours, designs, and finishes. In consequence, the region's clothiers had to be able to adjust both what they made and how they sold. For their part, merchants were increasingly turning to bespoke production and even putting-out as a way to secure their supply in this complex commercial world. Those who did not choose to go down that route, or those who could not–for example some of the large London wholesalers active in the Yorkshire trade–developed close commercial arrangements with their regional counterparts to solve the same supply problems.

There is also evidence in many entries for a noticeable increase in the scale and pace of manufacture in the West Riding's wool textile industry: changes in the mode of production which could be accomplished without factories or steam power but which nonetheless had important implications for the history of the region's industrialization. The development of a new kind of hot press with removable, heated, plates which allowed journeymen to press 16 (or 24) shalloons a day instead of 12 is a classic example of the kind of 'speed up' and 'stretch out' which intensified production in the absence of machinery or factories, and Brearley's description is all the more evocative of this fact since it notes that they were paid the same wage both before and after the change.[9] We also get a sense of the kind of scale on which some individuals were operating. One merchant who supplied London's biggest woollen merchant with cloth for the army kept 26 or 27 croppers at work in his shop during the summer months–a very large establishment.[10] Mr Lumb, a dyer in Wakefield, had the capacity to take in as many as 400 to 500 shalloons at a time to be dyed scarlet and crimson; the merchant he worked for, Mr Mills, might buy and ship as many as 1500 or 1600 of this one kind of cloth in a season.[11] And everyone, clothiers, dyers, croppers, millers, and merchants, had to be prepared to work nights and Sundays when the trade was busy, forces which made these individuals adept at streamlining the production process and managing a large workforce.

This kind of commercial environment invited inventiveness. Brearley constantly comments on how to make new kinds of cloth using cheaper materials. He also took notes on recipes for dyeing particular colours, remarking in bold letters if it was the 'Newest and Best Way'.[12] Since he was a miller, new technological devices were of course interesting to Brearley, and a good many of them were directly related to the

[9] Vol. 2 f. 108r; see also vol. 1 ff. 181r and 204r for other examples.
[10] Vol. 2 f. 113r.
[11] Vol. 2 ff. 81v and 163v.
[12] Vol. 1 f. 121r.

needs of the market, whether they were the flying shuttle, the gig mill, or moveable plates for hot pressing shalloons. Other inventions, more fanciful, anticipated the directions in which the industry was going to go, the most notable example being two diagrams for a mechanical shearing frame drawn half a century before the Luddites broke real ones apart.[13]

NOTES ON THE TEXT AND TRANSCRIPTION

As noted, the two volumes of John Brearley's memorandums are leather-bound octavos, the one measuring 113 × 177mm and the other 100 × 168mm. It would appear that the volumes were created, after the fact, by binding up separate paper-covered booklets. The inks, pens, and to an extent handwriting vary from folio to folio, and the entries are not obviously made in chronological order. One result of this fact is that the folios were not numbered originally. Volume one has had folio numbers entered, in pencil, at a later date, and since these make it easier to find one's way around the book, I have retained them.[14] Volume two has no folio numbering, but I have numbered the folios as they occur in my transcription. Readers seeking to find particular passages in that volume, however, will have to use these figures as a rough guide as to where in the volume the entry occurs.

Although only subsequently bound up into complete volumes, it is clear that Brearley made his entries onto the individual pages as we see them, for in many instances the words are squeezed into the space remaining, or continued in the margins. These marginal entries are indicated by footnotes without any other mark in the text if it is clear that Brearley was simply finishing up his thought. Interlineated letters or words necessary for the sense of the sentence are also included with only a footnote marking the addition. Words or phrases which were interlineated or placed in the margins and which are parenthetical additions to the train of thought are transcribed using parenthesis and a footnote.

Not surprisingly, given its age, there are places where the text is illegible, either because the edges of the sheets have eroded away or the ink has faded. There are also places where the subsequent binding has obscured some letters. In transcribing these sections, I have filled in missing letters where the meaning is obvious from the context and indicated the additions with a footnote giving the text as it appears in the manuscript. Where the damage is more extensive or the meaning is potentially ambiguous, I have indicated the presence of missing letters or words with ellipses and used a footnote. The only exception to this rule is when a whole page is damaged along one edge; in such cases I have indicated the damage in an initial footnote and entered additions in square brackets to avoid cluttering the text with notes.

I have retained Brearley's spelling as it appears in the manuscript except that I have spelled out common abbreviations. The most common of these are 'Wakefld' or 'Wakfld' for Wakefield, 'Hudfld' or 'Hudsfld' for Huddersfield; 'ps' for piece or pieces; 'yd' for yard; and a halfheartedly superscript 'd' for the suffix 'ed'.

Brearley's notation for currency was highly erratic; at times he used the symbols '£', 's', and 'd' next to the numbers or superscript above them, while elsewhere he simply assumed the numbers would make sense or used a variety of different punctuation marks. Thus for convenience I have rendered currency in one of the following two ways: as numbers with the symbols '£', 's', and 'd' (£1 3s 4d) or as a

[13] Vol. 2 f. 91r.

[14] There are a few mistakes in the numbering noted where they occur.

string of numbers separated by colons and preceded by the '£' symbol (£1:3:4), depending upon which of the two is closest to Brearley's use in that instance. This practice has not been followed, however, when Brearley entered numbers in a tabular form as he did frequently when calculating costs and profit; these have been entered in a way which retains the original format.

Brearley wrote almost entirely without punctuation and with highly irregular capitalization. For the convenience of modern readers, I have added full stops and an initial capital letter to break the text into sentences. However, I have not added other punctuation to delimit his endlessly run on 'sentences', except to use commas to separate items which Brearley wrote down in a columnar list. I have also changed the capitalization in the text to conform to modern usage, removing initial upper-case letters within a sentence unless it is clear they were meant for emphasis, and adding upper-case letters to proper nouns.

There are many of Brearley's diagrams in the text. A handful of the more interesting of these are reproduced in the pages that follow. The existence of the remainder is indicated by a footnote placed where the diagram appears in the text. Where it has seemed possible to give a sense of the diagram using words, I have attempted to do so in the footnote, but many diagrams are either unintelligible or indescribable, and the note merely indicates their existence.

Finally, as noted above, the text which follows only contains a selection from the original. A complete transcription would have been about 70% larger than the present volume. To give a sense of the complete train of Brearley's thought, the first 50 folios of both volumes are transcribed completely; however, only selected entries on the remaining 165 folios of volume 1 and on the remaining 137 folios of volume 2 have been included, approximately 45% of the complete text on those folios. The following criteria were used in making these selections. I excluded obviously repetitious entries or topics already covered in previous entries. I also excluded most of those entries which gave 'recipes' for dyeing particular colours, or specific instructions on how kinds of cloth were to be milled. Given that a sense of Brearley's interest in these topics was already present, it seemed to me that this was information which would only be of interest to a specialist. I have also excluded most of those entries in which Brearley records information on where particular products can be purchased or found, as this too struck me as esoteric. What remains are those entries which deal with personal issues, the broader social and economic context in which Brearley lived, science and technology, and the production and marketing of cloth. Such criteria, of course, cannot be perfectly applied nor will they meet the approval of every reader; however, what is published here will give all readers a sense of what is in John Brearley's memorandum books and direct them to the kind of information available in the original documents.

Glossary

The spellings used are modernized, but if Brearley's spelling is consistently different, that is given as well. I have not, as a rule, included entries for words which Brearley consistently misspells except in a couple of instances where confusion can result. In particular, Brearley tended to use the word 'the' to mean both 'the' and 'they'; he also often added an initial 'h' onto the word 'as'.
Some entries are grouped under a common heading.
I have checked all of these entries in the *Oxford English Dictionary*; some meanings, however, are purely conjectural based on the way in which Brearley uses the word in the text.

Act (ackt): When used without other reference, Brearley means the Acts of Parliament of 1725 and 1738 which specified that Yorkshire broad and narrow cloth had to be examined and stamped as to its length and breadth before being sold.

Archill (archol, argoll): In most instances the word refers to the dyestuff made from a kind of lichen used to create a blue or violet colour, see vol. 1 f. 22r. In some instances, however, Brearley may be using it to refer to the substance from which cream of tartar is made, see vol. 1 f. 34r.

At after: After. The initial 'at' seems to be a colloquial addition by Brearley.

Banians: A type of loose fitting coat.

Baulk (bauk or bawk): A reference to cloth in its unfinished state, i.e. before it was dressed and dyed.

Bay (baize or bases): A type of cloth made with a worsted warp and a woollen weft. See vol. 1 f. 27r for the distinction between cloth and bays. The cloths which Brearley refers to by their weight, 38 weight, 42 weight, etc., appear to be bays of some kind.

Bespoke: When a merchant arranged with a clothier to have a piece of cloth made to a particular pattern.

Blackwell Hall (Blacketh): The major market in London for broad woollen cloth. Mostly used in Brearley's time by West Country clothiers who sold their cloth by consigning it to Blackwell Hall factors.

Boking: A type of bay taking its name from the village of Bocking in Essex.

Broadcloth: A type of woollen cloth which was between a yard and a half and just over two yards wide.

Burl: The process of removing any small irregularities or foreign matter from a piece of cloth, see vol. 2 f. 45r.

Calimanco: A type of very thin worsted cloth, woven with a twill, which was often highly glossed when finished, see vol. 1 f. 118r.

Camblet: A type of worsted cloth, thicker than a shalloon or calimanco, with a plain weave.

Castle soap: Castille soap.

Clew: Brearley uses this term to describe something which is being acted upon to move it through a confined space. Thus clew could refer to a piece of cloth going through rollers (vol. 1 f. 9v) or to water going through a millrace towards the wheel (vol. 1 f. 62v); probably an adaptation of the meaning of the word which refers to a thread.

Cloth: A very long piece of woollen cloth, 40 to 50 yards long, usually cut into two pieces when sold. Also used to refer to woollen as opposed to worsted cloth.

Clothmaker: A master clothier of the West Riding woollen district.

Combers cast: See Noiles.

Coperas: A dyestuff made from iron sulphate used for the colour green. Also known as green vitriol.

Cottons: When used to describe a type of cloth as opposed to the fibre, as in Kendall or Shrewsbury cottons, Brearley uses this term to refer to a kind of cloth made with a mixture of worsted and woollen yarn.

Crop: The finishing process for a piece of woollen cloth in which the fulled piece first had its nap raised with teasels and then was sheared. The more times this process was repeated, the finer the surface of the cloth.

Drab: A colour of cloth, which, from context, would appear to have been a dull light brown. See, for example the following entries: 'blewely coalard drabs inclineing to a lead coalars' (vol. 2 f. 77v); a 'sandy drab' (vol. 2 f. 65v); or a logwood blue which, 'with wearing the weare to a drab' (vol. 2, f. 116v).

Druggits: A type of narrow cloth made with a worsted warp and a woollen weft, woven plain (without a twill), see vol. 1 f. 27r or vol. 2 f. 136r.

Duffils (duffels): A coarse woollen cloth with a thick nap or frieze.

Fine draw: The process of repairing any small imperfections in a piece of cloth, see vol. 2 f. 45r.

Finish: See Crop.

Flannel: A type of bay.

Flocks: Woollen fibres created either in the process of milling a piece of cloth (mill flocks) or finishing it (shear flocks); other types of flocks take their name from the kind of cloth from which they came, see vol. 1 f. 194.

Frize (Frise): A finishing process done in a frizzing mill which involved pulling the cloth across a rough surface–usually sand glued onto a board–in order to create a raised nap.

Frieze: A woollen cloth made by frizzing.

Fulling: Part of the finishing process for a woollen cloth in which the cloth was put in the stocks of a mill where the action of the mill and the water felted the fibres together so as to make the individual threads indistinguishable.

Fustian: A type of cloth made with a linen or cotton warp and woollen weft.

Gauger: Excise officer.

Gort: The channel of water carrying water away from a mill wheel.

Guttion: The pin on the end of a cylindrical mill part on which it turns and which bears the weight. A variant of the word gudgeon. See vol. 1 f. 141r or 168v.

Has: As. The initial 'h' appears to be a colloquial spelling of Brearley's.

Headend: The end of a piece of cloth, often woven or dyed or marked in a distinctive fashion, see vol. 1 f. 124v or 179v or 197r.

Hoowster: Worcester.

Jaks: The cards used to hold teasels for raising the nap on a piece of cloth.

Josephs: A long coat worn by women.

Kersey: A type of coarse narrow woollen cloth. Also denotes a twill weave in woollen cloth.

Kig mill: A gig mill. A device for raising the nap on a woollen cloth, see vol. 1 f. 32v or 124r.

Kimick: A mixture of oil of vitriol and indigo, see vol. 1 f. 15r.

Lant: A mixture of urine and dung used in washing cloth, see vol. 2 f. 117r.

Leck: To apply a liquid substance; probably a derivative of a usage meaning to leach out by adding water.

Lape (lap): Fold or turn. Also probably refers to the outside face of a cloth.

Light of: Find.

Lincey: Probably Brearley's term for linsey-woolsey, a type of cloth made with a linen warp and woollen weft.

List: The edge or selvage of a cloth. Often the list of a particular kind of cloth had a particular and distinctive design. In some cases, lists, or the ornaments in them, were sewn onto a cloth after it was woven, see vol. 2 f. 9v.

Logwood: A dyestuff made from the heartwood of a tree found in the Americas, used for making the colour red.

Long ells: A type of cloth similar to bays and serges, made of a worsted warp and woollen weft.

Milled: See Fulling.

Mixture (mixter, mixt): A type of cloth, usually a woollen, made with two or more colours of wool scribbled together before being spun.

Moatey: Having small imperfections or foreign substances in the wool, as in 'mote'.

Moks: A kind of bay.

Moowter: The portion of flour kept by the miller as a charge for milling grain.

Mort eat: The exact meaning cannot be reconstructed; however, Brearley clearly uses the word to describe a degradation of woollen fabric, perhaps from some organic action such as mildew or from a chemical residue left over from dyeing or finishing, see vol. 2 f. 31v.

Noils (noyles): The short fibres of wool left after the long fibres were combed out for use in making worsted cloth. Noils were typically sold to woollen cloth manufacturers.

Pack: A quantity of wool weighing 240 pounds; conveniently, the price of the wool per pack in pounds sterling is equal to its price in pence per pound weight.

Pattern: A small swatch of cloth sent from buyer to manufacturer or vice versa as a sample of the design, colour, quality, or finish of the piece.

Pennyworth (peneworth, peniworth): Value, as in 'money's worth'.

Perching mill: A device for raising the nap on a piece of cloth; probably similar to a gig mill. See vol. 2 f. 77r.

Perching (perking): A pole or pair of poles used to hold cloth so it can be examined or raised.

Planes: A type of woollen cloth (made near Saddleworth and Huddersfield) which was usually just under a yard wide; the quality of planes varied from cheap to fine.

Plush: A type of cloth woven with two sets of warp threads so that the weft threads can be cut to leave a pile of varying thickness. Different kinds of plush and shag were made with different materials, see vol. 1 f. 20v or 34v.

Porige: Adding flour (oat or wheat) to a piece in order to give it a better finish, see vol. 1 f. 63v.

Press papers: When cloth was pressed as part of the finishing process and in preparation for shipping, sheets of paper were placed between the folds.

Press: Many kinds of cloth were pressed as part of the finishing process. Two different kinds of press mentioned are 'stang press' and 'screw press'.

Printing: Embossing a design upon a cloth by putting it through a roller engraved with designs, see vol. 1 f. 97r.

Quarter: A quarter of a yard. A cloth's width was typically measured in quarters, hence entries such as '5 quarters and a half', vol. 1 f. 3r.

Raper (rapering): Wraper or wrapping.

Ready money: Cash in hand at the sale, as distinguished from any term of credit.

Reed: Part of the loom.

Save: The process of keeping the list or headend of a piece of cloth a different colour from the rest of the cloth, see vol. 1 f. 106v or 115v or 121r.

Scarlit (scarlet): Generally refers to the colour, but sometimes it also has the sense of the kinds of cloths which were dyed scarlet or of cloths which had been so dyed. One particular reference (vol. 1 f. 126r) makes a reference to scarlets of a yellow colour, but this refers to the particular shade of red.

Scribble: The process of mixing different colours of wool or types of fibre together before spinning.

Serge: A type of narrow cloth made with a worsted warp and a woollen weft woven with a twill, see vol. 1 f. 149r or vol. 2 f. 136r.

Sewk: A liquid, usually, that used for dying; probably a variant of soak.

Shagg: See Plush.

Shalloon: A type of worsted cloth, relatively thin, typically used for linings and such.

Shear: Part of the finishing process for woollen cloth in which the raised nap was cut off with large shears, leaving a smooth surface.

Shepherds: A kind of mixed cloth (see above) made in earth tones.

Shudes: The husks of oats after threshing.

Shumak: A dyestuff made from various members of the sumac family, used for the colour black.

Slays (sleays): Part of the loom which holds the warp threads.

Spanish brown: A kind of earth having a reddish brown or ochre colour, used as a pigment.

Spanish white: Finely powdered chalk used for cleaning – or, as Brearley notes, in bread! (Vol. 1 f. 212r.)

Spows: Spools or bobbins, usually used in reference to weft thread.

Stock (stoke, stok): The part of a fulling mill consisting of a wooden compartment into which a large wooden 'hammer' fits where cloth was milled and sometimes washed. Brearley refers to two kinds of stock. The 'falling' stock apparently worked by having the gears pick up the 'hammer' and letting it fall on the cloth; a 'driving' stock, in contrast, had the hammer work directly with the power of the mill. To 'stock wash' was to wash a piece of cloth by putting it in the stock and using the action of the hammer in the water to help get rid of dirt or dyestuffs.

Stop list: A particular kind of list made of black wool or other fibre, used in cloth which was dyed after being woven, see vol. 1 f. 107v.

Stoving: A finishing process usually used on worsted cloth, see vol. 2 f. 182v.

Sudderick: A place near London, perhaps a corruption of Southwark.

Swanskin: A type of bay but made with a linen instead of worsted warp, see vol. 1 f. 159v.

Teasels (taisels): The spiky seed pod of a plant used by croppers to raise the nap of a piece of woollen cloth before shearing.

Tenter: The process of stretching a woollen cloth after it has been milled or dyed in order to return it to its original size or sometimes to stretch it. The piece of equipment, a wooden frame fixed with hooks, used for this process.

The: A variant spelling of 'they'.

Twined: The degree of twist put into yarn or the process of winding two strands of yarn together.

Waltron: A unit of measure for yarn equal to 6 pounds, see vol. 1 f. 72v.

Warp: The lengthwise threads in a piece of cloth.

Water length: A small portion of a cloth's value held by the merchant purchasing the piece and paid to the maker once the piece had been proved to be the correct length when wet, see vol. 2 f. 39r.

Watering: Creating a wavy surface on a cloth by using water and pressure; it could also be accomplished with rollers, see vol. 1 f. 97r.

Weft (waft, woof): The crosswise threads in a piece of cloth.

West of England: Refers to the cloth-making districts in Gloucestershire, Wiltshire, and north-eastern Somerset. This region produced fine broad woollen cloth.

Wheel shuttle: Brearley's term for the flying shuttle.

Whisked: To brush.

Widow: A dyestuff used for the colour yellow, perhaps a local name for the European Geranium whose leaves had a dusky colour; possibly also a reference to a kind of willow.

Wool, types of: Brearley distinguishes between many different types of wool. One crucial distinction he notes is that between 'fleece' wool taken from a living animal, and 'skin' wool taken off the dead animal's skin. Other kinds of wool are distinguished by where on the sheep's body it comes from, a factor which affected its quality, see vol. 1 f. 38r.

Woollen: A kind of woollen textile, often referred to as 'cloth' and the yarn from which it is made. Woollen yarn is made by carding wool in order to create a thick mat of interlocking fibres which were then felted together when the cloth was fulled. Woollen cloth was then usually dressed or finished using teasels and shears to create a smooth even nap. Both broad and narrow woollen cloth was made; the former was usually of higher quality.

Worsted: A kind of woollen textile and the yarn from which it is made. Worsted yarn is made by combing wool in order to align the long fibres in the same direction and remove the shorter fibres (noils). Worsted cloth was not fulled nor was it usually dressed in the way woollen cloth was.

Wowlds: Meaning is not clear except from context where it is used to indicate a substance used for dying; perhaps a variant spelling for 'widow'.

THE MEMORANDUM BOOKS

Volume One

Where to light of good press papers at Sheffeild paper makers or att Halifax. f. 3r[1]

All blak and blew and drab shalloons to be stoke washed and scarlits and light blew or comon greens and reds so tentered and befor taken of tenter to be whisked over both bakside and foreside.

Hamocks.[2] Blankets to bee made of skin wool[3] and corse noyls mixt and to bee weell raised that side thatt is lape[4] outwards to bee more raised then the inward side and to bee cutt into pares the lentgh to bee 3 yards and 3 quarters long the breadth to bee 5 quarters and half brood to bee sold at 3s 6d per pare or 4s per pare for shiping. 1757.

Waste will make these sort of blankits and verrey good ones . . .[5]

Shalloons when prest to bee made up on a board and to bee stiched after this manner[6] f. 3v
and before you fast the end put them in press.

Blak and all blue shalloons to be stok washed and all after to bee run thorough a hott lead butt blews espesaly with archol.

Shalloons to bee washed in gort before the are stok washed and after stok washing.

Shalloons to bee scowred with hogs dung and lant hot in a tub and att after take them to the river and pos them weel with your feets so there swill them clean.[7]

Att Wakefild or for Leeds markets low prised white brood cloath cheifly goes well f. 4r
espesally war time. Cloath betwixt 2s and[8] 2s 6d per yard in bauk is called middles and all above 3s or 3s 2d[9] or 3s 4d or 3s 6d is called better sort[10] Butt cloath betwixt 2s to 2s 6d in bauk[11] cheifly goes well and the cloathiers gets most money bye this sort.

Plases where the make a deal[12] of cloth in the West of England is has Somersetshire Wiltshire Glostershire. Worchestershire and in Devonshire the make a deall of planes like Saddleworth and Hudersfild[13] peices. Observe att the above shires the frize a deal of goods some mills goes by watter other some by horses allso in the South of England the frize a deal has in Kent Surry and Sussex and Hartfordshire the frise in France some by horses and some mills is turned bye the . . .[14]

1 Folios 1 and 2 too faded to read clearly.
2 Word interlineated above.
3 Ms reads 'wo'.
4 Remainder of word torn, probably 'laped'.
5 Remainder illegible except the word 'waste.'
6 Diagram of a zigzag line.
7 Ms reads 'cl'.
8 Ms torn, 'and' implicit.
9 Word missing, presumably '3s 2d' was intended.
10 Ms reads 'sor'.
11 Ms torn, meaning implicit.
12 Ms reads 'de'.
13 Ms reads 'Hudfi'.
14 Remainder of page illegible except the phrase 'two men works'.

f. 4v Brazil is in America itt is belonging to the Portuguese and when the Brazil fleet comes to Lisbon in Portugall the take of abundance of all sorts of goods has brod cloath drugits bayes of all sorts long ells calimancoes tin lead leather fish and corn. All these comoditys the Portugues purchases from England the Dutch allso furnish them with woollen goods and naval[15] stores. Besides the trade prettey well with France for woollen goods. Butt the English have they greatest share of trade att Lisbon has apears by the number of ships wich is double the number to either France or the Dutch. 1758.

Cheif Towns in Portugal[16]
Lisbon, Coimbra, Braga, Porto, Miranda, Braganza, Evora, Tavira. 1758.

f. 5r In Holland the make excelent fine linen att Harlem and att Leyden the make brood and narrow[17] cloths serges and camblets but s. . .[18] infeirior to to those of Britain or else the would not purchase ours to export to other nations. Theire wooll the have from Spain and Germany and Turkey the likewise make fine silk gauses coarse flowerd velvits gold and sliver brocades and other rich stuffs butt theire silks not[19] so good has those of France or Italy but the are cheapar so that makes them go of better. The Hollanders has a prodigious trade in most of the nown parts of the world and are verry industrious people. England takes from Holland linen thred fine Holland tapes inckle whale fins brass battery madder argol lint seed. Theire is and advantage to England.

Cheif[20]
Amsterdam, Rotterdam, Hague, Leyden, Delf, Harlem, Dort, Hoorn, Enckhysen, Medenblick, Alemaer, Sardam, Utretcht, Daventer, Dam, Groll, Flushin, Amersfob, Davent.

f. 5v Att Kendall the frise abundance [of][21] coarse cottons and some is dyed blew [re]ds and greens butt cheifly a deall [in] the white. Now sopose all after [th]ese coarse goods are milled and hanged to dry so then weett them over with soap mixt up in warm watter just has much has will weett itt over then putt itt in the stok and crush the soap evenly [i]n to the cloth itt will make them handle strong and frise a great deall better because that these sort of coarse goods are apt to bee spungey and seldome will make handsome frises you must use castle soap so shafe itt thin with a nife into a kitt then pour warm watter on and beat itt up to a lather.

To dye black best way. Boyl in logwod and shumak att night for 2 or 3 hours pull the fire out and let the botom [of] the kettle cooll for one hour. So [p]ut your cloth in to the liquor and [let] itt stay all night so in the . . .[22]

f. 6r The globe is deveided into 4 parts Europ Asia Africa America.[23]

15 Ms reads 'nav'.
16 Entries in list along bottom margin.
17 Ms reads 'nar'.
18 Remainder of word faded.
19 Word interlineated.
20 Ms reads 'Che', remainder of line torn. Entries in list along bottom margin.
21 Left margin torn, initial letters of most words at the beginning of each line are missing. Additions in brackets.
22 Remainder of entry illegible except the phrase: 'up the kettle and saden'.
23 Entries on the following three pages are made in tabular form.

Countrys belonging to Europe is	Cheif cyties
Spain	Madrid
Portugall	Lisbon
France	Paris
Italy	Rome
Germany	Vianna
Holland	Amsterdam
Denmark	Copenhagen
Sweden	Stockholm
Russia	Petersburgh
Poland	Warsaw
Turkey in Urope	Constantinople
British Isles	London

Asia	Cities
Turkey in Asia	Bursa
Arabia	Mecca
Persia	Ispahan
India	Agra
China	Pekin
Tartary Chinese	Chynian
Independent	Samarch
Muscovite	Tobols

f. 6v

Africa	Cities
Egypt	Grand Cairo
Barca	Tolemeta
Abex	Erguiko
Fex and Moroco	Fez and Moroco
Taslet and Segelmesse	Taslet and Segelmesse
Algier	Algier
Tunis	Tunis
Triopoli	Tripoli
_dulgerid[24]	Dara
_ara	Tagessa
_roland	Madinga
_unia	Benin
_ungo	Loango
_ongo	St. Salvador
_ngola	Mochima
_nompa	Monomotapa
_noemu	Chicova
_uffers	Cape of Good Hope
_assa	Saffala
_anguba	Mosambiqua
_ian	Brava
_king	Caxinmo

[24] Initial letters of many of the 'countries' on this folio are missing.

_ba	Daneala
_	Angela

Ethiopa African Iles these two above has no cities

Square Miles[25]
200,340
27,500
275,000
234,000
378,000
264,000
184,900

f. 7r

America	Cheif Cities
Carolina	Charlestown
Virginia	James Town
Maryland	Baltimore
Pensylvania	Philidelfhia
New Jersey	Elisebeth town
New York	New York
New England	Boston
& Scotland	Annapolis
Iles	Kingston

Spanish Empire in America	
Old Mexico	Mexico
New Mexico	Sanekta
Florida	St Augustin
Terra Firma	Cartagena
Perru	Lima
Chili	St Jago
Paragua	Assumption
Land of Amazons	unknown
Magellanica	unknown
California	unknown
Isles	Havana

French Empire in America	
Lousiana	Fort Louis
Canada or New France	Quebeck
French Isles	

The Portugues Dominons
are Brasill and thats all.[26]

f. 7v The quantity of wooll the . . .[27] for a man to scrible of one d[ay] is 36 pound if itt is for mixt[er] aney coalar else that they call 36 pound a comon days work for one man. Leeds 1758.

[25] Referent for these figures not given.
[26] Remainder faded.
[27] Right and left margins of page torn, some words missing and additions in brackets.

[Th]e quantity of wool they use to putt [in] a peice of brood white cloath [is] 48pd. For warp about 16 or [18] pound. They cheifly have small [w]arps and well spun all of a [thi]kness so 18 pound of warp and 30 [p]ound of weftt is 48 pound of y[arn]. [N]ow sopose this 48 pound of yarn takes

50 pound of wooll to mak[e] [u]p att 10d per pound is	£	2	[5]	[0]
Then grease		0	1	6
[3d] per pound spinning warp 18 pd		0	4	6
2½d pound weft 30 pd		0	6	3
weaving and warping		0	6	0
milling		0	1	0
this peice will contain		3	0	11
. . .[28] at 3s 1d per yard is	£	5	12	0[29]

How to make mixt broods that are a dark mixter a cheap and nise handsome way first f. 8r
dye your wooll blak that you intend for warp so scrible a little white in and gett it combed[30] so spin itt into woosted and make your warp of woosted. Then sise itt and do itt the way has boking warps are. So dye wooll black for waftt and scrible the same quantity of white in has you did for the warp. Lett your warp[31] bee made of fleece wooll or broken wooll. Sell for 3 shilling per yard.

The make fine white brood cloath in the West of England and some is woven in the twiled way has searges is or druggitt so if itt is slender milled itt will cover the thread and look close.[32] They are seven quarters wide within the list when frised.

And some the make has blews or drabs or clarrits wich are dyed in the wool so frised wich looks well.

A deal George Charnock byes logwood blew and white inclining to ash.[33]

Observe that all shalloons for blaks they will do better unscowred then if the was f. 8v
scowred. The take a better blak and presses to a better gloss.

Lett all blaks bee stock washed in a driveing stok and the will look much better and shine clearar when the coperas[34] is washed out.

The prise they give att Wakefild for stoking moks that are dyed blak.[35] The give 4 pence a stokfull for them if[36] the miller washes them before the are putt in stock and att after[37] the come out or if the dyear sends a man to do them the are only 3 pence per stokfull. The allways put two moks in att a time or two brood cloath. Moks are cheifly dyed blacks bokins are dyed gold coalars.[38]

Aney wool you intend to make into a bloom coalar lett itt bee cleane scowred before f. 9r
itt dyed and itt will take a better coalar bye a greatt deall. If you scrible bloom coalars

[28] Figure for number of yards illegible; calculation suggests it is about 36 yards.

[29] Remainder of entry, presumably the calculation of profit, is illegible.

[30] Ms reads 'com'.

[31] Ms reads 'war'.

[32] Ms reads 'clos'.

[33] Entry in margin.

[34] Ms reads 'copera'.

[35] Ms reads 'bla'.

[36] Word illegible, meaning implicit.

[37] Ms reads 'aft'.

[38] Last line illegible except the phrase: 'reds pink'.

and white wooll and some red floks[39] make a prettey mixter or pe. . .[40] coalar and red looks well. Scarlitt or red shear floks will do to put in.[41]

How to dye a Masareen blew.[42] First dye itt in the fatt a comon blew then wash it weell so then finish itt up with logwood in a boyling lead and itt will look brighter[43] then done all with indigo. Let[44] itt bee stokwashed then gorted.

The reason why the Leeds and[45] Wakefild cloathiears cannot[46] dye a clarritt nor bloom coalar (that will stand but fade)[47] nor pearle because the[48] do nott boyl theire wooll in. . .[49] The call pearl coalars point . . .[50]

Theire clarritts or blooms fade with a hott sun or little rain.[51]

f. 9v The maner of drawing a large clew bye a rowler is after this patern.[52]

Observe number 1 is to bee att end of and axell tree and number 4 to the end of the same axis. The work deescribed is thus. Number 1 and 2 is two wheels with iron prongs in for a rope to ride in and by this rope you pull bye[53] when you draw the clew to stop itt. 3 is the wheel with cogs in fixed to the rowler and[54] that draws up clew. 4 is a little cog wheel that is fixed to shaft end that number 1 is. 6 is rowler to have a chain round to[55] pluck up the clew. 5 is the clew. Number 1 and 2 are to bee fixed on two axis.

f. 10r Or to draw a clew the common way bye a rowler is this way.[56] The work is thus. Number 1 is the rowler with holes mortised in to put the iron crow in. 2 is the clew with a chain fixed to itt and laps round the rowler. 3 is a man puling[57] by the iron crow. 4 is the crow.

Floks allways sells well when trade goes well at Leeds or Wakefild.[58] The cheif time of trade being att best is in the spring and all the sumer season. Wakefeild 17__.[59]

There is most deceitt in Hudersfild cloath of aney cloath lett it bee in what country itt . . .[60] for itt is one half dirt if itt is of a low prised sort. When milled with earth . . .[61]

f. 10v At Ackworth 2 miles of Pomferat there is a foundling hospitall for children that comes down from London (or country).[62] The are brought down bye weet nurses and so leftt att this hospitall. For so much a week the take them att one Rich Hargreavs from Roseindall in Lanckeshire. He is governer of this hospital. Nov 1759.

Att the above plase the are for teaching theire children to spin and are setting up 3 pare of looms to weave in the wheell shuttle way and theire is men and women comes

39 Ms reads 'flo'.
40 Word illegible.
41 Ms reads 'pu' and 'i'.
42 Ms reads 'bl'.
43 Ms reads 'bright'.
44 Ms reads 'L'.
45 Ms reads 'a'.
46 Ms reads 't'.
47 Phrase interlineated.
48 Word illegible, meaning implicit.
49 Rest of word illegible.
50 Remainder illegible.
51 Entry in margin.
52 Diagram in text with numbers indicating parts.
53 Ms reads 'ye'.
54 Ms reads 'nd'.
55 Word illegible, meaning implicit.
56 Diagram with numbers indicating parts.
57 Ms reads 'pu..ing'.
58 Ms reads 'Wa'.
59 Last two digits missing.
60 Word missing.
61 Remainder torn.
62 Phrase interlineated.

out[63] Saddleworth to instruckt them to[64] spin and the only think to make cloath for theire own use for the are 300 in number betwixt the age of 10 years to ¼. 1759.

Att Wakefild new corn mill or att aney plase where the have FRENCH stones they cheifly make 5 sorts of flower has superfine has common fine and has seconds and thirds and 4ths and 5ths and one sort called pola. . .[65] wich is drest outt in bran that is mixt amongst oatmeal to make haver bread on. Itt is mixt 3 hours before you bake itt with a little yeast in and itt makes the dough raise to a deal more to by thirds of flower. Att Wakefild mill itt will pass for fine flower in some country towns. f. 11r

Theire woollen looms at Wakefild theire sleays hangs at top as thus.[66] So rides on a pin wich is sharp[67] att point and makes itt go easy.

How to order to grease Hudersfeild peices to make them frise to a hard nap. Gett some shuitt either of beef or mutton and render itt down. So blow itt on while it is warmish then raise your peice and shear itt has useuall and doing this way is better than oil. f. 11v

Some men is and opinion thatt if light drabs that is Hudersfeild cloath was to have a little chalk mixt amongst earth and soap itt makes them look bright. Give them a little soap just att last to hold the chalk and earth down for dusting.

Sopose all dyed drabs that is dyed in the cloath was to have soap given them so crushed well in then to bee drest att after itt would make them handle strong.

The way that some covetous cloathmakers goes on with theire prentises in the winter season. They keep them with saltt beeff or saltt pork wich makes them dry all that day and they are obliged to drink watter all that day wich keeps them for being hungry that day. f. 12r

The properest to frise Hudersfild goods or Rochdale narrow cloath. Frise them first in a single mill first one peice at once. So frise them in a double mill att after two att once because no mill can frise two peices att once to do each place evenly. So a single mill is best for first time and then finish in a double mill.

A proper thing to be observed bye all mercers and woollen drapers that when a customer has bought quantity of goods above 5 shillings to have a dram bottle so give them a glass and itt is a thing that pleases people and will make them keep to your shop better. f. 12v

How to sharpen a friseing board when worn sliperey without washing. If you have a dark mixture blow it over with oyll so frise itt and it will cleanse your board and take grease or slipperiness of itt.

All in the west part and south where they make fine brood cloath the frise them 4 or 5 times over and are well drest. The west part is in Wiltshire and Glostershire and Somersetshire the south is down towards London and behind.

63 Word missing.

64 Word missing, meaning implicit.

65 One or two letters missing; probably 'pollard', see vol. 1, f. 54r.

66 Diagram in text.

67 Ms reads 'shar'.

f. 13r Observe that when a stok is sharp and works hard up itt keeps cloath to a better length. Now sopose them hard Hudersfeild peices att after milled up with earth was to have a little oyll layed on so worked well in itt would make them soft and keep them from dusting. Some will use soap in stead of oyll. Sopose shalloons att after scowred and wrung the watter well outt was to have a little soap squesed in itt will make them handle strong and itt might do well for blews or blaks.

The way some mills mixt broods att after scowred and the watter well[68] wrung outt they take a quantity of wheat flowr and mixes itt up in cold watter so then shaves 3 or 4 twopeney balls of soap in to a kitt. So pours hott watter on and beats itt up to a lather. Then mixes soap and and all together then starts itt on from end to end and doubles itt inwards[69] if itt is broods or some sla. . .[70] itt on in the stok.

f. 13v Observe that the Wakefild merchants keeps Hudersfild market and some of them seldom misess a market day in a year but goes winter or sumer and the allways pay ready money for aney peices that is under £2 10s 0d per peice and them that is above the are made by Saddleworth men and the trust 3 month and some more. Hudersfild cloath sells exceding dear and there is verry sharp markits just now. November 24th 1759.

The wheel shuttles that are made in Lanckeshire the wheels are shoed first putt[71] in a throw and turned to a truth rond the wheel.

f. 14r Pres papers to bee 3 quarters and ½ quarter long and ½ yard and . . .[72] quarter broad for to pres shallons in. When you paper shallons you must keep wattering each other paper if the bee blaks or drabs all other coalars to have less watter and when presed make them up on a board and lap them first in blew paper then in[73] strong white paper with your[74] coat of arms printed on and your name under and att the head end to bee stamped upon a blank of lead your name round the edge and your coat of arms in the midle and everey shallon or serge or aney sort to have three stiches of a side[75] to be tufted with silk.

f. 14v All dyed frises to be . . .[76] planed over as soon as ten[tered] or when dry of tenter if you . . . them of tenter blow them over with oyl then plane . . . down to work the oyl in and . . . make itt have a good bottom. Then sett the wool upon the end by planeing it bak . . . frise it.

All mottalls frises or planes . . . bee weel burled and att after to bee fine drawn if the n. . .

All merchants that deals in frises to have their name stamped round a blank in . . . circle round the edge and . . . lenth of the peices stamped . . . in the midle of the bla. . .

f. 15r The maner how Mr Lumb of Wakefild dyes his saxon greens. Hee first boyles one hour in chipt fustick and allom. So then puts in his kimick that is oyll of vittrol and indigo dry ground. So mixd together and stired for one hour in a mug pott upon the

68 Ms reads 'we'.
69 Ms reads 'in. . ..rds'.
70 Word illegible.
71 Ms reads 'utt'.
72 Word illegible.
73 Word illegible; meaning implicit.
74 Ms reads 'r' superscripted.
75 Word missing.
76 Folio torn along right margin; some words illegible, additions in brackets.

night before. Itt is used so when kimik is in lett it keep boyling for and hour and ½ and allways keep turning your peices over. The wen[77] only for 3 or 4 minuits you lett itt stand att after you have[78] turned itt the first ½ howr so[79] itt is finished in same liquor the fustick is in so kimick allom and fustick is all in one lead. Wakefild 1760.

Old comon green best is to dye itt first a middle blew so wash it[80] then . . .[81] itt with fustic and kimick.[82]

Lett plush thatt is cutt in [to] parts lett the two outtmost parts bee 2 inches longer then f. 15v[83]
the two inermost parts so you may frise broods better on this sort of plush then when the are cutt exact all of a length. Butt itt is best for broods to have the plush in two cutting itt in middle so turn the grain toward[84] each spindle. Butt for two narrows att once cut itt in 4 and lett two inwards parts draw inward and parts[85] outwards to draw outward towards the spindles for a single mill to frise on . . .[86] att once cutt has you do for a brood.

The maner how Mr Lumb dyes his ½ scarlits and and 3 quarters scarlits is first hee f. 16r
boyles them in ackofortis and allom so then hee madders them with good madder and some hee does with cropt madder wich is best madder. So then washes itt and finishes itt with scutconell and ackofortis and these are best grounded scarlits of aney sort. His spirits is killed the over[87] night with grain tin and stires for and hour with a good handfull of salt in so stired well up in the morning before itt is used. Hee flings his scarlits has soon has finished into cold watter for a scarlitt will burn att after dyed if itt lyes hott together and all coalars beside he flings into cold watter directly has soon has finished for if a peice lyes hott together 4 or 5 minuits itt will crimp and the crimp will stay in att after frised. 1760.

Places where cast iron work and rowls iron into plates of aney sise or thickness is has at f. 16v
Coln Bridge near Healland in Yorkshire and att Wotley near Peniston (5 or 6 miles of Peniston)[88] and att Rotherham. 1760. The rowll iron aney where where the make tin has iron for saws or aney other branch wich is needfull for rowled iron. Itt is rowled on and engine all tin is rowled iron before covered.

The have gotten a method of rowling press papers in some places and the do much better for fine planes then if the were[89] glased the are not glased at[90] all them that is rowled this[91] way is for Saddleworth planes.

To inquire of shops you may now where tin mills are of them shops that sells tin or them that casts or runs iron inquire att them shops that sells iron pots or weights. . . .[92]

How to make a nise sort of flanell lett your warp bee spun of cotton and your weft to f. 17r
bee small spinning of fine wooll and to be woven in a verry close fine geer so scowred and just covered in mill then raised a little of one side. This sortt is cheifly used for

77 Word faded.
78 Ms reads 'ha'.
79 Ms reads 's'.
80 Word missing, meaning implicit.
81 Word missing.
82 Ms reads 'kim'; remainder of entry illegible.
83 A second entry on this page omitted, too faded to transcribe.
84 Ms reads 'tow'.
85 Word interlined.
86 Word illegible.
87 Ms reads 'ove'.
88 Phrase interlineated.
89 Ms reads 'w'.
90 Ms reads 'a'.
91 Ms reads 'thi'.
92 Remainder of line illegible.

womens smock coats and look excellent well. Some is whitned lin warps and some cotton warps. 1760.

How to order a woosted shagg when put on new. Att first mist itt well on the shaged side with watter so then dry itt. So when dry brush it over on the bakside with strong glew. So dry itt then when itt is putt on to your board take a flatt smoothing iron and and heat itt hott before fire so singe your plush evenly over with itt and itt takes all the long coarse hairs of and makes it sharp and free from being spungey. Iff all shagg for shops was singed on and engine before dyed so dyed itt would look fine tho your wool is coarse. Bespoke itt made and you may have itt cut aney lowness in loom.[93]

f. 17v The prise of making a mixt brood the wooll costing £7 pound per pak and fine white base floks att 6d per pound. Now say 40 pd of fine base flocks and 40 pound wooll

So flocks att	£	0	10	0
40 pd wooll at		1	3	4
spining of warp 26 pound at 3d per pound		0	6	6
spining weft 34 pound att 2d per pound		0	5	8
weaving and grease		0	10	0
milling and soap		0	2	3
flowr to mill with		0	0	6
dyeing and scribling		0	5	0

now this peice will sell att 3s per yard in bawk and will hold 30 yards att least and milled to 1 yard 13½ inches brood when sold in bawk

so 30 yards is	£	4	10
the charge of making	£	3	3
the profit is	£	1	7[94]

These are never small spinning.[95]

f. 18r The prise of a Hudersfild 24 yard peice the wool costing 7 pence per pound and floks att 6 pence per pound.

Now say 20 pound of wooll att 7 pence is		0	11	8
10 pound of fine base floks		0	10	0
spining 16 pound of weft at 2 per pound		0	2	8
14 pound of warp at 3d per pound		0	3	6
scribbling and grease		0	4	0
milling and milling with soap and flowr		0	2	6
tentering and going to markitt		0	1	0

Now this peice will sell at £2 2s 0d att least and to bee milled to 24 yards long and 30 inch brood	£	2	2	0
		1	13	4
profit	£	0	7	4

Wakefild 1760. And Mr Yeald and Mr Mills byes brood cloath. Mr Fracis Maude and Mr Daniel Maude byes both broods and narrow. Wakefild. Mr William Naylor and Mr Charles Steer byes a deall of mixt brood and Mr Tenent Mr Norton and Mr William Charnock byes Hudersfild cloath.[96]

93 Sentence in margin.

94 Figures for pence in these last three rows of the calculation are missing.

95 Entry in margin next to the prices.

96 Entry in margin at bottom.

There is some places where the fix engines in the maner of paper mills to grind old f. 18v
rags of aney kind has all woollen rags into floks. So dryes them and swings them up lofty. They have of these mills in Kentt and about London that works bye tide water has att Deptford and Dartford in Kent. There is friseing mills att Deptford 5 miles behind London. These sort of floks are for soldiers when lyeing in the baracks or for shiping for saylors hamock. Them men thatt makes saylcloath can tell where to dispence with these floks or aney low prised floks whattever has one Mr Humphrey Heyden White Chappell London. Hee byes a maney and many more . . .[97]

Floks for barracks or hamocks must bee shortt shear floks and itt does not signefye f. 19r
what coalar for when a soldier has lyed on them 2 or 3 year there is men thatt makes a trade of them att after so swings them up lofty and makes them loftey for sale again so shortt floks are best for this way because the will nott clod together has long floks will and they are cheaphar in long ones.

The best way of dyeing drabs to pattern coalars is to examine your shalloons you intend to dye that day. So begin with your light coalars first so keep forward till you have dyed all and all in one liquor only adding more wares has you keep working.

In and about London there is men goes to farmers or gentlemens house of choping straw for young horses or cows to eat in winter season.

Some millers when the grind shilling for to make oat meall the will grind down a f. 19v
quantity of horse beans and pease mixt all up together and the make finear bread and comes in much cheaphar or if beans and pease was dryed on a kiln so ground down with mallt itt would make fine ale stronger a great deall then if of all mallt. Boyll a little treackle in the liquor and itt will look fine and good coalar.

How to make treackle drink that will keep itt head. Boyll your watter in a few hops and some raisens of ginger so putt your treackle in and yeast when itt is coolled just as it is blood warm.

To bake a pudding under meatt is best to have it in a fryeing pan so you may now and then . . .[98] on the fire to bake it under.

How to dye for a blewlye bloom coalar wich is a coalar thatt mixt broods are dyed f. 20r
oftens for the Wakefild merchants. First boyll your wooll in allom then in logwood and redwood and shumack. So sadden a little with coperas. Some uses madder instead of redwood.

For dying a logwood blue boyll itt in allom first and your logwood and your coalar will take dye much better. Allom makes logwood strike and makes a bodey of coalar.

How to dye a buff coalar. First boyll itt in allom then in chipt fustick or young fustic and wowlds so finish itt with ackofortis. A gold coalar is dyed with same sort of stuff only the double quantity of fustick and wowlds. Straw coalar is dyed with same sort of stuff only useing no wowlds to itt only allom fustick and ackofortis.

Att Leeds and att Sheffeild the make rugs that are pretty nise dised coalars and are f. 20v
woven in the maner that plush is woven in. The low warp is lin the higher woollen so the are cut about one inch assunder for to make the thrums stick up and this is a

[97] Remainder illegible.

[98] Word missing.

currious way of makeing rug. The are verry prettey thyng and sells at 16 or 18 or 20 shilling per peice them that is made att Sheffild are woven in the brood way and them that is made att Leeds are woven in narrow way and sewed up the middle. 1760.

Places where the make plush and hair shagg att is att Leeds Hallifax Manchester Bristoll and about Coln and Burnley.

Wakefild is only for corn and wool. All other things sells has dear as aney place in England.

f. 21r The way Mr Whitelock of Leeds goes on for plush for his friseing milns. Hee buyes strong buttok wooll of the skiners wich comes of Lincolnshire sheep wich has a staple 6 or 8 inches long. So gets it combed and spun. So weaves itt in for weft wich the shagg is cutt on and the bottom is of strong woosted and this holds cloath verry well and is much like hair shagg and comes in cheap. All other frisears in Yorkshire frises on hare shagg of 7s or 7s 6d per yard. Leeds 1760.

For friseing mixt broods lett them bee frised once over with a board that is not fine or close and then chawk them evenly over so frise them twise over att after and itt makes them clear and to frise hard and makes a peice cover the thread and look clean.

f. 21v Mr Danill Maude of Wakefild byes a deall of bases and broods wich is dyed blew and frised and mixt brood frises wich goes to Norich to Mr James Smith. Bases are flanills and goes in the white itt is in the month of July wich hee sends most on. 1760.

Hee has bought goats hair and made them into fearnoughts wich goes to Norich and is coarse strong stuff for saylors watch coats.

Camils or goats hair or long young cows hair or calf. Supose itt was dyed black and some wooll scribled in. So spun and woven into plush so when dyed again and dry dress itt on barrill cast over with sand and itt will make itt shine and take coarse hairs of and would look like hair shagg. It is to bee bought of the taners is the hair. 1760.

f. 22r All in the West part of Yorkshire the are hard working people and works for little wages and comon working cart or chair horses horses are used extreamly hard has aney part in the world. For in some places all the sumer season the roads are seldome free neither night or day att 10 of clock att night the are going one way. So bye two in the morning the cariges are going the other way. Some with one carige goods some with other sorts. Wakefild 1760.

How to dye a massereen blue. First boyll itt allom and peachwood so dye itt in a good fatt then stokwash itt so run itt through a hott lead with archill in.

Lett all coalard mixt broods to have a ¼ of the grease left in when for frises or if for press not to bee to cleane scowred but observe that itt must bee loosned to the heart[99] for no peice can scowr to well only you may take the watter of when you think proper. A little sweet soap mixt amongst your lant att first when you weet itt make aney cloth. . . .[100]

f. 22r[101] Mr Floodshire London merchant near Blakweth Hall byes a deall of mixt broods and dyed broods wich are frises from Wakefild. Hee trades with Mr Daniel Maude and

[99] Ms reads 'hear'.

[100] Remainder of line illegible.

Mr Frank Maude and Mr Naylor both with Jere and William Naylor all of Wakefild. Hee likewise byes a deall of Rochdale goods both basses and peices wich are shorn and goes in the white so are dyed and frised att London. One Mr Lintaill frises a deall living in Sudderick. Hee frises a deall of them Rochdale goods wich goes shorn in the white wich belongs to Mr Floodshire liveing near Blacketh Hall wich is a hall for cloath. John Clegg att Heights of Rochdale trades with Mr Floodshire. June 1760. Mr Floodshire Samuell and Thomas partners.

The frise either by horses or wind cheifly att London. Mr Lintaill goes by horses 2 in att once.

The reason why there is so few dyed drabs goes in the country that are frised because f. 23r
dyeing a peice drab makes itt look bare and handle thinish. Now sopose a white peice was dyed drab before itt is drest then when it is dyed wash itt in a stron[g][102] stream then putt itt in the stok and wring the watter well outt then pull itt ou[t] and leck on some soap putt itt in the stok again work the soap well in and tenter itt and dress itt. [So] frise when itt is dry and itt will look much bet[ter] and handle strong [and] . . . thread. If you was to . . . them a little in the w. . . itt would do well before you tenter itt. All Hudersfild . . . thats milled with earth th. . .

Now this engine[103] is worked bye a screw that is itt is the first movement of your f. 23v
friseing mill and all the weight lyes on the upright shaft and a new thing that rides on a pin will turn great weight with much ease. You may use a square. . . .[104]

The work is. Number one is the upright shaft. Two is the worm round itt. 3 is the wheel working in the worm. 4 is another wheel on the same axis. 5 is a little one to give number 6 a quick motion. 7 is a trindle head fixed . . .[105] then end of your frising mill. 8 & 9 is two wheels turning the spindle. 10 and 11 is the spindle.

Woosted trade is and profitable and improving trade has in different branches of itt has f. 24r
making woosted shagg or stoking shalloons and serges and a deal of wosted stuffs for womens ware and itt goes well now in the year of 1760.

A cloath maker that makes strong stout cloath and getts a corospondance with a merchant and his goods turns out well the will bye of him before aney other pearson for the know his goods to bee honist and has tried them before and will not bye of aney other pearson all tho the could have has good good and something cheaphar a corospondance[106] and can trust his goods. These cloathiers getts most money. Hudersfild market 176_.[107]

For Leeds markett if a man has butt the coalar and can suit a merchant to his pattern hee stands the best chance of selling his cloath to profitt and a cloathiers best chance is to mind whatt coalars and what sorts goes of best att partickular seasons of year for the merchants will not bye except the have orders for itt for brood cloath if coalard is much given to mort eatt and some cloathmakers when the cannot sell theire cloath the bring itt the mill each 7 or 8 weeks so freshens itt up and itt keeps mort out.

101 Marginal entry on this page illegible.
102 Margin torn on remainder of page; some words missing, additions in brackets.
103 Entries on this page refer to diagram in text.
104 Remainder faded.
105 Word missing.
106 Ms reads 'corospondan'.
107 Last digit illegible.

Some times a cloath maker has to bring his cloath to mill 2 or 3 times. Some for being a little greasey. Other times being to cleane and sometimes so is not even but cloudy.[108]

f. 24v Itt is a very bad method to bale frises for itt crushes down the nop and if itt goes a greatt way when the are unbayled you can scarce see aney nop on att all and bee verry good frises to when the was bayled att first and most of frises if the go in prest goods and in bayles to London the cheifley frise them over again to raise and freshen the nap and the frise with coarse bords. I am shure for resons because the list is oftens cutt up to a high ground nop and sadly murled. This I have seen bye goods returned from London to Wakefild for being over charged and to dear and some not coalars wich sells well of a deal of frises goes bayled from Wakefild all parts of the world. 1762.

Now in these days the shopkeepars wants soft pressing that is hard screwing and fired easily and thus a peice when itt comes to bee wetted a little on the back does nott shew spottey and there goes thousands of planes drest from Wakefild wich are drest has if for press so goes unprest and are worn so and these are called lambskins bye some others calls them hunters others shorn duffils. The look well thus.

Itt is dry weather cheifly about Wakefild sometimes 5 or 6 weeks no rain.

f. 25r The Leeds and Wakefild merchants are the cheiff men in England for furnishing the London merchants with brood cloath of all all sorts for soldiers cloathing. 1762.

Supose one of them mokins cheifly called moks was made of fine sort of good stapled fleece wool. So dye blew and when dyed take some sewk wich comes out in a white cloath so leck itt well over and mill itt and hour. So pull itt out in stok and leck itt over with blak earth and mill itt well in so itt will handle strong and not dirty the hands has cheifly all dye house blew does. Butt observe that before you leck on your sewk coalar itt with indigo so itt will not strike your peice pale butt make itt bright and lively and lett all sewk and earth stay in nott to scowr it out and observe to make both your woosted warp and weft of fine fleece wool and dres your piece in coalar blowing itt over with a little oyll before you raise itt and frise itt handsomely to a wrank low sharp nop and to cover well in bottom and these will sell well to merchant taylors or brokers shops. 1762.

To order scarlits after the best way to make them keep the coalar and frise handsome is dres them well and when dyed strike them on . . .[109] tenter so when dry blow them with a little oyl so turn the . . .[110]

f. 25v A man might make a scribling mill or a mill for carding wool on has thus. Sett 8 or 9 cards round a barrill so have two cards for these to work on and observe that in them 8 or 9 cards round the barrill have one card oposite that is with the teeth different way from the other cards. So this card will doff the wool of the two other cards. So lett itt go round like a perching mill barrill and have a method of layeing the two cards to work on closar or further of acording has you think proper bye a screw. This method will do well to[111] card wool or waste first time over.

108 Ms reads 'clou'.
109 Word missing.
110 Line missing.
111 Word missing, meaning implicit.

To make allakar have a fine flavour put[112] slice a lemon into a barrill of allaker and itt both makes itt sowrar and gives it a pleasant taste. 1762.

The butchers att Wakefild in sumer time when beef does not sell well of the take itt and sallt itt so sells itt out in pickle and when boatmen comes up the oftens buy a deall of itt and is good beeff out in pickle.

The way to dye leather black for breeches or wayscoats is boyle your liquour with logwood and shumak . . .[113] lett itt cool till milk warm then[114] lett your leather stay all night so boyl your coperas and putt itt in . . .[115]

Mr James Norton sends a good maney Hondly planes into Wales wich are dyed blew f. 26r
and frised and sends them of att shillings per yard and maney Hudersfild and Saddleworth prest goods. Wakefild 1762.

Likewise hee byes from Rochdale red blew and green cottons wich hee gives 14 and 15 pence per yard for. These hee uses for rapering and goes cheifly into Scotland to raper up prest goods with and lin raper outwards. Edmund Dawson sends him cottons at Rochdale.

A rule to bee observed bye cloathmakers wich weaves with weet spows is when you have woven each 5 or 6 yards to pull of the beam and hang itt up or else the will heatt and change the coalar whether itt is white or coalard. Besides itt will scowr better when pulled of and hanged up. A lad will weave a white brood in 5 days cheifly wich sells att 3s per yard in bawk. Wakefild 1762.

Att Ailsbury in Buckinghamshire the make a deal of broads 7 quarter made has a serge is woven and is much much worn for gentlemans banians or josephs and cloaks for women and maney is drest and frised and dyed a full blew some dyed in wool some in the cloath and wears very well.

Some of the above broods is wove plaine and made like druggits and looks well. 1762.

Peices wich are oyled mixt cloath when the are chawked the allways in 3 or 4 months f. 26v
turns spottey for the cropers all of them oyls them with theire hands pulling itt over the shear board and some places gets more oyl then other some and when the are chawked and lyes in a shop a while where the oyl is most it sucks in chawk and shews cloudy and spottey only if nott chawked itt would not shew spotey. Butt if a man could mist oyl on out in his mouth and do itt even on itt would not shew spottey if itt was chawked for chawk is and excellent thing for to make a hard clear round nop and shews a piece cleane and fair. Wakefild 1762.

Some men when a Hudersfild light drab getts spottey will send itt to dye blew and some of these drabs are middling cleane scowred and stuffed with earth and when the come from dyeing all the earth is gone out and the are supriseing thin with weeting out and washing and the like some grease milled in will not come out like earth does.

To raise all Lanckeshire bases or skins or thin goods itt is best to raise them with hand not on a mill for a mill is apt to fraye them and pull them narrow.

112 Word missing, meaning implicit.
113 Word missing.
114 Ms reads 'en'.
115 Line missing.

f. 27r When aney buff coalars att Wakefild or drabs gets spotey in dyeing or presing the weett them over with earth and watter so lets them lye 5 or 6 hours and letts them go ½ and hour in the stok. So scowrs the earth out and itt will bee cleare.

Aney sort of woolen goods wich is called cloath is brood cloath or narrow goods that is stout miled butt aney thing wich is thin and flanilly cannot properly bee called cloath has most part of Lanckeshire goods is.

The best way to spin cow hair and wool mixt is lett itt bee well carded or scribled together so spin itt on a line wheel has you spin line. So spin your weft has soft you can gett itt up.

There is a deal of men liveing about Hudersfild wich goes into the country and drives some 2 paks other 3 or 4 into the country so goes from town to town and sells itt amongst shopkeepars some times the sell cheap and some is sold verry dear and these sorts of men are called higlers.

The Halifax tradesmen are judged to bee right sharp men about bisness and takes a deal of pains to engross trade in a maney branches.

All dyed blews mist them over with oyl and itt keeps them to the coalar and will not bee so apt to frise white in bottom.

Att Wakefild all brood cloath of a low pr[ise][116] sort the raise butt a little so itt kee[p] stout and strong for bye no means th[e] will have no brood cloath made . . . with dresing butt kept stout and st[ong].

Druggitt is woosted warp and wool weft woven plain 3 quarters broad.

f. 27v A cloathmaker that must gett good spinning hee must seek good spiners out if itt is 5 or 6 miles distance and fetch and carry itt and keep certain days of takeing in each fortnight and hee will find itt much to his advantage in the way of makeing of fine cloath. May 18th 1762.

Them 17 yards white Hondly planes when dyed blew and frised the Wakefild merchants sends them of att 2 shillings per yard and a good 42 weight made about Rochdale will do much better if strong miled butt makes them Hondly planes goe the are made of floks and noyls or floks and wool and strong miled and good coalars. The dye att Wakefild or else these 17 yards sorts makes butt verry bad frises shear floks allways murls out. 1762.

Mr Frank Maude Wakefild merchant trades with Saddleworth planes all over the West of England amongst the shopkeepers. Hee keeps a ridear wich has 40 pounds per year and his charges allowed whilest traveling abroad. So hee goes from Wakefild through Manchester and all down into the West so comes through Lincolnshire . . .k.[117] Hee trades all over Lincolnshire and all into the North of England. 1762.

Prise of milling att Leeds and Wakefild brood[118] cloath is 3 shillings for a[119] couple of brood comonly called a cloath. Att Dewsbury 2s and 6d and some two shillings.

[116] Right margin of entry torn; some words missing, additions in brackets.

[117] Ms torn, possibly 'York'.

[118] Ms reads 'rood'.

[119] Word missing, meaning implicit.

Observe that except a man . . .[120] a sober quite temper hee can never do bisness wich lyes a brood and if hee can do bisness with soberiety hee needs not to fear of getting money and trade with good safe chaps. f. 28r

All them shear floks wich William Goth used to bye att Rochedale hee sold them again att Hudersfild markitt and att Hondley to cloathmakers to make Hondley planes on and Hudersfild planes and the will make low prised 17 yards pieces of noyles and shear floks and the Hondley planes are all white and cleane scowred because the are sold in bawk and when the are dyed and frised you may wisk shear floks out a handfull out in one peice and the are exceeding bad to frise seldome makeing a good nap of the 17 yards pieces. Then there is some of good sorts will make handsome frises. 1761.

Att Leeds or Wakefild cloath mills the generally keeps milling day and night and the miller is some times six weeks and never goes to bed only sleeping 2 or 3 hours bye the fire at nights. 1761. f. 28v

When cloathmakers pay for theire milling the pay one shilling at each cloath milling has soon has milled then two shilling more is booked and this the pay each ½ years so master of the mill makes a feast of meat and drink gratis so the cheifley all come and pays of and this is called mill feast or payday.

There is no low prised Hudersfild cloth will keep above 12 months before itt mort eats and some will eat in six months if sumer season.

Att Hudersfild markit in latter end of October and November when itt is bad dryeing weather pieces are oftens scarce and bad to come att and except the Wakefild merchants goes of on a Monday night to bee there readey all the choyce of pieces are licked up and cloath market over bee 10 of clock and some of richer sort of cloathiers will give readey money to others for theire pieces so the can keep up the market and have theire full prise when the have engrosed cloath into theire own hands and sometimes the will send itt to Manchester cloath hall and lett itt lye 3 or 4 weeks and if the cannot sell itt to theire advantage the will bring itt to Hudersfild markett again. November 1761. f. 29r

Country dyears allways are bisey from betwixt Mickelmas till Crismass both in dyeing and shearing has dyeers att Sheffild and att York and att Nottingham and att Thos Buxtons dyear in Retford in Nottinghamshire dyear att Selby and a dyear at Stamford Brigg wich has two stoks and a dyear att a town called Rasden in Lincolnshire has two stoks and a friseing mill and a dyear att or near Peniston James Air both dyes and trades into the country with Hudersfild frises and blews broods and narrows hee grinds his indigo bye a wind mill all the above dyears does country work. 1761. f. 29v

There is wool breakars at Wakefild wich byes fleece wool has out in Norfolk and Suffolk and sorts itt into 6 or 7 sorts so cloathmakers byes of such sorts has the have occasion for and is verry ready for them. For the can bye of these breakars has small quantitys has the please and of aney sorts. Mr Norton Mr Lumb Mr Zouch are wool breakars and keeps cropers and trades into the country. Mr Norton byes a maney frises from Manchester wich are them sorts called peticoat frises dyed blew reds or greens and hee byes a maney Hondley plane wich goes dyed blew and frised wich hee sends into Wales. 1761. f. 30r

[120] Word missing.

The Wakefild merchants are cheiff men att Hudersfild markitt. The bye a deall of Saddleworth planes there and Hudersfild pieces more then all the men wich keeps that markitt besides. 1761.

f. 30v In a general way theire white brood cloath made about Rochdale is too hard spun and not milled in driveing stoks wich makes them handle loose and spungey. Neither are the milled with soap butt are cheifley of a raw thin hand with them. When the bye aney to Wakefild the allways mills them over again and gives to each piece a pound of soap and the look quite another thing. One Mr Joseph Willis byes oftens from Rochdale and Mr Zouch byes a maney of Openshaw swanskins so shears them over again and dyes them and frises them so sends them to countrey shops and are used for josephs. 1761.

f. 31r Lett all spindles and bushes bee made taperish the bush holes to bee wide in bottom and narrow att top and the spindles fitted to the bushes so bye raiseing the will fitt to a hairs breadth and thus the will make a round nap and make a little noyce when working. 1761.

Att Leeds the perk all theire frises att after frised to see if aney spots bee in. Att Wakefild the seldome do perk aney except the mistrust there is spots in. This perking is drawing a piece ofer a perch pole faceing the light so two men draws over hand of either list and another stands att a distance and looks for the spots and this the do att Leeds bye all brood frises. November 18th 1761.

To make plush is and excellent bisness and make itt of buttock wool so dress itt on a barrill cast over with sand.

f. 31v Att Aberforth 8 miles of Leeds the make a deall of pins and a deall of bad cheese wich the can aford to sell itt att 5 farthings or 1d per pound. 1761.

The Wakefild merchants trades a deall into the North with narow cloath has to Newcastle Sunderland Alston behind Kendall and all over the North of England.

There is abundance of wool combers employed att Kendall and the make a deal of noyles there wich the make theire Kendall cottons on with a little wool mixed in.

There is abundance of fish of all sorts in and about Lancaster and all in the North part. Likewise butter sells cheap about Settle and them part.

f. 32r The way the go on with makeing a white brood cloath in and about Wakefild. First the sise theire warps and wea[ve][121] them with weet bobins. The weet their bobins over the head about ¼ of a minit. So to wring the watter outt the putt [it] on a spindle so gives the wheel a sh[arp] turn and the watter will flye out of the top of the bobin. So the bott[om] of the bobin is has weet as [the] top. So then itt weaves even and some strews theire yarn beam w[ith] dryed nocked clay so the yarn ke[ep] hard and cool free from heating. The weave in a fine geer and theire cloath is hard nock up in . . .

f. 32v To make divers kinds of plush is good bisness has plush made of long buttok wooll or mingled or mottled plush or long cutt shagg made of goats hair or hair shagg made of mohair or sopose you was to make of silk noyles. All is grett profitt.

[121] Page torn along right margin, additions in brackets. Second entry on page too torn to transcribe.

Lett all plush for friseing on bee made of strong buttock wool and not to small spining itt should bee about 12 hancks in a pound. So when woven dipt over head in watter for 5 or 10 minuits and itt makes itt thickar and strongar and sharphar to hold[122] the piece better. If a shagg bee stout and strong for sale the do not[123] mind the coarsness of itt does not shopkeepars but to make itt[124] fine and shine work itt on a barrall cast over with sand in the imitation of a raising mill bye some called a kig mill.

To[125] dye a bloom coalar that d. . .[126] take ripe elderberrys . . .[127]

The London merchants meets each day att the change in the afternoon transackt bisness and if a man is 4 days and does not come to the change except hee is badley itt looks has if hee was fayling with[128] world and people begins to take nottice of his comeing and judges hee is behind in the world. 1760. f. 33r

It is profit to bye coffee att Liverpool so burn itt your self and sell itt again to country shopkeepars itt is bought at[129] Liverpool unburned att 1s 8d per pound and some times at 1s 4d per and to bye itt at Wakefild out in shops itt is sixpence and ounce att 6 pence per ounce itt is after 8s per pound wich is extravagent for profitt and burning it. 1760. My wife had a pound att twenty pence from Liverpool to Wakefild brought bye a freind.

Observe that aney man that finds aney new invention that is a thing not[130] nown before and answer well there 50 pound allowed for his pattern.[131]

How to kill spirits for dyeing scarlitt with. First give the ackofortis has much grain tin has itt will take so keep stirring itt over night for one hour while the tin is quite melted. So pour 2 or 3 quartes of watter into your spirits with a handfull of sallt. So stir itt well up together and lett itt stand whilest morning before you use itt. Mr Lumbs way Wakefild 1760. Stronger your fortis and better it is.[132] f. 33v

Some kills spirits without sallt or watter and them dyears cheifly . . .urns[133] the cloath so has itt will not rise. Lett all scarlits has soon as dyed bee putt over head in cold watter or indeed aney coalar else ought not to ley hott together.

When you weett outt pieces for blew. Lett your lead not boyll for if itt does itt is apt to brown itt in places and them places will be dark cloudy spots when dyed. But to prevent this put some archill in or logwood and itt will prevent itt.

Lett all scarlitts bee stok washed and itt mends a coalar and take the argoll out and makes a piece handle soft and glovey and is a means to keep itt for friseing white in the bottom. Wakefild 176_.[134] f. 34r

Wowlds for dyeing of yellow with are grown about Wakefild has near new mill adam and about Criglestone and about Pomferatt. The farmers grows them so sells them att so much per hundred or by the stone to dyears. There is no widow is used att Wakefild 1760. The dye all yellows with wowld or fustick.

122 Ms reads 'ho'.
123 Ms reads 'no'.
124 Ms reads 'i'.
125 Word missing, meaning implicit.
126 Word missing; Ms reads '..d'.
127 Remainder illegible.
128 Ms reads 'ith'.
129 Word missing, meaning implicit.
130 Ms reads 'n'.
131 Remainder illegible except the phrase 'society att London'; see vol. 1, f. 161r.
132 Sentence in margin.
133 Margin torn, perhaps 'burns'.
134 Last digit faded.

Wowlds sells att 14 pence per stone and finest and best only 16 pence. August 4th 1760. And some at 12 pence.[135] In the yare of 1762 the sell at 8 pence stone.[136]

Widow is bye some called weeds grown[137] near Wakefild and down in Lincolnshire. The grow a maney they are but[138] little used in these days since wowlds[139] are gotten so cheap only when a green is save listed the use . . .[140]

f. 34v How to sharpen and clear and cleanse a friseing board when itt is sliperey. Have allways by you a peices of cloath that is white. So mist itt over with oyll and frise itt and itt will take the nastiness of itt so keep itt by you for a nother time and when itt is exceeding nasty gett itt stok washed so itt will do again for 10 or 12 times. Observe that you may clean with either side of your cloath whilest both are muckey.

Hair shagg is cheifly a woosted bottome and mohair for weft wich the shagg is cutt on and some has lin bottoms for warp such as long cutt shagg made att Manchester.

There is cow hair comes to Wakefild wich comes outt in Ireland and is sold att Wakefild att 7d per bushell and is quite cleane from lime or dust. Itt is used for plastering and some makes pompilion on itt . . .[141]

f. 35r Att Kedderminster the make a deall of carpets. Some are diced and figured verry handsome and some is woven in the plush way like a coarse thick plush. The make all sorts of changeable stuffs has silk and woosted for womans gowns and silk gowns all of silk. 1760.

Att Leeds and Wakefild the cropers when the find a coalard brood cloath greasey or clamey . . .[142] itt and raises itt with gall old lant and walkers earth so itt brightnes the piece and make itt shine and handle soft. So when raised the take itt to the gort and . .osses[143] all the muck and dirtt out and clears itt so then the tenter itt and strikes itt on tenter with a jak card. The keep posing itt with the end of a pole when itt is in gort so itt drive dirt out.

Cloath called thunder and ligtning is woven as thus with tyed yarn. First itt is made into long hancks so tyed in white and then dyed yellow. Then when dyed yellow it is tyed again then dyed a snuff coalar. This is for weft. The warp is dyed same way only not tyed att all.

f. 35v Young fustick is used in dyeing scarlits and gold coalars the use itt for and some uses cropt madder for gold coalars. All gold coalars or straw or buff or pink or crimpson or clear yellows lett them bee finished with sprits and the look much better clearar and brightar.

How a man may gett watter to turn and over fall mill. Sopose hee has the conveniance of a soft brogly place in a hillside. Bye cutting that place cleane open you will find a good spring. So if you have 2 or 3 of thes places bring the watter all together sett your mill below and give your watter what fall you can.

135 Sentence in margin.
136 Sentence in margin in different ink and pen.
137 Ms reads 'grow'.
138 Ms reads 'b'.
139 Ms reads 'wow'.
140 Last line torn.
141 Remainder illegible.
142 Two words missing.
143 First letter or letters illegible.

How to dye a purple in grain is first dye itt a middle bright blew so stockwash itt cleane then boyll itt in cream a tartar scuthoneill and ackofortis. Mr. Lumb way of Wakefild 1760.

Narrow Hudersfild frises goes best in August September and October. Mr William Charnock and Tenant byes a deall this 3 months. Broods goes best in May June July att Wakefild 17__.[144] Mr William Naylor byes a deall of mixt broods wich goes to London.

How to order to make a stone for a friseing board. Gett a stone of that sortt of greet (to be coarse greet) you think proper. So with a chisill work itt to and even fase then take another flagg stone and rub itt over from end to end has the do when the scowr flags to a fine fase for flaging with all the fix a flag in a frame so keep puling itt forward and bakward and letts watter keep pering one and now and then throws some coarse watter sand on to make it scowr faster and so work itt to a true face and fix your bushes . . .[145] att end has usuall and you may make it answer verrey well to frise with and will last a long time. f. 36r

The prise at Wakefild for presing shallon if the are fild and presed of both sides the are 9 pence per piece and if not filled the are 6 pence per piece. A journeymans work is 12 of one day pressing and what hee does over he has 1½ per piece is 9 shill per week.

How to order chalk for rubing on light drabs or mixtures. When you have itt in make itt one streight flatt side so to make itt flatt take a saw and saw itt in to pieces and itt will bee streight so itt does nott waste so much has rubing itt to a streight fase so then dry itt before fire to harden itt before you use itt lett bee well dryed to harden itt well. f. 36v

How to order the back rowler of a friseing mill best way in doing this way you need no slideing rowls only one solid beam with card nailed on to hook the end on one row of card leaves will do. Lett your rowler bee holden after this manner.[146] The work described thus. Number 1 is a round solid piece like a cheese of 14 pound weight fixed on to the rowler. 2 is the rowler. 3 is the long leavear with a sadle fixed under to lye on the round wheell. 4th is the lead weight hung on the leavar and near on the end itt hangs and harder itt hold the pices . . .[147]

Mr George Charnock byes a deal of mixt broods about 2s 2d or 2s per yard in bauk wich are cheifly frised and the are made of a deall of floks and coarse wooll and are dark blak mixtures otherwise called shepards att Wakefild. Hee sends them to Holland. Likewise hee byes a deall of low prised whites att 2s 2d or 2s 4d per yard in bauk. These whites is made of coarse wool and long floks and shear floks all scribled together wich are made at Hightown Robertown Heckmonwike and them parts. Coarse mixtures are made at Dewsbury Battlee Carr and them parts wich the are allways greasey and seldome make a good frise. Now if the was cleanar from grease and a pound of soap worked into each peice and some poridge in the would do a great deall better and frise much handsomear. 1758. f. 37r

That sort of stuff that the cloathmakers puts in the list called stop lists itt is called eastrick bye some cloathiears and by some Irish wooll. Itt is selled for 12 or 13 shillings per stone att Wakefild to the cloathiears and that stuff wich is cheifly thrown away f. 37v

144 Last two digits illegible.
145 Word missing.
146 Diagram in text.
147 Last line illegible.

that hatters skims of theire kettles or what settles to the bottom of theire kettle take this and dye itt blak and stokwash itt well itt will answer as well has aney of the former.

Another way to gett money is to bye bokin floks att Rochdale and shear floks so have a large pare of cards and turn or card them together so the will sell alltogether for long floks and the cheif plase to sell them att is has att Hightown and Roberttown (or Hudersfild or Dewsberry)[148] or Heckmondwike and all them parts to the white cloathmakers the will sell at 6s 6d or 7 shilling per stone a 15 pound stone or att Hudersfild the bye itt.

f. 38r 1758

Names of the Friseing mills in the West Riding of Yorkshire has att

Halifax Mr Laycock	5 boards
Mr Boyes	3
Mr Carter	2
Mr Haighhill	3
Atkinson at Hudersfild	5
Mr Forth at ditto	4
Howmforth mill	2
Hondly	2
Loewood	2
Dewsberry	6
Sir Lyons att Wakefild	4
Horse mill att Wakfild	2
Mr Whitelock at Leeds	4
Mr Banks att Leeds	2
Frising mills	46 in all

Besides one att Nottingham and one at Retford in ditto both turned bye hand.

Skiners in Yorkshire pulls 5 or 6 sorts of wool has fine head wooll second wooll middle wooll third wooll buttocks wooll tayles and shanks wool fine blak and common green.[149]

When wool staplers breakes fleece wooll the make 6 sorts.[150]

French stones they make 5 sorts of flower out in one parcle of wheat. 1758.[151]

f. 38v In Holland the make brood and narrow cloaths serges and camblits. Theire woollen manufacktures flourish most att Leyden butt the fall short of the English for goodness or they would not purchase ours.

Plases in Frances where the woollen manufactory is caryed on mostly has Olim provincia and Narbonensis Secunda. Itt is said from hence are exported yearly 6000 bales of cloth serges and other woollen manufactures to Italy.

The comoditys exported out of France are cheifly wine brandy vinigar sallt innumerable sorts of silks and woollen goods allso hemp canvas linnen paper glass

[148] Phrase interlineated.

[149] Entry in margin.

[150] Entry in margin.

[151] Entry in margin.

saffron almonds olives capers pruneloes chesnuts soap and the like. This is to foreighn countrys. Theire is a deall of goods from France comes by the way of Holland that wee bye and at Oblivila.[152]

The British Iles contain	104,701 square miles	f. 39r
Great Britain contains	77,244	
South Britain or England	49,450	
North Britain or Scotland	27,794	
Ireland contains	27,457	

Countries belonging to the English in America are[153]

1. Virginia
2. Carolina
3. Maryland
4. Pensylvania
5. New York
6. New Jersey
7. New England
8. Newfoundland
9. Jamaica
10. Barbadoes
11. Antegoa
12. St. Christopher
13. Nevis Montserrat

Belonging French is

Louisana or Florida	Martinico	Anticoste
New France or Canada	Guadalupe	Quebeck
Part of Hispaniola	Breton	

Belonging the Spanierd in America

Old Mexico or New Spain	Chili	Cuba
New Mexico or Granada	Paragua	Hispaniola
California	Land of Amasons	Porto Rico
Terra Firma	Magalencia or Patagonia	Florida
Peru	Terra del Fengo	

The Portugese has only Brasill belongs them in America.

In most of the friseing mills in Yorkshire the frise on a strong hair shagg costing 7 shillings per yard with a coarse board. The hair shagg holds the cloath fast and stiff but itt is very aptt to tear the cloath. The hair shagg holds the cloath or else theire coarse boards would nott frise att all and except a piece is greasey or chalked the seldome make a handsome frise or some blews will do well in their way butt the are apt to frise them white in the bottom if the come to mottalls of fine wool and low shorn the allways leeave them soft. f. 39v

In the year of 1728 there was no watter friseing mills att all in Yorkshire only two horse mills at Wakefild John Dewist and Jon Hewitt and the had 4d pence per yard for broad cloth and peney narrows.

What a narrow list base cost the wool costing £8 10s 0d per pak. Now wee will say 24 pound of wooll att 8½ per is 17 shillings. Now oyll making milling and raiseing 12 shillings.[154] f. 40r

152 Sentence in margin.

153 The following lists down f. 39r were in single vertical columns.

154 In the margin is the calculation, in vertical format, 17 + 12 = 29.

Now this piece will sell	£	1	18	0	in Rochdale market
		1	9	0	
		0	9	0	profitt

and if you make them of jersey warp itt is more profit and looks full as handsome.

Whitned lin or cotton will makes handsom warps for fine narrow list basses.[155]

Them sort of peices that Mr Samuel Stead of Rochdale was used to make called TSB if they was made in the brood way the would sell att Wakefild in bauk for 3s 6d per yard or 4s when wooll sells dear some mills with soap and some does not.

There is good spinning in Lanckeshire has Haslingdin and about Bury and in Roseindale and in Rochdale parish for small Haslindin cheif.

f. 40v Shires in England are[156]

Devonshire	Kentt	Herefordshire	Buckinghamshire
Cornwall	Lanckeshire	Glostershire	Oxfordshire
Dorsetshire	Yorkshire	Worchestershire	Stafforshire
Somersetshire	Durham	Warwickshire	Derbyshire
Wiltshire	Cumberland	Leistershire	Shropshire
Hampshire	Westmoreland	Rutlandshire	Notinghamshire
Barkshire	Northumberland	Northamptonshire	Cheshire
Norfolk	Essex	Lincolnshire	
Suffolk	Middlesex	Huntingdonshire	
Cambridgeshire	Hertfordshire	Bedfordshire	

Ilands are the Ile of Man and Ile of Wight

The length of England is 380 miles in breadth about 300 miles.

f. 41r The weave in France with whett[157] shuttles and has friseing mill maney and works their cloath into duffilds or presd goods has well has the English.

Sopose one them fine moks made att Rochdale the warp (woosted)[158] was spun of a fine short stapled wooll. Likewise the weft and made of broken wooll worth £10 per pak and milled up nisely with soap and dyed either blew or green or scarlitt or stoved and frised white would look excedeing well for womans Josephs and would sell has well has aney brood cloath att 7s 6d per yard. All scarlits to bee taken of tenter att after the dew is fallen on them so cuttled up and itt makes them handle soft and frise better. 1759.

How to mill mixt brood or Sadleworth planes for frises. When you scowr itt do not scowr to cleane but leave a little grease in so att after scowred lett itt go ½ and hour then shave some ball soap (a pound) into a kitt then pour boyling hott watter on and beatt itt to a lather with a wisk then in a nother kitt mix flowr and of cold watter so leck itt on the peice att 2 different times or once.[159]

f. 41v How to order a friseing mill to work and make butt little noice. Lett your wheells that turns the spindle bee thick sett with cogs and to have 48 or 50 in one wheell and 6 wrong staves in your trindle heads that turns your spindles and your spindles to fitt close in the bushes and this mill will work and make has little noise has any corn mill. 1759.

155 Entry in margin.

156 The following list was in a single vertical column.

157 Ms reads 'whe'.

158 Word interlineated.

159 Words 'so leck itt on the peice att 2 different times or once' are in margin.

Some will make wheels for friseing mill of ash fellix and thinks the are has good has oak and comes in 5 times cheapher considereing the working and cheapness att first

Some will make a waiscoatt of strong lin then gett itt painted or varnished and itt is good for rain wether.

Fustians are made in and about Manchester and are worn much by country people all f. 42r
over England and is good handsome ware. Itt will rise to a nap with wareing very much like frise.

Setlins or skimins of hatters kettles would make low prised Hudersfild cloath provided itt was stok washd so dyed some darkish coalour inclining to bloom coalar.

There is a kind of hair shagg made about Manchester wich is of a long cutt. The length is ½ and one long of a shagg. This sort is cheifly worn in wayscoats and lasts very long in wareing.

Observe that the brokers shops in and about London they bye a deall of frises wich are sold from Wakefild. Mr. Charnock and Tenant byes a deal of frises and sends them to brokers. Wakefild 1760. They make them into cloaths does. . . .[160]

David fell into the River Calder April 8th 1760 like to been drowned. f. 42v

Mary fell into the River Calder April 11th 1760 but receiving little damage being helped out soon.

Wakefild is a plentifull place butt itt is carryed on bye men thatt every thing is has dear and bye itt bye little deals has aney place in England.

There is a deall of gentlemans seats about Wakefild and a deal of gentlemans sons comes from a broad wich come to schools there and a deall of merchants and cropers wich will give a good prise for aney eatables that suits theire fanceys.

They make files in Liverpooll and the neighboring towns has att Prescott Newton in Willows and that circuit. They run iron att Liverpool.

Trade carried on att Wakefild. First for gardiners the will carye theire stuff has far has f. 43r
Dewsbery Helland and Hallifax and sell itt has cheap or cheaphar then the will att Wakefild.

Likewise all flowr or meall is to bee bought 20 miles of and bye itt bye small quantitys has att Wakefild and is send from Wakefild so by mallt itt is.

Likewise ale is verry short measure and no better then att 20 miles of and mallt send from Wakefild the brings pints in glases and in pint pots wich wants ½ a gill of a pint of full measure. Some has silver and thats best measure of aney. There is no pewter measure. Wakefild 1760.

Flesh sells cheifly dear at Wakefild, spesaly veall wich never under 3½ per pound and whey itt butt itt is sold by hand not by weiht.

Memorandums. The make coperas and press papers at Heland in Yorkshire. f. 43v

[160] Remainder illegible.

There comes from Rochdale to Wakefild Rotherham and Shefild and them parts to bye skin wool. Mr Bavison John Taylor of Crankeshaw Robert Wolfinden trades with Mr Zouch for skin wool of Wakefild wich hee gets out in Norfolk and Suffolk. Cheif place att Wakefild to by skin wooll is in Blak Bull Bakside att top of Westgate. The skiners all about comes there on Fridays. 1760.

Master dresers and some of the merchants at Wakefild puts out wooll to make into cloath and the pay so much a yard for making when itt is milled. The maker finds oyll and gets itt milled but the allways are verry naveish oftens stealing a deall of the wooll. All coalard brood cloath to be mild with soap. Let your cloath bee well opened and streightend att finishing.

f. 44r Stuff that Spanish brown is made on is called oaker. Itt is gotten in coal pitt sows near Wakefild and a horse load is sold for 2s 6d or so. Then the burn itt and itt is called Spanish brown itt goes up to London and send down into the country wich makes itt to bee selled att great prises. The gett a deall of money bye this sortt of stuff because itt is bought in so cheap at first.

Att after blok tin is mellted in a lead pan lett itt drop into watter then put itt in ackofortis to kill the spirits and lett them stand to kill for 12 hours and the will do much better then if you use them direcktly.

Att Blackath Hall in London near Guildhall the keep a markit for cloath wich the south clothiers brings to sell in bauk . . .[161]

f. 44v The prise of Hudersfild pieces that are cheifly frised att Wakefild are from 28 shill to 36 or £2 2s 0d or £2 8s 0d is the highest cheifly except some od peice bye chance. There is good handsome pieces att 1s 6d per yard and att 2 shill good stout strong cloath. The Wakefild and Leeds merchants byes all theire narrows att Hudersfild markett both Hondly planes and coalard narrows.

Some of the Wakefild merchants cheifly marks theire pieces 10 shillings over the prise they bye them att. Some mark them in the head end some in the tayll end after this manner

+ + + L | – or + + 0 L | |
1£ 16s 6d or 1£ 7s [162]

this mark cypher 0 is a blind mark.

f. 45r The way that in some places the catch eells or indeed aney sort of fish that hapens to bee in when you find a standing of watter has a pitt or under some weir when the watter does nott run over. Put some quicklime in thatt is fallen of itt selff and all the fish will swim att top so take a wire riddle and when the swim att top put the riddle under them so you have them because eels are sliperey and nott good to hold with your hands.

The Wakefild merchants byes a deall of Hondly planes. Some are 24 yards pieces some 17 yards and some 36 yards long. These last are called double ones the 17 yards are of a coarse low prised sort cheifly made of floks and noyles and never makes

[161] Last word illegible.

[162] These two lines of text aligned so that the numerals come under the marks.

handsome frises butt cuts and grinds in friseing.

A rule to bee observed that when you go abroad to aney fair or horse rase to take notice what people wares cheifly most has coats or womens cloakes or them things wich is cheifly of the woollen kind. If you observe att a horse rase you may see 1000 scarlet cloaks so that needs must bee a thing that sells well and a thing to gett money by provided you make itt and gett itt finished your selff. f. 45v

There is a country shopkeepers that byes a deall of Hudersfild frises and Saddleworth planes has att York Hull Lincoln Beverly Hawden Scarbrough Tadcaster and maney places more in Yorkshire and Lincolnshire. Norfolk and Suffolk are both great plases for sending frises to.

Some blankitt makers they will mill theire blankits with soap and Spanish white and itt makes them look clear and white. Some will scowr them and mill them up so raise them in the weett then hang them to dry then weett them over with sap and Spanish white and watter all mixt up together. Or some will do itt they first time has soon has the are near thick they will laye itt on in the stok so work itt in then scowr the soap and white cleane outt and the will look clear and white. 1759. f. 46r

Things bought att Wakefild that comes up bye watter are fullers earth callys and Spanish white chalk whall plaister iron rotten wood besides all sorts of dyeing woods and corn of all sorts.

There is a kind of stuff gotten near Wakefild that is called Spanish brown or oker. Itt was used to bee gotten upon Wakefild out wood butt the cheif plase is some where on the south side of Wakefild within one mile or two of the town. This stuff is sold verry cheap att the plase where itt is gotten and some times itt is send to London and so selled from there all over the country and so itt becomes dear. There is a way of burnin itt att after itt is gotten to give itt the right coalar. A horse load is sold att Wakefiled for 2 or 3 shillings. Shackleton groser in Wakefild byes deall. 1759. f. 46v

The cheif time of frises going att Wakefild is from betwixt July to latter end of October.

Whall plaiseter to bee weel burned and then knocked small with mallat so made into mortar for plaistering. Itt exceeds aney lime for fine work and for white washing. Itt comes to Wakefeild by watter. f. 47r

Where to light of sand to cast either bras or iron or aney sort of mettall in att Sheiffeild or att Wakefeild key of the boat men. The right name of itt is called Trent warp.

Before you cast with itt you must work itt with bottoms of ale baralls and betwixt every cast work itt together with the said liquor with a wooden bealle.

Where to light of pots to cast aney sort of mettel in att Sheffeild or att Birmingham from 4d to 8d or shilling per piece. When you putt the mettal in the pot so put itt in the fire and cover itt over the head with . . .[163] f. 47v

[163] Remainder illegible.

f. 48r How to make a furnase to cast aney sort of mettall in after this manner.[164] This place to be covered up with tin. The fire hole to put the pot in. The vent hole. The long drawing hole.

When you cast bushes for a frising mill you must put a iron pin in the sand for the hole where the spindle runs your pin to be fitted to the hole of the pattern.[165]

The first drawing place to have a large sheet of tin to hang before itt to make itt to draw better and to bee so as you may take itt down when you will. The fire hole to put the pot in must bee a four square hole and to have a grate under the compas of the hole. Then under a little above the grate to have a brick breadth out to make itt draw better. The grate to stand a yard and a half of the ground. The ashes to fall down the long drawing hole.

f. 48v How to make a watter wheel go with with a little watter. First if there is conveniance for an over fall wheel bring your watter in to a sestern so lett the sestern bee just over the center of the wheell so lett the watter turn the wheel the same way as a breast wheel goes. So draw your clew has you pull out a drawer in a dreser.

Then if watter be scarce fix another wheell below the first as near as you can conveaniantly then fix a pump to return the watter into the first wheel or into the dam so when the first wheel is a gate the watter may work the second. The pump to stand lower then the wheell so have a lodge for your watter when you pump has worked as high as you would have itt carey your water in troughs bak.

Where to by super fine broods with John Whitehead a dealer in Sadleworth white brood cloath.

Broods to have a stript list of blew either one 2 or 3 stripe.

f. 49r 1758 Where to by Manchester waste att att a rag mans att top of Mount.

At a rag mans in a collet att corner of Key Street.

Mr Brooms near New Church in Parsinidge.

Mr Hawkers in Marsdin Square.

Mr Blinkhorns near cokpitt top of Market Street Lane.

Att a mans in Salford going towards Joseph Smith dye house.

Att a mill near Mr Blinkhorns.

And of them people that winds worsted.

And of them people that doubles worsted.

Att a mans with large lye in millgett bottoms.

f. 49v How to mill white brood cloth. First sap them well and lett them go two hours to scour them. Then lay on earth so thicken itt up when near thick pull itt outt and lay ½

[164] Diagram in text with labels. Remainder of entries refer to diagram.

[165] Words 'of the pattern' are in margin.

pound or a pound of castle soap or sweet soap. So lett itt go till quite thick then shoot itt outt clean. So swill itt in the gort. Some thinks soap and earth does not agree together.

Coalard cloath to bee scowred when have mild then lay on wheat or rye flower made into paste. Lay itt on with a whisker. So mill itt up and keep starting earth on when itt is turning in the stok so finish itt up with sweet soap or castle soap. Leave some greace in.

Spanish white to lay upon white cloath[166] to give itt a good coalar.

Otherwise to mix itt in . . .[167] when grinding.

All cloth both coalard and white broods or narrow . . .[168] miled thick enough to be f. 50r
taken out of stok and cuttled up so put in streight with cuttles so lett itt go about 10 minutes and that will take outt all the scrimples.

Coalard cloath to bee scowred when itt has gone about 4 hours then lay on your earth and your soap and when mild nott to lett the watter on butt keep the earth and soap in. So swill itt in the stream.[169]

White cloath when that you have a mind to have itt clean shoot itt outt as clean has you can and some Spanish white layed on. Butt if you have a mind to have it to handle stout and strong mill itt has you do coalared cloth onley swill itt in the gort after mild.

How to have a pres the best way. First to the sides to bee made of barr iron well fixed at f. 50v
the top and bottom and the screw to bee a strong one with a fine cutt worm and your iron crow to be near 4 yards long. Then you may sett hard and with much ease. Your pres plate to bee a strong one and the front of the plate for itt to lye on bee all . . .[170] a piece made of cast iron with arches for the fire holes and iron holdin out to lay your planks on when you pull your cloath of. Plate to bee all cast in one solid lump. Wakefild 1758.

Shalloons are handsome for womans gowns and dye them dark browns or claritt f. 51r
brown. If them thatt you intend for gowns thicken them in the miln or if the are for linings or quilted coats the must bee scowred by the hand and some coalars to bee firstt scowred by the hand so then dryed and then you mustt earth them and putt them in the stok one ½ hour to cover them a little. Those coalars are as bloom coalars light drabs scarlitts or aney coalar thatt shews bareish. When dyed shalloons mustt allways bee prestt with two fencins.

In Yorkshire in sumer time the eatt abundance of cabage littice to roated lamb or f. 51v
mutton or beeff. The always eatt them raw as the are getten and has them cutt in to 4 partts on a dish.

The maner of makeing haye in Yorkshire. All grass thatt is mowed att after diner the shake itt abroad and letts itt lye all night till ten of clok day after and if the mow on Setterday all thatt is mowed after dinner the shake itt abroad and letts itt lye till Moanday lett the weather bee how itt will hapen.

166 Ms reads 'cloa'.
167 Ms reads 'w^{t} Feb^{r}' or 'w^{t} Tib^{r}'.
168 Word faded.
169 Ms reads 'str'.
170 Word missing.

Corn iff itt hapens to bee to rank you mustt turn sheep in aboutt a week when itt is well sprung up or a month beefore itt sho. . .[171] mow the tops of. Yorkshire.[172]

f. 52r Some Leeds mearchants when the bye cloath in the baulk they have a yard alowed att a peice and pays ready money only alowing 20 or 30 shillings to keep in their hands while the cloath bee finished and this is called the watter lentgh and some pays all ready money.

Att Leeds the give 2s a yard for verey coarse cloath in the white and in the baulk.

f. 52v Mearchants att Leeds or Wakefild would have theire cloath if the bye itt in the baulk to be 5½ quarters brood. You must nott bee under you may bee one inch or two over. But itt will do if itt be 5½ brood. If the bye cloth finished itt mustt bee six quarters brood.

f. 53r Cream of tartar is good for childern after pox. Itt refines their blood and makes them healthfuler. You must make tea of itt and sweeten itt with shugar candey. Dyears uses cream of tartar.

Godfrey bottles are good for children thatt is in the measels or smallpoks.

f. 53v There is a sort of coarse flower att Wakefeild to be bought that is called measlin (or mashonger)[173] wich makes good loaf bread and is healthful bread. Mashonger is wheat and rye ground together.[174]

f. 54r How to make haver bread a cheap way. Take one pek of oatmeal and one pek of bean flower and one pek of wholson so mix all together as you do oatmeal. So in the morning mix a good qantity of yeast and lay your board that you ridle them on with wheatt flower and oatmeall mixed.

Wholson (some calls it pollard)[175] is dressed outt of bran. Itt is about the same roundness as oatmeal is ground.

f. 55r How to makes cakes for a cough or cold. Take Spanish duice and treackle (and duice of liqorish)[176] and sougar so boyl itt together then cast them in a mold aboutt the largeness of a crown peice with some sortt of a descrption on itt to bee sold att 2d or four penneys per peice.

f. 55v How to have frisings mills the old sort the best way to stand in a chamber. The room to bee seven yards square and your watter wheel to go in the midle of the low room. Your frisings mills to be two double ones and two single mills from your watter wheel to have a upright shaft to come in to the chamber with a wheell to turn all the four frising mills and the cogs downwards in the low room to have a raising mill att one side of the mill wheel att the other side a falling stok or a driving stok.

f. 56v Dyers att Wakefild have 4 shillings for dying brood drab and carries them home in the weet untentered.

How to make stripet lincey to have two piks of red two of yellow and two of blew and so weave forwards.

171 Word illegible.
172 Ms reads 'Yorksh'.
173 Phrase interlineated
174 Sentence in margin.
175 Phrase interlineated.
176 Phrase interlineated.

Them people thatt spins weft att Rochdale for moks will do to spin for fine brood att 3d per pound weft and 4 pence warp.

How to dye coalars that is called modes or points or to dye for a mixter for a bloomey f. 57r
mottal either in the wool or in the cloath. First boyl them weel in allom and then in logwood. So putt to a peice a pound of peachwood then finish with a litle archill. Itt makes a butifull coalar.

All the dyed peices (broods)[177] lett them bee whatt coalar the will to bee saved att the f. 57v
headend and blews greens or red and scarlitts to be save listed.

How to have spindles and bushes the best way for frising mill. The lower bush to bee the hole of itt taperish and the spindle fitted to itt as to the top bush to have itt butt a verrey little taper and the neck of the spindle fitted to itt your spindle to have chase ½ inch or[178] ½ quarter of an inch your spindles necks and bushes to bee made of German steell.

Names of the frisers in Yorkshire Mr Walker of Crownest Mr Whitlock att Leeds Mr f. 58r
Banks Mill att Dewsberry John Hunt att Wakefild Horse Mill Sir Lyonell Mill att Wakefild Hondley Mill Abraham Roberts friser Mr Atkison att Bradley Mill att Hudersfild Mr Forth att Hudersfild Mr Boyes att Hallifax Mr Laycock att Hallifax Mr Grime att Hallifax Daneill Heigh near Hudersfild a man thatt comes from Carlisle James Carter a friser att Hallifax Mr Banks mill att Leeds Richard Haykil att Halifax Lockwood mill Holmforth mill.[179]

How to make a mottal that sells best for mens coats clarit brown and white mixt or f. 58v
blew and clarritt mixt. Scarlitt and peach coalar is a butiful mixter pease bloom and white mixter scarlitt and blew mixter coper brown and white mixt blew noyls and white mixter raven green is prettey mixter lead coalar and bloom coalar mixter light and dark drabs and midle drabs dyed blak and three pounds of white in a peice mixt raven. All the above cloath to bee made in the Sadleworth way.

For coalared cloth att Leeds markitt begins in sumer att 5 of clock and is over at seven in f. 59r
the morning. In winter the begin att seven and is over att nine. Tusday is markitt day for white cloth two markitts for coalard. Setterday and Tuesday for coalared cloath.[180]

White cloath markett att Leeds begins att two of clok in the afternoon both sumer and winter.

How to bye cloath the chapest way att Hudersfild markitt. Enquire outt the masters dressers att Hudersfild and the will shew you the best peniworth such as James Walker or James Booth.

Names of the places to sell frises att both Hudersfild cloath and Rochdale bases frised f. 59v
or blankitts for watter Newcastle, Durham, Chesterfeild, White Heaven, York, Lincoln, Norich, Edinborough, Inverness, Dumfries and in most towns in Scotland and Lincolnshire and Yorkshire.[181] Att Sheffeild, att Birmingham, att Scarborough, att Neasborough, att Tadcaster and Rotherham, att Peniston, att Hull, att Newcastle, att Carlile in Scotland.[182]

177 Word interlineated
178 Word illegible, meaning implicit.
179 Last three entries in margin.
180 Sentence in margin.
181 Entries in list form.
182 Entries from 'Sheffeild' to 'Carlile' in margin.

The Wakefild merchants keeps warehouses has att London Norich att Hull Lisbon and in some parts of Scotland.[183]

f. 60r Peices called Rushias broods to bee made of wooll aboutt 4 or 5 pound a pak and spining to bee 2 pence weft and 3 pence warp per pound. To sell att 1s 10d per yard in the baulk breadth is one yard 13 inches brood to be mild white and clean scowred to have a white strip listt. The lentgh is 24 or 25 yards.

f. 60v How to make a cartt to run on four wheels to teach young children to go soon. The wheels to be made as the will turn of aney one side of the round to bee angled to open and shutt to put the child in and take itt outt att a model of the same. The heightt of itt to bee justt a have a yard high from the floor.[184] This is beeter then a siday for children.[185]

f. 61r The names of the blankit merchants. Mr Ridghill Mr Mills Mr Willis and Way Mr Norton Mr Charnock Mr Daniel Maude Mr Frank Maude Mr Nevison Mr Naylor Mr Robinson Mr Zouch Mr Rickaby Mr Steer Mr Anison Mr Yeld or . . .[186] Hull is a great place for blankits to sell.

These merchants above bye cloath both broods and narrows and some of them byes bokins and bases.

These merchants some trades into . . .[187] and some over watter has coun. . .[188] to Hull Lincolnshire Scotland London Ile of Whight and all country plases in England and Wales over sea . . .[189] to Holland Lisbon Ireland Port Rico to Brassill and maney plases more into America.

f. 62r Blak tin and coper mixtt rings weell. Otherwise ½ tin and silver looks butiful and rings well.

Coarse blankits sels best from betwixt Micelmas and May Day bestt.

f. 62v The ladles of a water wheell to bee after this maner. The one[190] to lye flat to the wheell the other to stik outt as other ladles.

If the mill bee a breast you must lay your watter on after this manner and your clew to go sloap down as your wheel is. The watter strike when draw exact . . .[191] Your clew to go neck in ashlar stone. [192]

f. 63r Mixtt broods goes for frising well towards latter end of July. Geo Charnock and Mr Daneill Mode byes a deall and maney more att Wakefild and att Leeds. The call them dark shepards if the are a dark mixture and light shep if the are light mixtt. There is of these sort of broods from 3s 6d per yard to 1s 10d per yard. These low prised ones are poridge in the mill and made of coarse wooll about £3 10s a pak. Observe allways lett your white wool bee fineer than the dyed wooll bee. 30 shillings a pak for mixtures. Observe to dye your wool a good blak for a dark mixture.

183 Sentence in margin.

184 There is a diagram with the text: it shows a square with small circles at each corner and a small circle at the centre connected by lines to the middle of each side.

185 Sentence in margin.

186 Word illegible.

187 Word illegible.

188 Remainder of word illegible.

189 Word illegible.

190 Diagram in text.

191 Word illegible.

192 Diagram in text here showing water striking a very rudimentary mill wheel at its mid point with a line labelled 'clew' going diagonally down and around the wheel.

There is some mixtt broods thatt sells att about 1s 10d or 2s a yard bauk thatt are made f. 63v
of floks and buttok wool. The are poridged and a good deall of grease leftt in. The are to bee 30 yards long and 5½ quarters brood in the baulk. Butt if you sell them finished the must bee six quarters brood. This sort are all frises.

Modes and points mustt if the are for press to bee always wetted outt in a softt watter. Hard watter is aptt to change the coalar. Scarlitt and point makes a prettey mixture.

Att Leeds and Wakefild the mill theire cloath with soap. Theire white cloath the use f. 64r
castle soap 1½ to a brood and if itt is coarse cloath mix a little barley flower along with your soap. Coalared cloath the cheifley use casteell soap and sometimes sweett soap. The leaff theire sewk and soap in coalared cloath only the gortt itt in a easy stream. The have a wench such as dyers has over theire leads fixed att top of the gortt so puts the peice in and windes itt up once or twise as you like.

Att Wakefild and Leeds the have their bell ropes tuffted with woosted thrums and itt is verrey easy of theire hands.

The way thatt the mearchants bys cloath att Leeds when the bye itt in the baulk white f. 65r
cloath the have 6 months criditt coalared cloath if itt is under 3 shillings a yard the have 3 months criditt and if itt bee above 3s they have 6 months. Butt the cheifly pay some in hand and leave some whatt the call watter lentgh.

The spin all theire fine yarn of Dutch wheels. This sortt of wheels has verry large rims and stand high.

Lincey. How to make linceys strong for mens waiscoats wich sells best. Piks have two of f. 65v
blak two of white and two of blew and two of red or two of red and two white or two blew and two red or three white and two red or to make diamond lincey of blew and red squares or make all of woosted of blew and red diamond or two red and two green.

This sortt of linceys to bee made of good fleece or broker wool and to bee small spining and to bee mild weet so tentered and bakshorn of both sides so easily prest.

The Wakefild merchants has orders for white brood cloath that is to bee double f. 66r
milled. The are dyed blews in the wooll and are for coachmen or chair mens coats att London. These peices are milled has strong as a hatt and sells att 4 shillings per yard in bauk.

There is a some peices made att Wakefild white broods that are stop lists wich are stoped with white coarse wooll and headed att both ends with white coarse wool. They are milled to 6½ quarters brood and made of wooll worth 15 pound per pak and sells at 6 shillings per yard in bauk. These sort are dyed black and cut in the middle when dyed. The go in imitation of the West of England brood cloath. These sorts are cheifly bespoke of the cloath makears.

And easey way of catching eells. Gett one of them piches such has people catch f. 66v
minnows in only lett itt bee twise has large. So gett some live fish has gudgeons or roch or aney small fish. Putt them in the piche and sink your piche in a mill dam and tye itt to some willow that you may find itt again. So the eells will go in to eat the small fish and when the are in the can not itt the same way bak and you may catch 10 or 12 pound of a night this way. Wakefild 1758.

A thing to bee observed in seling woollen cloath or indeed aney thing else to trade with them that are good chaps and mind to keep in with them and when a man gets a freind that hee may get money bye hee his has good to him has and estate.

f. 66(a)r[193] A rule to bee observed. Lett a man go where hee will in England that where poplar tress grows the allways yeild or lean towards the east bending from the west.

The prise of dressing frises att Wakefild 1758 for mixt brood the are 10 shillings for a couple of broods wich is called a cloath or some goes bye the yard that is 2d per yard for master dreser and one peney per yard for journimen. For white broods the master has 9 shilling for a couple of broods dressing. The men has allways one half of the profitt that the master dresers has.

Some gives 4 pence per yard for dresing and friseing at Wakefild . . .[194]

f. 66(a)v Att Norich there is merchants that keeps warehouses for woollen cloath has Mr Richard Pratt and Mr James Smith and maney more the sell wholesale and retail. Wholesale to foreighn merchants retayll to master taylors and shopkeepers. The bye theire cloath of the Wakefild merchants.

f. 67r The prise of a white brood the wool costing £8 pound per pak

	£	s	d
48 pound of wooll att 8d per pound is	1	12	0
makeing	0	16	0
oyll for greaseing	0	1	6
milling	0	1	0
	2	10	6

Now we will sopose that this peice to sell att 3s per yard att lowest and to contain 25 yards long so 25 yards at 3 shillings per yard is £3 15 0

	£	s	d	
Now take	3	15	0	
or substrackt	2	10	6	
So there is	£1	5	6	profitt.

There is men fomerly has gotten 4 pound by a couple of mixt broods makeing about the yeare of 1728.

f. 67v Itt would bee proper for aney man that has the conveniance of a watter wheell to sett and engine up for sawing of timber. So have your saw to keep working up and down and has itt cuts for your wood to keep thrusting forwards by some screw like a rasping mill or to be contrived to thrust itt up by rowlers. This is good bisness.

f. 70v[195] The maner how Atkison brushes his cloath for press. He has and engine sett with brushes has after a raiseing mill is sett with taysails and this is a good way of brushing peice to a good face.

193 Two folios in original are numbered 66.

194 Last word illegible; sentence in margin.

195 Folios 68 and 69 located between folios 71 and 72.

New wooll that is new clipt in the latter end of June or May if itt is made into cloath soon after clipt itt is allways bad to scowr and selldome make handsom cloath till wool has taken sweat itt never does well.

The length and breadth of Hudersfild peice is cheifly a 24 yards peice is cheifly 30 inches brood and a 17 yards peice is 28 or 29 inches brood.

The prise of Hudersfild peices wich are cheifly frised are from 2s per yard to one thats lowest highest.

The comon breadth the mill theire white broods and coalard for Leeds markitt is to 1 f. 71r
yard 13½ inches brood and thats full breadth that the ackt runs to. But if the are one yard 12 inches brood the will pass. Mixt broods are cheifly 30 yards long and whites betwixt 24 and 28 yards long.

1758. It is thought the Saddleowrth cloathmakers exceeds aney part of England for good nise fine cloath. The keep Hudersfild markit wich is cheif markit for them.

At Southwell in Notinghamshire the make abundance of stokins. There is one man f. 71v
keeps 60 looms agate and itt is a proper plase to bye broken wooll and noyles att both white and coalard.

In Lanckeshire the are not confined to the ackt of Parliment has the are in Yorkshire f. 68v[196]
and maney shires besides. The ackt for breadth and length in the watter so that cloath made in Lanckeshire are called outlaws because there is no ackt for them.

In the West Rideing of Yorkshire itt is the lowest place for wages of any part in f. 69r[197]
England for journimen woollen weavers. The highest is never above 5s per week and 4s 6d and some 4 shillings and no meat nor drinkings allowed them. Leeds 1758.

A rule to bee observed that in war time coarse woollen goods goes of verry well has coarse dyed white brood cloath or white kerseys and Kendall cottons both dyed and whites.

Itt is the opinion of maney cloathmakears that cloath sells better att Leeds bye a peney in a yard then itt does att Wakefild because the merchants att Leeds byes itt in the markitt and att Wakefild there is no markitt for cloath. The bye itt att Leeds markitt or else the makears brings itt to theire warehouses. 1759.

Merchants that trades over sea would have theire cloath to handle soft and glovey and f. 69v
them that trades in to the country would have itt to handle stout and strong for these last merchants you may poridge your coalared brood cloath a little in the mill.

1758. The prise the give for makeing Rushias when a man puts out wooll to another f. 72v
to make. The makear finds grease and gets itt mild and has many yards has itt is stamped the have 9d pence per yard for makeing. The have cheifly 46 pound of wool in a peice and some puts 5 or 6 pound of floks in a peice and itt makes them have a better bottom and look cloasear. The give 10d a waltron for spinning weft and 14d pence warp. A waltron is 6 pound. One of these peices cheifly holds 25 yards long so the prise for makeing is for one peice 18s 9d. Now recken

[196] Folios misnumbered in original.

[197] Folios misnumbered in original.

	£	s	d
30 pound of weft spining att 10d pence a waltron is	0	4	2
warp 16 pound is	0	3	4
weaving is	0	4	6
grease is	0	1	6
milling	0	1	0
	0	14	6
now take	0	18	9
subtrackt	0	14	6
profit	0	4	3

f. 73r All blankitts to have a pretty good plump thread and to be well twined on the wheell so the will abide tentering and raising.

f. 74v In some parts of Yorkshire the dry the oats or mallt on tin that is punched full of holes like a gratter and the sharp side of the tin upwards and this exceeds aney hair cloath or tiles for itt does not waste nor scatter aney and dryes itt much sooner and itt is a thing will last a mans life seldome needs repairing. Wakefild 1758.

In the South of England the make fine broods wich are woven in the kersey way and are dyed and frised. Blews the sell at 10 or 12 shillings per yard and when selled outt in the shops bye merchant taylors the will sell them at 16 or 18 shillings per yard. The South of England is in Hartfordshire Surry Kent the West is Glostershire Wiltshire Somersetshire the North is Norfolk and Suffolk the East is Yorkshire and Westmore-land.

f. 75r The prise the recken that a new watter wheell shaft and iron work wood and workmanship lyes in when new sett up is ten pound has so a new stok the recken 10 pound for wood working iron work and setting up. Wakefild 1758. So twentey pounds will furnish you with a cloath mill provided you have a plase to set itt.

All coarse Hudersfild peices to have a prettey plump thread and not to bee to small spun and the will mill to a stouatar board of cloath then if the was small spinning and coarse coalard brood cloath ought to bee spun same way.

Cloath sells well down towards London and all there abouts. There is merchant taylors that byes a deall of fine brood wich are made in those parts and sells att verry great prises. The like them fine and slenderish and small spinning so if the warp was fine woosted of a short stapled wool itt is the bestt for makeing these fine brood for womens josephs or mens banians. Gentleman like best fine slender cloath.

f. 75v There is one Mr Evison or Eveison mercer and draper in York byes a deall of low prised Hondly planes wich are dyed blews and saxon greens of Mr Daniell Maude Wakefild and low prised Hudersfild frises. Likewise one Mr Smith from Norich byes a deall of frises and aginst mid somer the gett him 40 or 50 mixt broods ready against hee comes to look att so them hee likes hee byes and sends orders when hee has ocasaion all the year over. Hee byes dyed shags.

Observe if a man has money hee may sett up aney bisness for hee may gett workmen f. 76r
of aney branch so by keeping them att work hee may soon have a notion himself alltho hee bee quite ignorant before.

Them that has wheel shutles about Wakefild the recken the can put 2 or 3 pounds of f. 76v
weft in a peice more than the could with weaving with old sorts of shuttles and itt makes theire cloth hold longer by 3 or 4 yards. June 5th 1759.

One of them fine moks that the warp is woosted made of good fleece wooll and weft of fleece wooll would look exceeding well frised and stoved for womens josephs or rideing jakits.

There is a deall of stoves att Halifax. 1758.

1759 The Wakefild merchants trades into the North has Newcastle Hull and all into f. 78v
Lincolnshire. A Wakefild merchant send a blew brood frise cost him 3 shillings per yard finished hee send itt at 4s 2d yard . . .[198] profit.

A receipt to renew a friseing board when greasey. Take a stone and scowr itt well so f. 79v
wash all the filth of cleane. So rub itt up to a face with your stone then sprinkle itt over with slender glew or good strong liquor that has been boyld so rub itt evenly over with your stone then sifft your sand on and rub itt well in and if your glew runs of lumps mist itt over with watter so rub itt in.

How to take up a friseing board both ends att once and all att one pull.[199] f. 80r

Described thus. Number 1 is round peice of wood about a foot over and 4 inches thick fixd on and axelltree that is number 3. Number 2 is a rope round the trindle head 4 and 5th is are two pullis for the rope to ride on and to bee fixd over end of your board. 6 and 7 are the links to put into the staples that are in the ends of your board. 8 and 9 is the rope rides on a pully that is fixd on a raill and that rayl is fixd on the axtree. 10 is a man pulling by the rope. 11 is the place to hang the rope end on.[200]

How to make a pare of shears to work by watter for to shear woollen cloath. A pattern f. 81r
of the work.[201]

Your peice to be shorn the length way on and to keep moveing under the shears and yours shears to bee fixed att the heell and point with screwes either end one.

Lett your peice come of one rowler so wind on to another and have a card beame has a friseing mill is.

Dyears att Leeds and Wakefild keeps presses to press thin goods has shalloons or serges f. 81v
calimancos and the like. A journimans work is 12 shalloons of one day then he does not make them up and all hee does above 12 he has 1½ per peice. His wages is 9s per week. 1759.

Itt is greatt profitt for dyears to keep markits a distance from where the live and take in country work 1758. One dyear at Wakefild clars £100 per year from Pomfreatt.[202]

198 Word illegible.

199 Diagram in text.

200 Following line faded in Ms.

201 Three diagrams in text.

202 Sentence in margin.

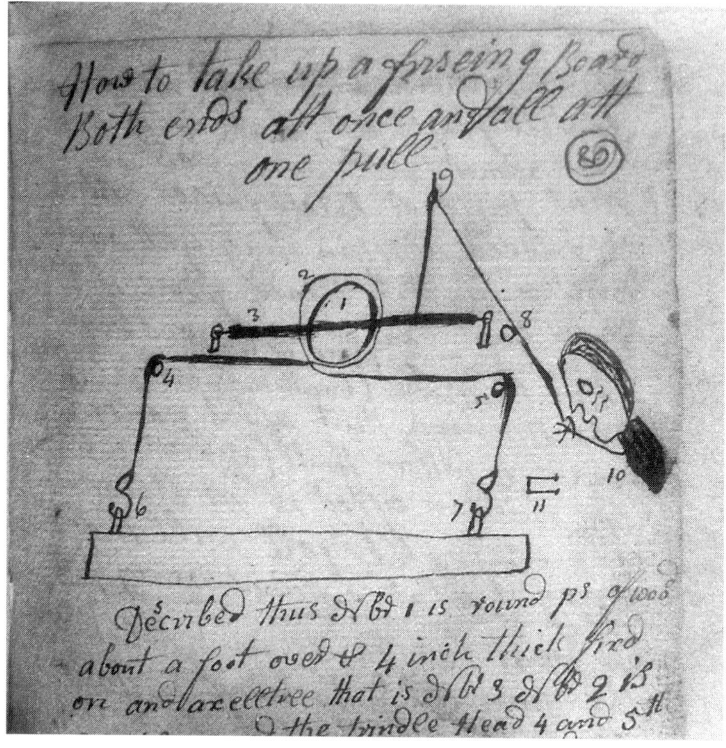

'How to take up a friseing board' (f. 80r)

f. 82r Observe that itt is best to sell cloath att markitt and not to sell itt att merchants houses. The gett more att market money.

f. 82v A rule to be observed that for working liquor if itt is winter time work your drink in a cloase streight vesell. In sumer time lett your vesell bee widear and not to be kept so cloase has in winter time.

Observe that rabits will feed in 24 hours if itt chance to bee a frost and will do better on a low grass that grows on comoning then if the was in good ground. Att 9d per couple the are cheap meat if itt is frostey weather.

Snuff sells att Leeds and Wakefild att 1½ per ounce out in the shops and that is lowest except itt be some that is of bad sort. Theire cheese comes all from Manchester cheifly. 1758.

f. 84v Taisills (not to be over ripe but greenish)[203] are sowed att mid sumer so transplanted att Mickellmas then the will be ripe by nextt midsumer after or in the latter end of July and if the are nott ripe by then the seldome prove good ones. Rapes are sowed att mid sumer so transplanted in two month after or some never does transplant them where there is large feilds of them the grow all winter and are ripe about same time has taisils.

[203] Phrase interlineated.

How to bye wool the cheapest way. Bye of that that is called combers cast that is short wooll wich combers cannot use. Now some men will bye this sort of wooll and sort itt into 3 or 4 different sorts and seell two of better sorts for has much has the give for the whole quantity. Att Nottingham and at Norich are greatt places for wooll combers. Some times if a man goes into the country and looks out and byes tyeth wooll that att belongs persons or priests hee may light of a good penorths. To sell blankits in country plases is good profitt. f. 85r

Leeds Wakefild Birstall Dewsberry and aney where brood cloath is made in Yorkshire the mill two broods att once in one stok and theire stoks are all drivears and works sharp up. 1760. f. 86r

Att Bristoll there is a deall of merchants wich byes Yorkshire cloath and Manchester wares of all sorts wich the send into America. Likewise there is a deall of merchant taylors wich byes a deall of cloath and shalloons and all sort of stuffs. The have all low prisd cloath out in Yorkshire has the English merchants to send into America. Yorkshire and Devenshire and Wesmorland are cheif in England for coarse cheap cloth. 1760.

Or get blak calf hair and scrible itt amongst blak skin wool so leck some soap and little oyll on so heep itt up in lumps and squeese it in a stok bitt to saden it. f. 86v

A curious way of makeing coarse wooll look fine. First spin your yarn and make itt into hancks. So dry itt then sett some straw of a blase and lett two people have hold of either end of each hank and keep pulling itt bak and forward over the blase and opening the hank while all the coarse hairs are swealed and so dye your yarn afterwards. 1760. f. 87r

All peices made outt in Yorkhsire has white broods made about Rochdale and mixtures planes made in Ashton parish and about Steayly Bridge are called outlaws by the Wakefild merchants because the Ackt of Parliment does not reach Lanckeshire and the merchants byes these sorts much cheapar then aney else in Yorkshire and wonders how the are aforded att prise. Hudersfild markitt most of the Wakefild merchants are there each Tuesday or sends some of theire master dressers to bye for them. Hudersfild markit is cheif plase for Saddleworth men to sell theire peices att and would bee properst for all Lankeshire men to sell white broods or mixt planes. Theire is only three markits for cloath in Yorkshire has Leeds Hudersfild and Peniston on Thursday. March 1760. f. 87v

Cheif time of skin wooll being longest is in the month of Aprill. Lincolnshire sheep has longest stapled wooll of any in England. The kill a deall of them both att Leeds and Wakefild. Skin wooll will comb verry well in this month and weys the lightest att this time of year of aney time. April 1760. f. 88r

Att Wakefild the press all Hudersfild strong peices in a stang press. The think itt is much better then a screw pres. Itt does the middle has well has the ends for the are so stiff and strong that a screw press does the ends quite too hard or else the cannot press into middle. Saddleworth planes are all done in a screw press. March 1760. f. 88v

f. 89r Yorkshire men are not loved in no part of England has work men for if a woollen dyear or a cloath dresser goes to London or to the west part of England the seldom will employ him has journiman if hee says hee is Yorkshire and if hee says not and is the can tell bye his speech. Yorkshire men are noted for bites and sharphars.

f. 89v There is blak and white fullers earth comes up to Wakefild bye watter. The blak earth is for Hudersfild and Saddleworth cloath. The white is for milling white brood cloath or basses. How sopose that fatty blew marle wich is gotten about Rochdale was taken and dryed itt would answer to mill Hudersfild cloath has well has aney other blak earth that sells att 9d or 10d per stroke. Att Wakefild there comes a deall of wadd for dyears to Wakefild out in Lincolnshire.

f. 90r A method for returning watter bak to work and over fall wheel.[204] The pattern above is described thus. Number 1 is and upright shaft. 2 is a worm round the shaft one spire may do has thus.[205] 3 and 4 is two wheels that the worm may work. 5 and 6 are two cranks to work two pumps. 7 and 8 are two iron rods to ride in two pulys wich is number 9 and 10. 11 is the leavar to work pump riding on the pin number 12.

Riding on the pulley is as great advantage has well has the leaver or whatt is called the purchase by some.[206]

f. 90v Carpets are made cheifly in Scotland (and at Kidderminster).[207] The are used in England for layeing on gentlemens floors and some are excellent good ones of divers coalars and strong made of strong woollen 2 or 3 fold yarn.

Lin and cotton gowns in the imitation of dark chynce are worn much all over England both by young and old women. These things are made in and about Manchester.

f. 91r Fustians made in and about Bolton are a thing that is worn verey much in most towns in England and is handsome ware. Both ribed cut fustian and what is dresed with shears called baragun fustians. Some fustians has lin bottoms warps.[208]

Frises are worn by few only bye farmers and in country towns and places a great distance from where a woollen factory is carryed on. Farmer for top coats and theire wifes has them for josephs wich takes largest quantitiys worn in England. Then there goes a deall over sea frised. (Saddleworth prest cloath best in fashion 1760.)[209]

f. 91v Soft watter is best for a dyehouse only for dyeing blak hard water is better then soft. Att Stroud in Glostershire theire watter is exceeding softt for scarlits. Itt is so soft itt will wash with verry little soap. The lett theire scarlits lye all night in clear watter att after dyed and washed.

f. 92r Cheif place for makeing fine coalared in Yorkshire is att Hunslitt near Leeds and in Sadleworth fine brood cloath is made both coalared and white.[210]

[204] Diagram in text with numbered pieces.

[205] Small diagram of a single spiral is placed in the sentence.

[206] Sentence in margin next to diagram.

[207] Phrase interlineated.

[208] Sentence in margin.

[209] Sentence in margin.

[210] Phrase 'and in Sadleworth fine brood cloath is made both coalared and white' in margin.

How to make wheels in the spur way best and cheaphest. Bye a strong bar of iron of 4 f. 92v
or 5 inches brood so peice both ends together and cut peices out in the edge has thus for iron cogs and these sorts of wheels will work easey and keep them oyld with cow foot oyll.[211]

The lay theire list 12 threads of one list of thick soft spining and puts itt through the reed and yells each other or if a fine geer each 3rd the skip for white brood cloath. Wakefild 1760.

Observe that aney woosted warp for woollen cloath can never look fine because f. 93v
woosted is made of the longest of the wooll outt in the fleece and more that woosted is milled and coarser itt looks. The best way to make fine broods is lett your warp bee of fine . . .[212] and small spining and weave your broods in the twilled way has a serge is woven and lett itt bee in a fine geer and if a peice is butt thin this way you cannot look through itt itt is so close or a fine woosted warp looks well.

If a man has a gardin hee may have green sawce all the year about and earlyar in the Spring then aney.

Att Wakefild there is cowslops grows in the meadows and wich smells sweet and is good to make wine on. Those in Lankeshire is caled . . . [213]

Butt my opinion is that if a man was to bye some silk noyls at Stockport silk mills or f. 95r
att Macksfild silk mills so scrible some of them in would look excelent well and white noyles are sold in cheap.

Printing rowls or watterin rowls may be turned bye a horse and is best except the was f. 96v
to go bye watter. The can print aney sort of goods prise is a peney a yard.

Printing rowls and watterin rowls are two curious sorts of engines. The one setting a f. 97r
curious print on goods the other seting a watter on. The are made like a hott calander only the middle brass rowll is curiously engraved. The print rowll is wrought full of flowers and the wattering rowll is worked full of a running worm and strokes cutt in betwixt the worm. Itt is my opinion that one of these rowls if the was punched full of holes itt would sett a good frise on cloath.

For cancker in the mouth or aney other scruff on the tounge take bole armonick and f. 97v
roch allom and nutmeg and honey and white of and egg boyled in a pot to a kind of elecktuarey. 1760.

How to take a leavell the best and properst way. Take a thing like a perspeckt glass but your glasses to be plaine common glas like spectackle glas and fix them in with wire has thus.[214] So when you have itt in the center you have a true levill and your instrument to stand on a steel has after this[215] maner and your instrument to ride on it axis has you may raise itt to aney height or to have to to raise itt bye a screw.

How a man may gett watter to work a mill. Observe if you have a place that is soft f. 98r
and quagmire and itt bee in a bank side where there is good fall clear all the dirt for 3

211 Diagram of a simple wheel with teeth is inserted in text.

212 Word illegible.

213 Line illegible.

214 Diagram of cross hairs.

215 Diagram showing stick figure man looking through a 'tube' on legs.

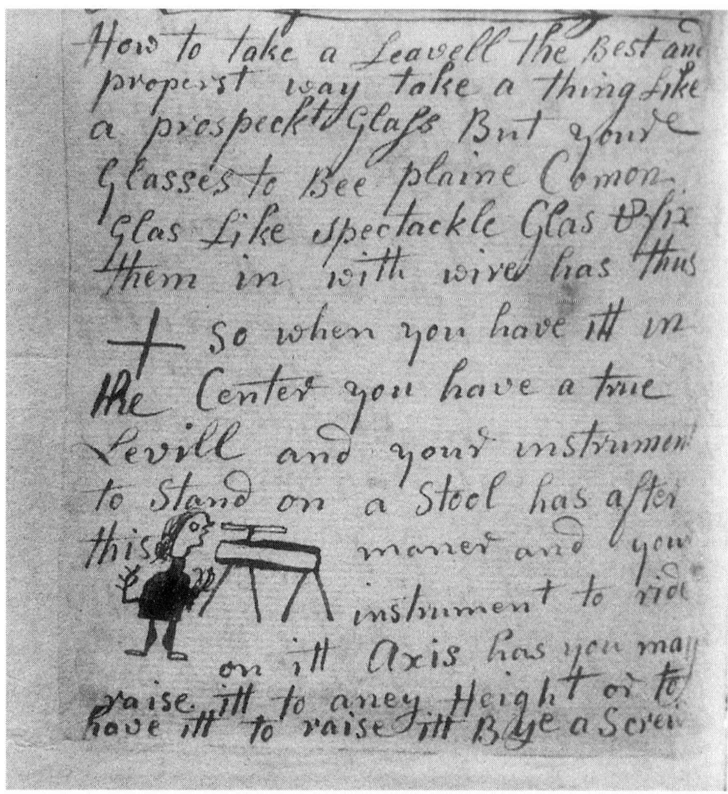
How to take a Leavell the Best an
properst way take a thing Like
a prospeckt Glass But youre
Glasses to Bee plaine Comon
Glas Like spectackle Glas & fix
them in with wire has thus
+ so when you have itt in
the Center you have a true
Levill and your instrumen
to Stand on a Stool has after
this manner and you
instrument to rid
on itt Axis has you ma
raise itt to aney Height or to
have itt to raise itt Bye a Scre

'How to take a leavell the best and properst way' (f. 97v)

or 4 yards deep out of the quagmaire and watter will flow out. Att cinamon hills near to . . .[216]

f. 98v Observe that to wind your cloath on to a bak rowler is nott so good has has if itt was to come through a rayll for when a peice is frised and going the second or third time over the bak rowler itt crushes the nap and flattens itt down. Likewise the rowll that takes of card beam itt is much better to have a lad to rowll itt up then to have a wedge for in the West of England the have lads to mind the rowlers for itt is apt to crush the nap of fine cloath and make itt lye down.

f. 99r The reason of a maney people haveing such a notion that a freese will not ware or last aney in and about Wakefild for 20 miles round is because the are ignorant of the spining and the wooll itt is made of and acording to theire expecktation itt does not last halff so long as the think itt should. When the bye itt the think itt looks handsome and fine on the frised side and the shopkeepars allways charges and sells them dear. In a comon way the are called freese by country people.

To chawk frises and will keep for spotting when the lye in a shop above 6 months. Blow them with good oyl evenly over so rase and shear them and frise them twise

[216] Word faded. Top margin reads: 'under bank near Rochdale Church'.

over so then chawk itt evenly and frise it over again once and some will need twise.

This machine is to turn a friseing mill with much ease itt being worked bye two cranks.[217] This works bye two pulleys and is better then the other.[218] f. 101r

Sopose you take woollen yarn and scour itt and tye itt when itt is in hanks ech 4 inches tye itt. So dye itt what coalar you please then weave itt for wefft itt will look weell and itt is called thunder and lightning. The name of it is. f. 101v

Woosted shagg woven has above looks well for mens coats or breches and is much worn. 1760.

A rule for cloath makers is to have theire weft all spun of a thickness and evenly twineed not to have some hard spun and some soft for that makes cockled cloth.

The shopkeepars att Wakefild byes all Saddleworth planes for narrow cloath and for brood cloath the cheifly bye the West of England cloath. Then the bye Rochdales basses and 42 weights wich the cutt out for singlits and Welch flanels the cheifly have a peice or two in shop to cutt on and a deall of divers sorts of Norich stufs for womens gowns and butt a verry few frises is sold in the shops att Wakefild. The sell a deall of all sorts of rugs blankits coverlids and fustians. 1761. f. 102v

The may bye and excellent good 42 weight att 16 pence per yard in the shops att att Wakefild. November 1760.

How to dress them hard stiff Hudersfild peices for pressing is first blow them over with oyll. Then with a quantity of watter so raise them to a face with jaks. So then give them one crop over if the are peice worth 30 shilling. So then cutle them up streight and laye a plank on them with 12 score weight on itt to press itt down. So lett it lye all night and the watter will bee sucked up into the heart of the peice. So then strike itt and give itt another cutt and brush itt and bak shear itt. f. 104r

Them broods wich are mixters wich Daniel Maude of Wakefild byes in May and June and are frises wich goes to Mr Smith of Norich hee gives for the better sorts 3s 4d so down to 2s 2d or 2s 3d per yard in bawk. Mr Smith cheifly comes into the country in letter end of June to bye goods. 1761.

The press all shalloons with plates wich are cast ones has thus. Your pattern to be made of wood to cast bye and cast of the best of mettal.[219] f. 104v

To sett down in some mens companey to spend money att the alehouses wich men are given to great drafts and will bee drunk in ½ and hours time. For sober wise men to sitt down in such companey except some way of bisness or engaged there the might has well give money out in theire pocket to them great swallowing drinkers. f. 105v

Them beasts called mules are verey servisciable[220] ones and is good to keep and good to dress. There is some men will gett has much work done with one of these mules has most part of great horses can do and what will keep one horse will keep two mules. These are gotten by and ass of a strong mares bodey.

[217] Diagram of mill wheel and cogs is placed in text.

[218] Diagram of mill wheel and cogs. 'Other' refers to the other diagram on the page.

[219] Diagram showing a long rectangle, twice as long as broad with a handle coming out of the short end.

[220] Letters 'vis' interlineated.

f. 106r Att London is the cheiff place for the Wakefild merchants to sell mixt broods both frises and duffils. Likewise to Norich and some into Scotland. The country shops seldome byes any mixt brod.

Light mixtures goes best and is liked best by the London and country merchants. March 1760.

f. 106v The maner of save listing has thus. Take your cloath and stretch itt out for 3 or 4 yards and lett itt be pretey hard stretched. So sew your web on or cord and when you have sewed 14 or 15 inches harden your band with a thing like shoamakers hawll. All peices for over sea are save listed and lettered with silk scarlit blew green and white silk.

f. 107r For a dark mixture sopose white silk noyles or a few fustian floks getten with raseing was scribled in itt would shine and look bright and exceed wool.

f. 107v The reason why that no dyed wooll or aney thing dyed blak will not answer for stop lists is because these sorts of peices are oftens dyed scarlits and when a dyed list comes into allom or spirits itt discharges itt selff and spoils all the spirits. For that reason the use selff blak and blak wooll thatt comes out in Ireland wich the cloathiers gives great prise for. 12d per pound for some of best blak.

That stuff has comes out in Ireland some thinks itt is goats hair[221] and itt verry likey itt is so and why then might nott blak cow hair do has well or any black animal but horses.

f. 108r To bye noyles and spin them into knitting yarn and sell itt to towns where the woollen factory is not caryed on is greatt profitt. Make itt up in pounds and ½ pounds.

f. 108v How to win womens favors. If she is beautiful the are to be won with praises if proud with gifts if covetous with promises if coy with flattery and fair speeches.

The man that has marryed a peacable and vertuous wife being on earth hath attained heaven being in want hath attained wealth being in woe hath atained comfort.

Trust not a women when she weepeth for itt is her natture to weep when she wanteth her will.

Itt is meet for lovers to prefer maners before money and honesty before beauty.

f. 110r Peices called white greays for Leeds markitt to be milled has coalared cloath. Is to have the soap left in. The cheifly scrible 18 ounces of blew[222] into 60 pound of white wool or 45 pound of wool and 15 pound of white flocks. The are milled to one yard 13½ inches brood and lenght is 28 or 30 yards long. Milled has strong has hatt with a list of yellow and white has all colared browns or drabs for Leeds markitt is listed.

f. 110v 1760.[223] Lett all mixt broods have 4 or 5 pounds of wheat flowr mixt up in your soap and to bee scowerd 3 parts outt in 4 leaveing one 4 part of the grease in and the will handle strong and frise handsome or else the will bee spungey and thin except you use the above method. Some rases the dim side of the letters and burls it[224] has soon has itt comes out in loom so itt takes all the coarse hairs of and makes itt cover. Itt is a great

221 Word interlineated.

222 Words 'of blew' interlineated.

223 '1760' a centred heading.

224 Words 'and burls it' interlineated.

advantage to a man to sell cloath to a man that has orders for itt or else the merchant will scarce look att a cloth and if the have orders the will give good prise for them. Mr Daniell Maude Mr Frank Maude Mr Naylor byes a deall in the month of March.

Itt is my opinon makeing mixt broods is has good gotten money has makeing aney sort of cloath for Leeds markitt. Mr Smith of Norich and Mr Floodshire London merchant byes a deall of mixt brood frises of the Wakefild merchants has Mr Daniel and Frank Maude. 1760. f. 111r

The reasons why theire mixt broods made about Wakefild are allways thin because the mill with white earth and itt does not stiffen like blak earth. White earth is a scowring cleanseing thing. Blak earth is sliperey and saddens cloath much better. 1760.

Cheif time of bokins being dyed att Leeds and Wakefild is in the spring has March Aprill and May and all sorts of Rochdale goods goes best then for sea trade.

The prise of journimen weavars about Leeds or Wakefild is 4s 6d or 5s most and no meat only one pint of drink of the day and the common prise for man when hee scribles is 9d per day and one drinking and this is full prise itt was never no more in the memory of no man. 1760. f. 111v

How to lay the watter on to a watter wheel either breast or undershut. When you lay the race att first have a modell the same sise of the wheell you intend to put in has thus.[225] So lay each stone within ¼ of and inch or less and turn your watter over top of and arch so itt will strik streight down. Lett your clew go sloaping down and to lett into ashler stone in a nick or into wood is better.[226]

Daffey elixer is made of anisseed watter and a little elder berry sirrup mixed in and cream of tarter dissolved in warm watter so mix all together with a quantity of loaf shugar. f. 112r

1760. Sopose one of them fine 38 weights made aboutt Haslingden in Lanckeshire the same wool and same spinning was woven into brood cloath. Itt would sell for 3s per yard in bawk or to to dye them the would make verry handsome womens joseps drest and frised well. There is a maney 38 weights and 42 weights and 30 weights and sayls dyed and frised att Wakefild wich comes from Rochdale milled and drest. The are 12d per peice friseing and 3d pence tentering. The dyears does not tenter aney thing butt shalloons and stuffs att Wakefild or Leeds. Mr Lumb in Westgate tenters for Edmund Smith bases for frises and moks or bokins and for maney more Lanckeshire men and bayls them and pays for friseing. Them 38 weights that Edmund Smith sends hee cuts the head ends of leaveing only one small barr for fraid of the Wakefild merchants noweing where hee byes them. The was 2s formerly then 1s 6d . . .[227] 1 shill friseing. f. 112v

Itt is allways pleasant liveing near a river that runs briskly or near weirs of watter. Some gentlemen lays out 2 or 3 thoursand pound to bring in watter to make a kenell f. 113r

225 Diagram of lines and rectangles, with the notation: 'this is to try each stone with'.

226 Diagram of mill wheel [numbered 3] with a horizontal line meeting it half way up and curving around below and breaking up into 'waves' [numbered 2] and a diagonal line [numbered 1] running between the wheel and the 'water' with the following annotation: 'Number 1 is clew, 2 is watter, 3 is wheell'.

227 Word faded.

or what is called by some a gascade and for no other profit butt to have theire fancy and better health.

f. 113v 1760. The prise of 17 yard peices made aboutt Hudersfild and sold att Hudersfild markit is 21 shillings or 22s or 22s 6d and used to bee sold at 16s 6d or 17s or 18s highest in the years of 1740 till 1755. The began to raise because wooll began to advance.

f. 114r Mr William Charnock and Tenant partners att Wakefild sends a deall of long Hondly planes to Ports Mouth wich are dyed blew and drest one cutt and striken on the the tenter so prestt in a stang press wich is best for long peices.[228] It preses the middle has hard has the ends or a screw press may do. Sopose you heatt iron plates in a stove or before a fire presing this way the are all done twise to break the cuttles. 1760.

In the month of March and Aprill there goes a deall of mixt brood frises to London from Wakefild. Mr. Frank Maude and Mr Daniell Maude Mr William Naylor Wakefild merchants does a deal of frise wich goes to Norich and London. 1760.

f. 115r And excelent receipt for cureing the rhumatism. To a pint of anissed watter bye one quarter of ounce of[229] ivy pikearey so put itt into the bottle with aniseed watter and shake all together and take a tea cup full att morning and nights or two cups in morning and one att night and gett a treackle positt each night just when you are gotton into bed so keep warm all night. This medicine is a perfect cure and never nown to faill. Itt is a good thing to drink now and then a glass of aniseed water when you are in health. Itt is and excellent thing for wind. The rumatism is nothing else but wind. This is a French docters receipt. March 8th Wakefild 1760. (¼ of and ounce of ivy pikearey is 3 pence att drugists.)[230]

f. 115v JB NEW METHOD.[231] How a man may dye the lists of brood cloath aney coalar and your peice whatt coalar you please. First double your peice list to list streight so have two streight even boards. Let one board bee of one side and the other of the other side so pinch them hard together with screws made porpose. So have and iron rod for your peice to hang bye the middle on. So dye your list in a vessel 10 or 12 yards long and 3 inches brood and 3 deep like a trough. So have a fire under at three different places. The merchants att London are great admirears of ornaments of the list and headin. All peices that goes into America are save listed [and] to Quebec.[232]

f. 116r Mr George Charnock Wakefild merchant byes a deall of them peices called 42 weights and fine 38 weights milled up thick as 42 weights bye some called swan skins likewise bokins and thin broods wich he sends into Holland has hee byes them and byes them of George Low and son and some of William Holtt of Town Mill Rochdale wich Holtt either sends of his own bottom or sels them to George Low so George sends them to Wakefild. Febury 1760.

It sould bee proper to make low prised white cloath att Rochdale and would answer verry well to sell itt att Leeds markitt or to the Wakefild merchants. The work theire cloath in the makeing much better in or near Rochdale att prise then aney where in Yorkshire.

228 'For saylers jakits' is in the top margin.
229 Words 'ounce of' interlineated.
230 Sentence in margin.
231 Emphasis in the original.
232 Words 'to Quebec' in margin, 'and' is implicit.

All them stop lists broods that is made aboutt Birstall Wakefild and them parts the are f. 116v
sold to the London merchants bye the Leeds and Wakefild merchants and from London the go to America and some is sold into Holland and from there into America bye the Hollanders. Febuary 1760.

To dye woosted and tye itt for the warp of woosted shagg so lett all your weft bee f. 117r
dyed same coalar and not tyed. It looks well for coats. Or some tyes both weft and warp and some makes mixt shagg that is the scrible blak and white wooll together so combs itt att after.

Mixt broods made about Leeds and Wakefild are 30 yards long and one yard 13½ inches brood in the watter before tentered. When the merchant byes them hee weets them and setts them 6 quarters brood and draws them 2 yards longer. The prise of a mixt broods is 60 pound of wool at 8d per or 45 of wool and 15 pound of fine long base floks

	£	s	d
45 pound wool at 8d per	1	10	0
15 pound of floks 6d per	0	7	6
dyeing and scribling and makeing	1	10	0
milling and soap	0	2	6
	£2	10	0[233]

This peice will sell att £4:10:0.[234]

1760. Itt is great profitt to dye a fine brood cloath blak and press itt so sell itt out. f. 117v
Wearing blak is verry much in fashion likewise full blew for second mourning.

The London merchants sends a deall of all sorts of goods into America and the French has settlements there and Dutch and Spaniards. The have all a part in America. November 1760.

Cheif part of theire goods made att Kendall goes into America and Leeds and Wakefild merchants trades to London so into America after by the London merchants.[235]

Calimankco is woven with four shafts in some places called treadles that is 3 up and f. 118r
one down or 3 down and one up and thus the weave some of their fine brood cloth in the West of England.

Hull is cheif place to bye dealls iron fullers earth chawk cally sand wad madder f. 118v
logwood fustick and maney other things. These things comes bye watter both to Leeds and Wakefild from Hull.

Att Wakefild there is money left by certain peoples that is dead to put out poor lads f. 119r
prentice to cloathmakeing and the master has 5 pound with[236] him and to serve 7 years and the lad has 20 pound in ready money when loose of prentise. 2000 pound left so the use is . . .[237] money is to put out lads to woolen factery and none else.[238]

233 Addition is incorrect in original.
234 This sentence in margin.
235 The phrase 'by the London merchants' in margin.
236 Word interlineated.
237 Word faded.
238 Words 'use is . . . money is to put out lads to woolen factery and none elese' in margin.

f. 120r Cheif places for trade in Yorkshire for woollin goods his Leeds markit Tusdays and Setterdays brood cloath.

Hudersfild markitt for kearseys and planes both white and coalard and Saddleworth planes. Markit on Tuesdays.

Peniston markitt for coalard kerseys of all sorts from 2s shilling to 4 or 5 shilling per yard the finish most of them before sold seldome selling any in bawk on Thursdays.[239]

Halifax on Setterdays for shalloons serges kamblits everlastings denims and all sorts of woosted stufs.

Wakefild is no cloath markitt. Itt is only for corn and eatables. Friday.[240]

Rochdale markitt on Monday for bases both thick and thin and bokins and rough dicks and some white brood cloath.

Fustians att Bolton and all sorts of wares att Manchester.

f. 120v 1760. There is one Mr Floodshire London merchant (he lies near Blacketh Hall London)[241] byes a deall of cloath from Wakefild both mixt broods frises and dufils and prest cloath. Likewise white dyed cloath of all coalars frises dufils and prest cloath and all sorts of Hudersfild and Saddleworth cloath frises and prest. In the spring hee has orders for coarse dyed frises broods wich the Wakefild merchants gives 2s 2d and 2s 4d or 2s 8d per yard in bawk and them low prised one are verry coarse. The are send into America by the merchants from London. 1760.

f. 121r How to dye common green the newest and best way. First dye itt in the fatt a sky or middle blew. So boyll itt up in chipt fustick (and kimick)[242] att after itt will bee a good lively green. How to save the end either yellow or blue. If you stich the web on before you dye itt blew so loose itt when you finish with fustick your end will be yellow and if you stich your web on att after it is dyed blew before you finish with fustick your end will be blew and not green. 1759.

f. 122r Breaking wool. There is men that breaks fleece at Wakefild and will make 9 partickular sorts out of one fleece. This is good bisness.

f. 122v A curious thing to bee observed by all men that is concerned in bisness and goes into company. First to refrein from drinking provided hee loves ale never so well for if is a lover of ale and lets his words go att everey thing. The count that man a foolish man and no one heeds him provided hee was talking good sense. Butt to help this remedy sitt in company and drink but little alltho not to never refuse aney because of people takeing notice. Then hee may place his words and learn other peoples bisness and bee counted a wittey man and if he loves ale lett him gett his skin full att home of his own drink then no one nows butt his wife and family.

Observe. The ruler of a house ought to shew good examples then the family is in better goverment.

[239] Words 'on Thursdays' in margin.
[240] Word in margin.
[241] Phrase in margin.
[242] Phrase interlineated.

There is a deall of men wich trades with cloath about Hudersfild and drives theire f. 123r
horses before them and goes from town to town amonst shopkeepars and some of them will take about two two peices on their back and go 20 miles to sell them below Wakefild.

The above men will change theire cloath when the cannot sell itt to theire mind for hats leather breeches or indeed aney thing wich can sell about home and when the swap this way the are shure to gett money for theire cloath is bad.

A curious method how a man may make woosted shagg lett the wooll bee never so f. 124r
coarse to look fine is when your peice is woven have a round barrill cast over with coarse sand like has a friseing boards is cast. Then work your plush on itt. Your barrill to bee fixed and a wheell to wind itt up just as a kigg mill is for raseing cloath. So work itt on the barrill whilest itt shines and looks bright and if itt is for dyeing do itt before itt goes and att after and if you blow a little oyll on itt will make itt shine so run itt on your barril.

The make verey coarse cloath in and about Dewsberey wich the are noated for itt and f. 124v
the have such a name on theire baks that the do not putt Dewsberry in the head end but Row the put in because each cloathmaker is obliged to putt his name in full length and the place where hee lives. The parson took his text att Wakefild in 1728 and said woe be to them Dewsbereians that makes cloath without wooll.

Things acted knaveishly in Yorkshire is when the mix swines grease in butter all winter time is wall[243] plaister in to ground flour when itt is burned and knocked so ground down and mixt in your flowr or Spanish white mixt in.

About Dewsbery and some parts of Hudersfild parish the are great cheats in makeing f. 125v
cloath.

Att Leeds or Wakefild the canott dye scarlitt has the do in the West of England lett f. 126r
them strive never so much. Theire West of England scarlits are allways of fine yellow clear shineing coalar lett the cloath bee butt coarseish. The are of good coalars and extroardnery good frises being a little small round nap. Now cloath made in Yorkshire is cheifly milled in soap and in driveing stoks wich makes itt boardy and solid in the hand wich is not proper for scarlits for if a peice his milled with soap itt is not so good for scarlitt. Now the West of England the mill in driveing stoks and theire cloath is soft clear and scymitt and open and seldome you can find one milled strong. The have and excellent trade of these things from the West sending to shopes all over England. Cloaks made up wich are made up at London so sells to shops in country.[244]

The ground aboute Wakefild is verry dear wich makes butter allways sell high in f. 126v
winter. Itt was used to bee 8 and 9d per pound and bad butter too because of cows eating turnips. But of late there is men comes 20 miles with fresh butter from Skipton and Coln and about Otley wich keeps down the markit. The bring 3 or 4 horse load in a week to Wakefild from them parts and afords att 6d or 5½ sometimes 5d. Jenuary 19th 1761.

For Leeds and Wakefild merchants the best time to gett orders of the London f. 127r
merchants for frises is in the months of Febuary or March. Itt is then when give outt

[243] Word interlineated.

[244] Sentence finished in margin.

orders for low prised brood cloath to send to Quabeck and into other parts of America. 1761.

The West of England tradesmen sends scarlitt brood cloath to the merchants att London so the sells itt to merchants taylors att London wich sends cloaks ready made up all over England both frises and prest cloath.

f. 127v Bag skins are to be[245] bought about Leeds Wakefild Pomefratt Doncaster and all the neboring towns about. So sell them down in Cheshire where cheese is mostly made. There is no cheese made in Yorkshire butt what is verry bad.

f. 129v There is shalloons att Wakefild wich goes over sea wich are verry coarse and thin and these sorts are bad to press. Now att Coventry and Gloowster the run the low prised sort through a hot lead with a little siseing in and some has a way of guming them. Butt if the was stoved has crapes are done the would pres hard or to bee run through a hott lead with a little sweett soap in would make them press hard. Butt to thicken these sort and make them to handle strong lick them well over with soap and put them in the stok for 10 or 15 minuits then tenter them and the will handle stout and press hard.

Observe if a man can aford a thing cheap lett itt be never so coarse hee needs not fear haveing a trade provided hee gets them well finished up and are strong and stout goods.

Observe the poor working people gets theire liveing from the tradesmen and tradesmen gets theire from merchants and shopkeepars.

f. 130r There is some men in Yorkshire that will make calf hair into cloath. The way the do itt is the scrible hair and wool together so spins to make low prised Hudersild cloath on or coverlitds and these men live about Dewsbery or Pudsey and when the go to bye hair of the taners the seldome will tell where the come from. The will saye perhaps the come from Sheffild or Rotherham and att same time lives att Dewsberry. This is to keep people blind for fear aney one should know what use the make of itt. There is goats hair and kids hair[246] to be bought in Wales wich will spin excellent weft and is sold cheap.

f. 131r Mr Atkison frisear att Huderfild has and advantage of byeing narrow Hudersfild cloath because hee cheifly frises some of each cloathmakers makeing and some makers puts a deall of shear floks in wich makes them bad to frise and these hee will not bye wich each nows.

f. 131v If a man observs there is no prosperity where drunkeness is carryed on.

f. 132r Observe there is most chatery[247] in woollen cloath of aney one facktory in England and take itt itt in each branch of itt. Butt Yorkshire exceeds all others for boughisness and naveishness.

How to order to make shalloons press hard and gloss well. Att after dyed and washed run them through a hott lead with a little sweett soap in and so tenter them. A pound of soap will do 40 or 50 peices. If shalloons are hard screwed and hott fired has the cheifly are the break in the wearing and never will last well.

245 Word interlineated.

246 Phrase 'and kids hair' interlineated.

247 Presumably 'cheating'.

Chief time of woollen cloath trade going at Leeds and Wakefild is from March to October butt best is in the spring for briskness. f. 133r

Whatt trades are rogeish wich are used cheattary in is has barbers when the use wooll in stead of hair for grey wiggs wooll and grey horse mixt. Shoemakers that cuts horse and dog leather and fitts heels up with shavins of leather. Cloathmakers milling theire cloath with earth or poridge and soap or frisears friseing mixt goods with chawk or dyears useing logwood for bluews and maney trades more. f. 134v

Wakefild. Mr Mills Richard and John and Pemberton all 3 partners sends a deall of bale goods from Wakefild to Manchester so the take shiping and goes down to Liverpool then the are boarded of a ship of theire own wich sayles into the East and West Indias. Wakefild 1760. (and to Bristoll.)[248]

The number of coalared cloathmakers att Leeds Hall in 1759 is 1800 men. f. 135r

Att white hall the number is 600 cloathmakers and there is a deall more in the West Rideing wich never comes att Leeds butt carryes to merchants houses. 1759.

North country wooll is oftens scurvey has Newcastle Durham and them parts. Itt is cheifly sold cheap. The have 4 cloath stoks att Durham wich are kept for country work. Skin wool is sold cheap in them parts. 1759. f. 135v

Att Durham the are begun of a facktory. The make fine brood cloath and makes both white and coalared. Seven quarters brood and finishes itt and facktors itt themselfs. 1760.

There is a sort of liney made of whitned lin and cotton for weft and woosted for red striping and the cotton is for the white and itt is woven red and white stripes two piks of white two of red and so on. Now if fustian floks was spun into cotton yarn a man might gett a good peney this way. The are worn for mens wayscoats and close woven butt none milled.

Invented in 1760. The have a waye att Wakefild and Hallifax of presing shalloons with plates heated in a stove so the can paper 6 or 7 peices together so when theire plates are hott the only need to stay in press for 3 hours. So shift into cold press if the are bisey and thus the can press 20 peices of one day in one press and never needs to screw or unscrew but three times. The maner of a stove is as thus and heat with sinders or coals.[249] f. 136r

A kind of strong woosted called bagin (5 hanks in pound spun)[250] wich is used for puting rape seed in when ground so to squeese itt in a press. Itt is made of for warp is 4 fold and weft is 10 fold of coarse strong woosted. Itt is wove like saking twiled and about same breadth. Itt is sold about 12 pence per pound has itt comes outt in loom and is verry strong stuff. f. 137r

[248] Phrase in margin.

[249] Diagram in the text with the following annotations: 'Your plates to be made att forges.' 'Your plates to bee ½ inch thick; it be made thus.' 'Number 3 is where the plates are to sett on the edge on a strong grate. 4 is where the fire is made and to bee all covered up with tin to ride on inges to take plates out.'

[250] Phrase interlineated.

f. 137v How to make a weir or bye som called dam. Stones to keep the weight of the watter of best way. Lett your weight of your watter bee baked off with large stones for 5 or 6 yards of the inside of your weir. So fill itt up with gravill then lay large stones upon all so the watter has nott such a force or weight on your dam head. Wakefild dam.

f. 138v Wakefild is a proper place to bye rape seed att. The send from Wakefild seed to Manchester and Stokport and to each town within 40 miles west of itt. Small parcils is sold for birds cheifly.

Mill shudes are a good thin for a gardin that is what wich is shilled of oates. Lett them lye while the begin to rott so sweep them on a heap and the will be fire hott in 2 or 3 days. So putt them in yours beds.

f. 139r There is a deall of striped blankits made about Dewsbery and Wakefiled. The are black and peachwood red stripes 4 each two yards space att each end has thus and two small stripes.[251] These goes of un cut all in the peice. The are strong milled and are 6 quarters brood and exceeding well raised. The are sold by weight att 15 pence per pound the are send over sea and is bought by the Leeds Wakefild Hallifax merchants. 1759. (This is a stolen trade from Witnay in Oxfordshire in 1745/_.)[252]

f. 139v Att Dewsbery markett on Wednsday there is country people bring warps for brood white cloath to sell winded on bun horns.

f. 140v How to order to have a watter wheel to work either in high watter or low watter.[253] Lett your watter[254] wheel ride on slideing head stoks to slide up or down. So you may raise or fall just has you have a mind and have the cog wheel above fixed to the watter wheel shaft and the trindle itt works in to have 6 quarters long of wrong staves so your cog wheel is always in the staves. (This method will answer for to turn any mill butt cloath mills.)[255]

f. 141r The maner of a worm round and upright shaft for turning the engine with much ease. The reason is most of the wheight lyes on the guttion and anything that runs upright will move great wheight with much ease. Number 2 is 4 spires round shaft.[256]

This is a good method to work a pump and lett the screw bee first movement for returning watter back to work it twise over.[257]

A leavear is a powerful thing or whatt is called a the purchase has this maner.[258] Pumps and presses are beholden this machine and maney things more.

f. 142v In Sudderick near London is cheiff place for woollen dyears and mills of divers kinds. Likewise att Deptford there is mills of all sorts and many more has tide mills.

251 Diagram as follows:

red red
| | | | yard space all white | | | | || | | | | space | | | |
blk blk cut blk red blk red

252 Sentence in margin, last number illegible.

253 Diagram in text.

254 Word interlinated.

255 Sentence interlineated.

256 Diagram of cog wheel and vertical shafts with worm gears; annotation as follows: 'number 3 is only one spire round the shaft wich will answer very well'.

257 Sentence in margin, refers to the same diagram.

258 Diagram in text of stick-figure man lifting a lever which has a pivot at the end farthest from him.

Itt is good profitt to make brood white cloath about 2s 7d or 2s 8d per yard in bauk wich the Leeds and Wakefild merchants byes a deal of this sort. Butt espesaly the Wakefild merchants. Now these sorts the makers puts long white and shear floks scrbled in theire wool. Now wee will recken f. 144r

	£	s	d
36 pound of wool at 7d per	1	10	
10 pound of floks at 5 per	0	4	2
grease	0	2	0
makeing	0	14	0
milling	0	1	0
	£2	2	2

This peice will hold 25 yards milled to 1 yard 13½ inch brood is the Ackt of Parliment for Yorkshire. Wee will say 25 yards at 2s 8d per £3 6s 6d

	£	s	d	
Now take	3	6	6	
Substrackt	2	2	2	
	£1	4	4	profitt

How to make a friseing board that will answer. Att Sheffild the make a deall of files and if a man was to get a plate of iron the lenght and breadth of the friseing board so gett itt cutt into a fine file the same sharpness has the files are cut for polishing so fix your plate of iron on to your wooden board with screws att each end. 1759. (Best to let plate bee rowled att tin mills.)[259] f. 144v

Some thinks a stone of right greet fixed on might do for friseing with butt the above method is has good or better.

The way the case harden files att Shefild is the mix saltt and yeast in some places called barm so when the have itt in the fire the keep starting the mixture in and coolls itt in the said salt and yeast.

How to press woollen cloath with out aney crisps in. Gett two hott rowls like callander rowls. So putt the cloath through them and has itt goes through lett itt lap on to a nother warm rowler. So lett itt bee on that rowll wilest itt is cold. f. 145r

Att London there is merchant taylors that byes abundance of frises has blew broods and narrow Saddleworth planes (and mixt broods)[260] and Hondly blew planes wich people gives order to have a coatt. So the furnish them with cloath and buttons and all things needfull wich the charge extragavently for. The genearly gett one ½ of the vallue bye the cloath. There is few people has taylors att home. All is done upon shop board. f. 146v

Itt is greatt profitt for a family to bye wheatt and gett itt ground and nott to bye flower.[261] f. 147v

[259] Sentence in margin below entry.
[260] Phrase interlineated.
[261] This entry set in context of discussion of prices of malt in Wakefield and Lancashire.

f. 148v The breadth of brood cloath both white and coalard in bauk the Ackt of Parliment is 1 yard 13½ inches brood in watter. So the cloathmakers seldome strains theire cloath because the searchars stamps the right lenght and breadth on the blanks when the cloath is in the weett. So the makers sells by the stamps. The length of white broods are cheifly betwixt 24 yard to 27 or 28 yards. Coalard is from 28 to 30 or 31 yards long. Wakefild 1760.

f. 149r If aney pewter or tin vesells bee placed up oposite a fire in a howse or kitchin the are a thing thatt refleckts a heat from them and keeps a house or kitchin much warmar and the bak part of a man placed in such a room is kept much warmar.

Some country people will scrible blak and white wooll together and has lin warps so the weft is mixter and looks verry well for coats. Others will have woosted warps and fine woollen weft woven plane for cloaks and looks well and some weaves itt twilled and that is called serge and drugitt. The last have all woosted warps and fine woollen wefts.

f. 149v A method how to work and overfall wheel with a little watter is has thus.[262] Lett your wheel go the same way has and undershutt wheel is turned and your wheel to run with in one ⅛ of and inch of your race bottom. So your watter works all the weight down and has to work under att after and lett your watter come outt in a large cistern or out in some large hogshead so itt will come out with the more force. If you observe when a barrill is full pull your spigott outt and itt comes with great force and lower the baril drawn and the weakar itt comes out. So by drawing out of a full barrill theres is both ye force and weight.

f. 150r Some will have narrow Hudersfild frises rased a little on the bakside. Butt the best way is to bakshear all the coarse hairs off so rase itt with a little mist of oyll on a raseing mill with dullish handles.

f. 151r Archimedes screw is made of a cyelinder with a nick cutt round like a screw and to bee cutt bothways to screw watter up instead of pumping when makeing of locks or bridges to work bye a horse has thus.[263]

f. 151v In Yorkshire the are verry loyall people to the king wich makes them have good trade for soldiers cloaths in war time and in peace. The send from Leeds and Wakefild a deall of brood cloath wich are blews reds and ½ scarlits wich goes to the London merchants. 1760.

The are verry hard working industerous people in the West Riding of Yorkshire has aney in England and for has low wages has aney in the world has all about Leeds Wakefild and all the west part. 1760.

f. 152v A rule to bee observed is has thus. For a man to keep his mind and his temper to himself and not to boast of his gets for a trade is not worth a turd when every body nows theire gett.

f. 153r Observe if a man can have a Hudersfild peice neatly frised for one shilling wich is comon prises. Itt is had cheap has provided hee had a mill of his own and take one end with another trouble and all of friseing.

[262] Diagram of a mill race and wheel in which the water flows over top of the wheel to the right, around the wheel, and back out under the wheel to the left, changing direction of flow while falling.

[263] Diagram with annotations.

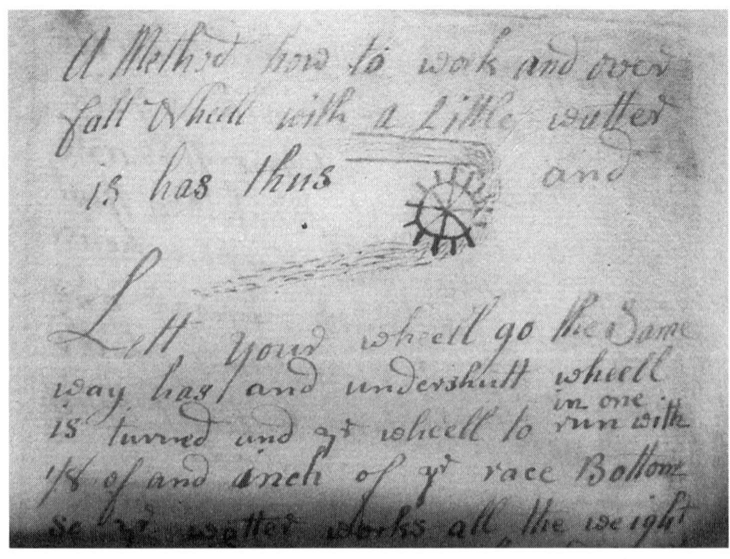
A Method how to work and over
fall Wheel with a Little watter
is has thus and
Lett your wheell go the Same
way has and undershutt wheell
is turned and yt wheell to run with in one
1/8 of and inch of yt race Bottom
so yt watter works all the weight

'A method how to work and overfall wheel' (f. 149v)

If a peice is a good coalar and strong milled and a good frise itt will sell aney where lett the wooll bee never so coarse. A fine low thick sharp nap is most admired in these days and to bee round has a marble. Wakefild June 1760.

Itt is the opinonon of maney that a square pump of 4 bords nayled together has thus f. 153v
will bring up the largest quantity of watter with most ease.[264] So work itt by a double leavear. Wakefild Navigation November 1760.

How to press cloath without aney paper and to have no crisps in. Have two iron iron f. 154r
plates and lett them bee 12 inches brood and has thick has can bee got. So have a cynder fire under the low plate and have a fire to the top plate. So have a screw to pinch them together and your cloath to wind of a rowler and on to a rowler and when itt is on the rowler lett itt stay 12 hours. So have more rowls for other cloath.

A rule to bee observed is to never negleckt going to church has often has conveinance f. 154v
permits for if a man negleckts this hee is nothing butt scoundril and a vagobond and is counted has such bye men that is good men.

Sopose a man sets potatoas in the month of December and mixes lime amongst the f. 155v
arth and covers them well with straw that you may have new tatoes in the month of May when some people are butt setting theirs then. 1760.

A rule for a man to keep his mind to himself and let no one now his bisness.

All the mills about Leeds or Wakefild or within 10 miles about espeasaly cloath mills f. 156r
the are allways att work Sundays if they have not work for all the week the cloathiers are shure to mill on that day. Wakefild.

[264] Diagam in text.

f. 156v How to make coarse woollen cloath look well on the backside. Gett and iron plate made arched as thus[265] so have itt breath of your peice and well pollished and let your peice slide over itt of a rowler and wind on to a rowler has itt does on a perching mill.

On the 11th of November there is a fair att Wakefild for fatt cowes and bullocks and horses and on the 12th men and women hires themselfs. (called stattues)[266]

f. 157r A curious to bee observed that is to know where itt is that the day spring the soonest is observe where the sun rises att first. There the daye springs soonest has in the longst days itt springs in the north soonest and in shortest days itt springs att south east soonest and so all the rest in proportion. In the shortest day itt is soonar daylight att Wakefild then att Rochdale bye ½ and hour then att nights itt is soonar dark bye ¼ of and hour att Wakefild then att Rochdale.

f. 158v In and about Wakefild itt is cheifly drye fair wether oftener dryeing tenters in the winter season then in and about Hudersfild or Saddleworth or aney where in and about Rochdale. Perhaps sometimes dryes two days in a week when the above places cannot drye one wich makes Hudersfild markitt scarce of cloath them times.

f. 159r Logwood at Wakefild windmill sells by single pounds att 2½

Shumak at 2

Redwood at 2½

Coperas is bought att Healand and about Hallifax where itt is made cheapest.

1760. Att Dewsberry mill the grind a deall of all sorts of dyeing woods.

f. 159v Sopose one of them fine narrow lists basses was made of warp to bee of small whitned lin or such has comon bleached yarn wich is used much att Manchester. So have small woollen wefft and nisely scowred and covered in the mill and raised. Itt will look excellent well. In some places this is called swanskin then other some base has wosted warps. The make both of these sorts in Wales with one brood list and one narrow and rased both sids.[267]

Some has woosted warps for fine brood cloath wich are to bee dyed scarlits for cloaks. In the West of England the have some broods woven with woosted warps and woven has a serge is woven in the twil way and if a peice is thin milled itt handles close and you can scarce look through itt.

f. 160r Observe if a man can do a thing within himself itt is much to his advantage for if hee gets a thing done and itt goes through 2 or 3 brances itt oftns gets mised in some point.

f. 160v Observe that all tradesmen liveing by theire trade in the first place the poor working people are what the gett theire money bye for tradesmens money if itt was not for poor people itt would not bee of 1/10 the advantage to them provided itt was putt out to other uses. Itt is working people that keeps up common welth.

If a man is content in is station itt exceeds riches without content for content and necercary usefull things is the hapyest station in this world. 1760.

265 Diagram showing half a circle.

266 Phrase in margin, probably the name of the fair.

267 Phrase 'with one brood list and one narrow and rased both sids' interlineated below.

Observe that the Society att London oftens publishes itt out 50 pounds or 60 for aney best pattern or a modell wich is of a new construcktion. Butt lett a man make the best thing ever invented sometimes another man gets the day by haveing a freind att the societey and perhaps his modell is nott so good has others. f. 161r

Take nettles and chew them and itt cures toothach.

In Lincolnshire and in maney places more the have a great notion for Devonshire planes wich are no good cloath att all butt in shortt these Devenshire plane is nothing butt Saddleworth planes and Hudersfild planes wich the London merchants byes so sends them down into the country and pases for Devenshire planes and itt is so for hats and gloves and maney things more. f. 161v

The best waye is when a man mills coalared cloath with soap to coalar itt the coalar of your cloth and itt makes itt look much better coalar or else soap of itt selff rather makes a coalar look dul. f. 162v

The Wakefild merchants are verry curious about haveing all the burlls pulled outt of theire cloath and the will have them all drawn. Burling and draweing is two different trades. Leeds and Wakefild 1760.

Itt is a silley notion to think to much of religon for if a man does right and has a good concience itt is better then a religous hipocrite and itt is no heeding the pearsons for the pretend to teach people the way to heaven and nows it nott.

In the West of England the work theire brood cloath to a good face butt never sheares them lowe wich makes maney of them when the go to London the merchants and shopkeepars will will gett them drest over again so sends them down to country shopkeepars and maney shopkeepars can tell wich has been drest over again and them the call a towns drest cloath and the like them sorts well. f. 163r

The above place [Hunslet and Holbeck][268] is proper to bye good old second hand cards has breakears and midlears and clearars. For observe where fine cloath is made the cannot wear theire cards so far has others thatt makes coarse cloath and in Saddlweorth cards are nott much worn were fine planes is made. f. 164r

A thing to bee observed thatt there is no woman in the world butt if shee is in want or if not if shee can butt come att a aney thing shee desires and cannot gett itt no others ways then bye playeing the whore shee will nott regard thatt thing whether the are marryed or single women. f. 165r

There is verry little brood cloath wich is made in Yorkshire that is sold in aney shops in England. For Yorkshire cloath in a generall way is acounted butt of a bad sortt. The shopkeepars cheifly byes the West of England broods and Saddleworth cloath for narrows alltho the make good cloath about Hunslitt and Holbeck near Leeds coalared. Butt in generall Yorkshire brood cloath has a bad name of its bak that is itt nott being fitt for a gentleman to weare. Itt is cheifly vented over sea because itt is aforded cheap.

Itt is a good thing to bring up theire children in the fear of God and to go to church to make them bee a little instruckted in the scriptures that the may discern good from evill. Butt has for heeding the pearson itt is vanity for hee thinks to shew people the f. 165v

268 Place names clear from context.

way to heaven and does not know one step of the road himselff and no man of understanding surely is so simple to heed him.

f. 166r At Norwich and Kederminster and Leeds and Hallifax the make a deall of woosted stuffs of all sorts and kinds. 1761.

The prise of makeing a Hudersfild peice and the weftt to bee made of waste or jersey hends.

	£	s	d
Now take 8 pound of waste 1½ per pound	0	2	3
12 pound of wool for the warp att 5d per pound	0	5	0
dyeing your waste and wool	0	2	0
grease and makeing	0	10	6
milling	0	1	0
	£1	0	9
Now this peice will sell in bawk for	1	16	0
	1	0	9
profitt	0	15	3

The bye a deall of low prised frises at Wakefild.

f. 166v Att Wakefild the cheifly mill cloath on a Sunday seldome mising one Sunday in a year. If there is not work each day in the week day the cloathmakers are sure to forecast for that day because each cloathier attends his own cloath att mill. 1761.

And the frequantly frise on Sundays at Dewsbery butt att Hudersfild the never do except on necesity and itt is not often and itt is so bye all other mills.

Att Whitby itt is thought there is the best corn mill in England. For a good contrived engine and the highest and best building of a mill of aney in England. Itt belongs mee Lord Cholomondly or Chumly. 1761.

Mr Atkison of Hudersfild has 3 boards to one mill and them hee has not att work hee lyes them flatt down with sand to sand and itt keeps them for scalloping and puts in dry place.

f. 167r Your friseing mill will go 12 times about for the watter wheell once and this engine moves by three cranks wich is moved verry easey.[269] The figures is number of cogs. Your pump will bee to swift here fix it to number 9 to have 24 staves in.[270]

f. 167v Some places the screw theire scribling cards on instead of nayling them on and doing so one stock will do for aney sort of cards and the can loose one pare off and putt another on in 2 minuits. Theire screws are like them wich screws a hand hook on for a pare of shears wich shears cloath has thus.[271] So itt hooks on to the side of the cards. 3 screws is anough or 4 att most.

f. 168r To make and Archimedes screw instead of a watter wheel and the watter to run in att top itt haveing has maney powrs has there is screws cutt round the cylinder and to

[269] Large diagram of mill wheel and gearing is placed in text, showing the numbers of teeth or cogs on each wheel.

[270] Sentence in margin.

[271] Diagram of a screw with a flat hook on the end and what looks like a wing nut.

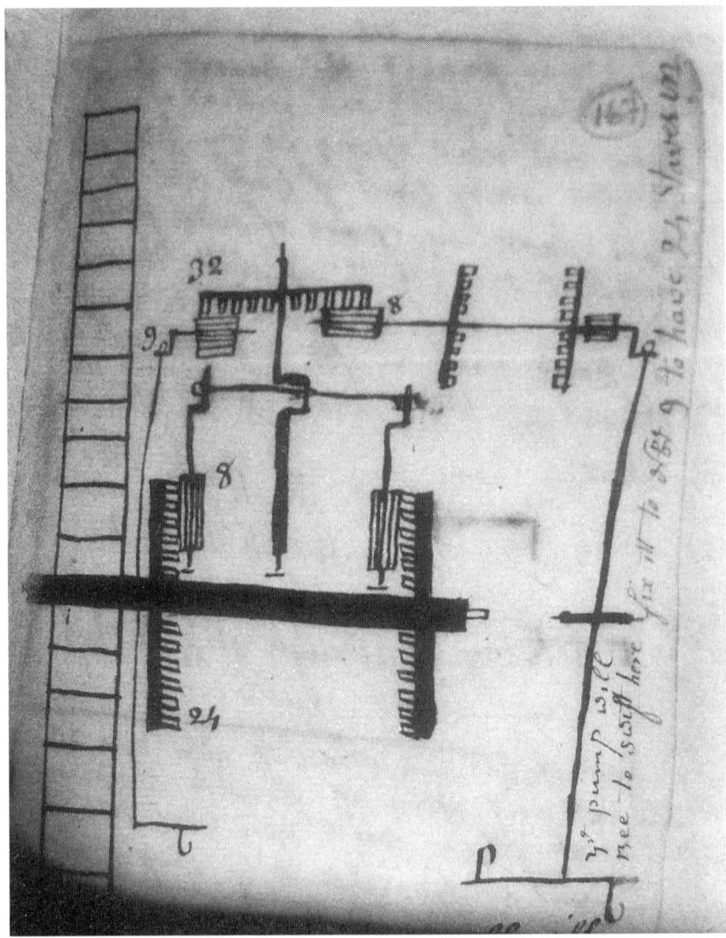

'Your friseing mill will go 12 times . . .' (f. 167r)

make itt large this is and extroardnery engine for to turn a great weight with a little watter has thus.[272] Number 8 is the watter strikeing on to the wheel.

A man may work aney engine by a rope and puleys to aney weight wich a horse is f. 168v
able to draw has thus.[273] If a man byes a large coach wheell by turning a nick in itt hee maye have and excellent pulley. Observe that all pulleys att after putt on their axis to be turned to a truth in the throw att after or to fix a handle on the guttion so turn it round.

Lett all pulleys bee turned wide at top and narrow in bottom when the are for turning a weight then the rope sitcks better.[274]

[272] Diagram in text.
[273] Diagram of two wheels connected by a rope.
[274] Diagram in text.

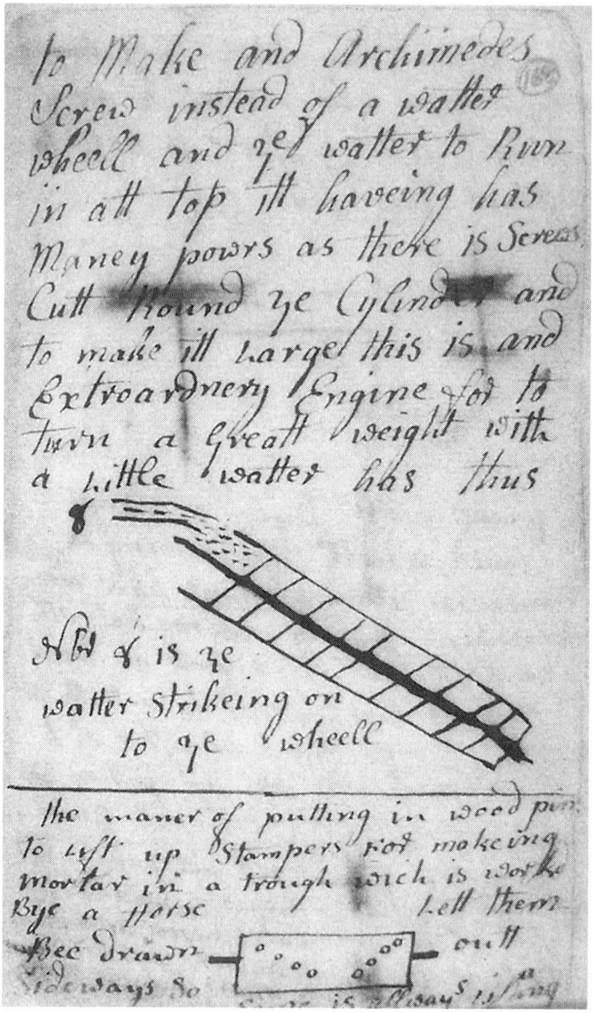

'To make and Archimedes screw' (f. 168r)

f. 171r Boyll in alom then take logwood and peachwoold and redwood and saunders and a quantity of old lant. So lett all boyl leiserly together for ½ and hour. So dye with itt and itt makes a prettey coalar for mixing white along in for making of mixters on.

f. 171v There is a kind of mixt cloath made for the Leeds and Wakefild merchants wich is the wooll for the redly coalar is dyed with peachwood and logwood and nott boyled in allom. Then for the blewly cast the wooll is boyled in allom then in logwood so saddened with old lant to strike in blew. So the mixter of itt when scribled together is a redly cast and a blewly cast. These coalars is cheifly bespoke by the merchants. 1761.

f. 172r In some parts of America their is a voyce wich is oftens heard wich cannot bee seen wich cryes Haowe. Some people is pleased to saye itt is the voyce of that greatt man

Columbus wich att first found itt outt wich hee oftens cryed out to his men when att a distance Haowe and this is what is called the American Haowe.

All cloath mills about Leeds or Wakefild sets att great rents cheifly 30 or 40 pound a year and no ground only mill.

How to make black crapes for womens gowns. Dye your woosted for warp all black f. 172v
and for your weft lett it bee two fold one white the other black both twined together and lett itt bee small woosted and well woven up. Some twines one fold of white silk and one fold of black woosted for the warp. Cheif place for makeing these things is at Norich. (Or white cotton twined in looks well.)[275]

Crape for mourning each third thread of your warp to bee of light blew silk and your weft to bee all black of fine wool and small spun woosted. (For warp or each thread twined blew and blak together.)[276]

Att Wakefild the allway recken that to a white about 3s per yard in bawk will take 12 hours in milling but coalard will mill in 10 hours.

Some of the Wakefild merchants gives orders for cloath to bee made and gives the f. 173v
cloathiers patterns to make bye has Mr Daniell Maude Mr Charles Steer both gives orders for mixt broods to bee made. Cloath about 4s per yard bawk is highest that is frised of mixt brood att Wakefild so down to 2s. Mr Frank Maude keeps men in Saddleworth that hee takes all the make constantly whether hee needs them or nott hee takes them so has some times 40 or 50 before hand so if and order comes hee has them bye him ready and hee nows there shure to go of some time. 1761.

Verry few frises worn in the west part of Yorkshire. The are cheifly worn abroad.

The prise of a mixt brood made of fine base floks and wooll costing 8d per pound. f. 174v

	£	s	d
Now wee will say 40 pound of wool at 8d per is	£1	6	8
And 20 pound of fine flocks at 5d per is (crops or first cuts flocks is best)[277]	0	8	4
dyeing 30 pound of wool	0	2	0
scribling	0	2	6
grease 3 quarts of oyl	0	2	0
spinning 40 pound of weft at 2d per pound	0	6	8
warp 20 pound at 3 per pound	0	5	0
weaving	0	6	0
milling and soap	0	2	0
tentering	0	0	6
	£3	1	8

Now this will hold 32 yards and milled to 1 yard 13 inches brood and will sell at 3 shilling per yard in bawk wich is £4 16s 0d. So the profitt is £1 14s 4d. (And this peice is sold verry cheap.[278])

275 Sentence in margin.
276 Sentence interlineated below.
277 Phrase interlineated.
278 Sentence in margin.

f. 175r The cloathiers att Leeds and Wakefild the cheifley sell a couple of broods together and a couple of broods is whatt is called a cloath. Leeds or Wakefild 1761.

f. 175v If a man observs thatt Presbytarians are of a covetous carefull hollow kind of people and will speak you faire and with a disembling heart and will look to you has if great freinds butt if the gett you into theire power the will shew you little mercey and the are of this kind of people all over the world where Presbytarians inhabits. 1761.

Observe if a man is abroad and gets his dinner and pays 6 pence for itt that itt is has cheap has if hee was att his own home and considering the noveltys wich is cheifley had att a tavern or and alehouse. For when a man is att home and has aney thing of a novelty sopose there bee 4 or 5 to dinner you cannot dine 4 or 5 less than 2s 6d and sett trouble of cooking aside.

f. 176r The gentlemen about Wakefild are of a covetouos carefull nigardley sort of men and does not care who sinks so the can swim seldome or att aney time releiveing aney time a poor pearson and in a generall way there is abundance of men both gentlemen and common working men wich are batchelors and never intends to bee maryed for fear of bringing themselfs to povertey for gentlemen is has Sir Lyon Pilkington Mr John Mills merchant Mr Ricard Buxton merchant Mr Frank Maude Merchant Mr Thomas Norton merchant and a maney more gentlemen besides 100 comon men in and about Wakefild. 1761.

f. 176v Some people will saye that such a man has a good trade and gets money fast and att same time there is others of same bisness wich perhaps cannot live of the said bisness butt in short trades are just has theire managed.

In the West of England the oyl all white cloath first thing the do so raises itt and oyling a peice makes itt raise much soonar and to a better bottom and keep a peice for flyeing and to itt substance.

f. 177r Mr William Naylor Wakefild merchant byes a deall of mixt brood for frises wich hee sends to London to Mr Floodshire and other merchants there. Likewise into Scotland hee sends mixt broods frises and duffills. Mr Charles Steer sends a deall of mixt brood frises into Ireland and a deall of Saddleworth planes. Mr George Charnock Wakefild merchant sends into Holland a deall of dyed blews and green frises and a deall of white broods wich are shorn for frises and are dyed and frised in Holland. Likwise hee sends a deall of mixt broods wich are dyed blak and a little white in wich hee gives about 2s or 2s 2d per yard in bawk and these are made of calff hair wich is dyed blak some are frised and some is prest. Wakefild 1761.

f. 177v Treackle drink is verry good wolsome in a familey where there is children for itt is a thing that makes people have a good apatite after itt and provokes hunger and aney thing that does so much must needs bee healthfull. If not perhaps so profitable itt is healthey.

Att Wakefild on a markitt day on a Friday people are genaraly all gone home att 3 of clock in winter and 4 in sumer and if you go up to the town att after then you can scarce tell itt has been the markitt day. All people is gone of. The are extroardnery sharp people in Yorkshire and much given to cheatery and deceiveing. 1761.

f. 178v In some places the use guttions for mills wich are of cast iron and the answer well.

In most towns in Yorkshire the have Lanckeshire basses to sell in woollen drapers shops.

Now in the years of 1761 the are begun of makeing low prised cloath in the West of England and can aford itt has cheap has the Yorkshire men and finishes itt up much handsomer. The used formerly to make no low prised cloath.

How to make morter for building with by and engine instead of treading itt. Have a f. 183r[279]
thing made has thus to work in a large[280] trough covered quite up with a door in att side to take outt mortar and putt lime and sand. You may have 4 or 6 stampers to work bye a horse or 3 is suficent to work bye hand and this is a quick way where a deall is used for greatt buildings. Let your stampers work in a trough has after this[281] so your mortar keeps in bottom. This works best bye rowlers.

Lett all stones for grinding on lett the lower edge run in a trough of watter so your f. 183v
stone keeps allways weet and grinds much better and faster and to a finear edge.

There goes a deall of frises to Norich both mixt broods and dyed broods from f. 179r
Wakefild butt now in 1761 the are begun to bye frises out in the West of England and thinks the gett better served with cheap penorths.[282] The Yorkshire men are greatt cheats in makeing of woollen cloath. Theire cloath is much better ware att prise.

The Leeds or Wakefild merchants have 6 months creditt with all white cloath above 3 per yard in bawk redy money for coarse.

About Leeds and Wakefild them peices called shephards wich are mixt brood the f. 179v
cheifley have one brood barr of white for the head end and the list is all white and the mans name thats name in full length and place where hee lives to bee sett in the garter. But if the headend was made of red and blew stripe like Lanckeshire basses and the list striped the would look much handsomere and the merchant would like them better. Bokin weft is spun about same smallness of a mixt brood wich sell for 3s per yard in bawk. All them thin broods made in Lanckshire att Rochdale are used for lineing of soldiers cloaths when dyed blews or greens or yellow acording to the companeys cloathing.

The merchants would bee glad to bye cloath has out in Lanckshire [so called outlaw f. 180r
cloth[283]] so the could have them sorts of cloath the want has mixt brood or white brood cloath. The ackt was made for Yorkshire because the are such knaves and makeing deceitful cloath. 1761.

Att Rotherham the will cast iron of aney shape provided the have a pattern made of f. 180v
wood to go bye. The will cast aney kind of cog wheels with cogs and all in or trindle heads with heads wrong staves and all solid has natturable has you can make them of wood. His name is Walker that belongs the forge. 1761.

For a tradsman itt is the cheif thing to have a corospondance abroad or else his trade is butt of little value if he has to hawk his goods.

279 Folio out of numerical order.

280 Diagram in text; last two sentences in margin around diagram.

281 Diagram in the shape of the letter V.

282 Presumably 'pennyworths'.

283 The context of this passage makes clear the reference to 'outlaw' cloth.

For a cloathmaker itt is proper to know where good customers lyes for thatt is a deall to his advantage.

f. 181r The prise att Wakefild for scowring and dying and pressing shalloons is has drabs blaks and take all together light or dark drabs (or browns)[284] is 2s 6d and used to bee 4s and then to 3s 6d so 3s so 2s 9d then att 2s 6d now in the year of 1760. Dyears scowers all bye the foott att Leeds and Wakefild. 1760.

To make a condry to gloss aney thing have a casten iron plate well polished so have a charcoal fire under so lett your peice slide over itt of a rowl and lap on to a rowler. Your plate to bee made arched.

f. 181v Mushrooms stewed are a thing eaten much by Yorkshire people and made in to catchup to keep all the year about to mix amongst sawce. September is cheiff month in a wett season for them.

When you roast a duck put some mushroms in with sage and onions in and itt makes excellent sawce or gravey.

Att Hoowster cyty is a great fair in September for hops has aney in England.

Wakefild markitt is has dear a markitt has aney in England for either butter flech or aney thing thatt that is bought by little quantiy. There comes butter from Coln and Burnley Otley Settle and Skipton to Wakefild.[285]

f. 182v Or there is a kind of claye gotton about about Wakefild wich will scower excellent well[286] and the country popole will make itt into cakes to gett spots outt in cloaths and is frequently sold in Wakefild market and yett still the millers makes no use of it att Wakefild 1760. The used to mill all with white earth butt blak will answer as well now. 1769.[287]

f. 184r[288] The maner of a crane made of wood for emptyeing watter outt of one hole into another where itt has not conveniance for runing is has after this model.[289] So fill itt full of watter and have a drawing slide to putt in att side att after itt is full. So when itt is in the watter you may pluck itt outt. Observe this slide must bee within side of the watter for iff there is aney air gets in above the watter itt will not draw aney att all. Therefore lettt your joints bee close and lett all the machine bee dawbed over with pitch and tar well boyled up together for and hour. Your machine to bee made 8 inches square of good deall and close jointed. This is conveniant in makeing of locks for navigation. Wakefild 1760.

f. 184v Observe that kersays are to bee drest on that side wich the twill comes towards the right hand has thus \ and serges are to bee done on the contrary side with twilling drawing toards the left hand has thus /. Or some will have them done on the side wich kersays is done on then the think that itt imitates German serge. Druggit is woven plaine without twill so either side of druggit will do to dress on. Wakefild 1760.

284 Phrase interlineated.
285 Word in margin.
286 Passage appears in the context of a discussion of substances to use for milling.
287 Sic. There is no evidence elsewhere in the book of it being used after 1762.
288 Folio 183 located between folios 178 and 179.
289 Diagram showing a long horizontal 'tube' with two short vertical 'tubes' extending downwards. One of these 'tubes' has this 'slide' in it.

Twinding weft into warp (on a mill)[291] is not a way to make cloath on for itt is apt to twind to hard. Lett your warp bee soft and kindley twined and sise itt to make itt strong and weave better. Likewise your weft to bee soft spun. Itt cannot bee to soft so has itt will weave. All peices for Hudersfild markitt if under 2s per yard in bawk the give no more for spining then 2d per pound so down to 1½ per. f. 169r[290]

Att Ackworth Hospital maney children is kept to the quantity 300.

Them peices called stop lists made mostly about Dewsbery and Birstall are used in foreighn countryes for womens petticoats and the list is and ornament for border of the bottom of the coatt. f. 185r

How to make coffee wich imitates right sort verry much. Take new barley and roast itt in a coffee roaster and lett itt bee well gresed with butter and itt will taste like aney other coffee butt if you grind some coffee beans down with your barley the best judges cannot tell so sell itt ground to country people bye ounces and ½ ounces.

Peice called white grays (sells att 3s 4d per yard in bawk)[292] are cheifly bespoke bye the Leeds merchants. The have 6 or 8 ounces of bright blew wooll scribled into 3 or 4 pound of wool so then that 4 pound is scribled into 60 or 90 pound of wool so out in that 90 pound the spin theire warp for a couple of broods then the remaining part the have about 4 stone of flocks in and so scribles all together (3 times over).[293] The floks and wool for a couple of these broods is 120 pound weight the must have a striped list of 3 stripes of blew and two yellow to bee one inch and ½ brood when milled has thus.[294] The are milled strong and breadth is to one yard 13½ inches brood or one yard 12½ is some. The are milled with castle soap and verry strong. The allways keep giveing itt more soap if itt ofers to tire. The soap is all left in milled in drivers. f. 185v

The Hallifax tradesmen are thought to bee has sharp and perlight men has aney in Yorkshire. The soyll is barren and good for little in and about Hallifax butt theire trade brings in great quantitys of money wich makes some of them exceeding rich. 1760. Woosted business is cheif trade. f. 187r

To keep a brokers shop with woolen cloath and coats and wayscoats and goods made up and redy out in new cloath is great profitt in country towns.

Att Leeds and Wakefild the shear all with heavey shears and greatt weights on and when the come to a thin peice the cutt itt in holes allmost each boardfull besides shearing itt low and uneven for low prised broods or Rochdale goods the now nothing att all about itt. f. 187v

The reason of mixt broods being called shephards is because the were att first a coalar thatt was inclineing to home spun greay butt now the are of diferent coalars but still the are called shephards. Wakefild June 1760. f. 188r

Making cloath is has good bisness has aney in England provided a man understands his bisness of makeing milling dresing and finishing.

[290] Folio out of order.

[291] Phrase interlineated.

[292] Phrase interlineated.

[293] Phrase interlineated.

[294] Diagram showing five vertical lines labelled: blue, yellow, blue, yellow, blue.

To putt 2 pound of coarse shugar into a load of liquor when boyling itt makes itt stronger finear and better. Observe to hop itt well after this manner of boyling. 1760.

17 yards Hudersfild peice will sell for 19 or 20 shillings lett them bee made of what sort of coarse wooll you can pik or aney sort of floks or hair.

f. 188v The best and shurest way of ordering new cogs when putt in att first is to pitch them outt with compases. Then saw them with a saw with a handle fixed to the lower end so two men may work a comon hand saw and saw streight. So pare them after wards with a cog nife to a right truth and the will look best and handsomest this way. 1760.

f. 189v Att Malton a 11 mile behind York is a great markitt for swine and maltt shells cheap there. Likewise itt is a good place to bye wooll att. The send bacon and maltt frequantly to Wakefild to sell. In and about Malton and Scarbrough and Whitby and all in the north part are good places to sell blankits and frises att.

f. 190r Mr Atkison frisear att Hudersfild has two sons partners. The trade both into the north and south. The make a deall of brood cloath both whites and mixters and the are cheifly one of them rideing outt for has soon as one comes of a journey from the north part the other takes into the south so keeps cheifly rideing out for orders and byeing wooll in. 1759.

Masereen blew is dyed a good indigo blew first so washed well then finished with logwood to give itt the right cast. (Dye itt with peach wood first so in fatt.)[295]

Them 28 weights and 30 weights and 34 weights called bases or flanells made aboutt Rochdale the are much used in some places for childrens lapings[296] and with washing the will thicken to bee twise has thick as the are att first.

f. 190v Chips of the heart of oak or sawings are a good thing for grounding copers or browns. There is men will bye whole trees for to chop into small chips and so sells them 3d per stroke to cloath makers. Observe this is to bee sound wood full of virtue and not rotten wood that is used for grounding drabs.

f. 192v Mixt broods looks well with a striped list of blew and red or if the had a blak list would look well butt the are cheifly all made about Leeds or Wakefild with a white list.[297]

It is proper to cover waggons with a tarpaulin that is coarse lin done with linseed oyll and oaker to colar itt. Itt is good to cover stalls or paks.[298]

f. 193r Saveing the listt and the head end of brood cloath is a greatt ornament to broods. The will look much handsomer and sell better bye 10s a peice. The are done att Wakefild bye women and the dyears gives them 9 pence a peice for stitching and and loosing and the dyears has 18 pence and some 2 shillings per peice. There is a new way of sewing a cord about twise has thick as peney cord is wich are sewed on cloath that has a thick blak list. The are called stop lists. The are done on the cloath in the inside of the list has this manner[299] or thus.[300] This is called a runing worm.

295 Sentence in margin.

296 Almost certainly means diapers or nappies.

297 Passage appears in context of discussion of West of England broadcloth.

298 Following words in margin: 'oaker to colar itt. Itt is good to cover stalls or paks.'

299 Diagram of a wavy line.

300 Diagram of a wavy line with much tighter undulations.

There is a deall of sham doctors goes about with pills and box of balsoms has the call f. 193v
itt. The green box is nothing but rosin and verdigrease and tallow. Theire white coalared box is rosin tallow and a little turmerick. The mellt all down so pours into a little round thing to shape itt round so laps itt up in paper. These men cheifly calls them selfs Doctor Green. Lett them come from where the will the right Doctor Green was a Doncaster man in 1740. Hee traveled all over England.

Price of floks at Leeds and Wakefild 1759 f. 194v

White mill floks 4d per pound

Coalared mill floks 2½

Raisings and shear white floks mixt together 5 pence some 6d

Coalard raseings and shearars mixt 2½ and 3d when wool is dear

The keep all coalars seperate and mixes shear floks and raseings together both whites and coalars except itt is a third cut then them floks belongs journimen. Leeds 1759.

Short shearars comes of third cuts. Whites used to sell att 2½ and 3d and now in 1759 sells att 4 pence per pound.

The prise the have (for frises)[301] for dressing broods att Wakefild for a white brood tho f. 195v
never so coarse the are 4s 6d per peice and and if of a fine sort some gives five shillings. The never give them but one cutt whether fine or coarse ones and coarse peices are rased not much but keept has thick has in bauk allmost because they allways have a deall of floks in.

How to make janock jingerbread. Take rye meall and oatmeall and knead itt with f. 196r
treackle and raisons. So bake itt in the oven butt nott to hard. This is selled bye wheight att 4d or 6 pence per pound. Cheifly the best cake gingerbread is made oatmeal treackle and shugar.

A rule to bee observed that when you bye a horse or cow or aney cattle bye a good one for itt is all has one keeping a good one has a bad one.

All white broods if the are to bee sold in the baulk to have a blew head end of two f. 197r
stripes and your name in the midle betwixt the stripes. Some makes a stripe listt of blew some all white most is white.

The butchers att Wakefild or Leeds the feed theire sheep with turnips. Itt makes them f. 198v
verrey fatt and theire flesh to look well. Also the farmers gives theire cows turnips to eatt and itt keeps them in good order and makes them give more butter only itt is of a white coalar. (Turnips are good and bean meall to feed cows or sheep.)[302]

Whatt meatt is profitable to keep a family where there is a deal of prentise lads. Bye flech and always eatt itt outt in the salltt or pickle and bye pork so hang itt and allways when you boyl itt have a quantiy of pease in. Also when you boyll beef haver bread is cheapest and when you wantt flower bye wheat and gett itt ground. Yorks.[303]

[301] Phrase interlineated.

[302] Sentence interlineated below.

[303] Page torn, presumably 'Yorkshire'.

f. 199r Observe that itt is profitt to for them thatt has a gardin to lett things stand for two years so thatt the may seed as onions brockalite beets turnips and the like. You must nott cutt them no time in the time of growing.

f. 199v There is a good deall of cloath made in Ireland and a good maney frising mills there and the frise a deall of goods. The frising trade and mills where invented att first in Holland so the gett them into Irland then into England so into Scotland then into Wales in 1742.

There is a deall of white cloath send to London and into Holland. The go drestt so are dyed and frised or prest at London or Holand. There is a maney shalloons that goes in the white to . . .[304]

f. 200r Rushia cloath for Leeds markitt is spun about the same as the spin rough dicks thatt are made in and about Rochdale. The wool the are made on is little better then rough dick wooll. The are milled stronger then rough dick are and nott much. The prise is near 2s a yard or some byes them bye the cloath that is a couple of broods att 4 pounds 10s.

The dye good coalars in Holland and has theire wares cheaper by far then the have in England. The sell a deall of woods into England.

f. 200v The Wakefild merchants sells a deall of fine Sadleworth planes into Ireland. The are of a good sort worth 5s or 6s a yard and the are very cautious about haveing burls picked outt. The will not send a peice with a burll in though itt bee never such a coarse one and the are all fine drawn.[305]

f. 201r One Mrs Wakefild att Kendall has frising milns and keep them employed with their own goods. 1758.

The have 10s att Wakefild for dyeing a cloath black thatt is a couple of peices.

f. 201v Veall sels dear att Wakefild. A fatt calf the give 26 or 28 shillings. The butchers sells all joints by the hand and for a loyn about 7 or 8 pound the will sell for 2s 6d if not more. 1758.

f. 202r Observe thatt you may sett a mill in aney place[306] where there is ¾ of a yard fall of watter and no less will do for a mill and undershott.

All mixtt broods or coalard broods if the are to bee sold in baulk or if the are sold to the Leeds or Wakfild merchants the must bee letered in the head end in the garter and nott in the bars because the merchants will send no letters in no peice of so the rive the letters of.

f. 202v All shalloons or linceys to bee weell wisked of both sides before the are taken of tenter to wisk the coarse hairs of.

f. 203r At Wakefild the always have 10d pence a peice for tentering and planeing down and bailing bokins. Journimen has and the master has 2s. One Mr Lumb in Westgate is the man thatt serves all Wakefild thatt way and for Lankeshire tradesmen his brother is a dyer of bokins.

304 Word missing.
305 One line missing below.
306 Word faded, sense is clear from context.

Itt is greatt profitt to make of them peices thatt are called dark mottalls for when you dye your wooll blak lett itt bee never so coarse itt will kill all the kemps and roug hairs so scrible some fine white wooll with itt and your pieice will look fine. f. 203v

Att Kendall the have only 6 pence a peice for frising theire 17 yards cottons. The where used to bee 10d pence. The frise a maney of them in the white and chalks them. The have an engine to chalk them with thatt is sett with chalk and theire raising mills are all sett with jak cards and itt answer well to raise with. Make a deall of blankits. f. 204r

Itt is greatt beneffitt to bye mild sheep leather so gett them dyed blak for waiscoats. The will last exceding weell or for breeches. York. f. 204v

Searge stripett with blew or red for waiscoats or peticoats to have two piks[307] of white and two of blew or red. Mill them with soap and the look weel.

All blankits to have 16 threads of one listt and the two out most threads to be of two fold yarn. Blankits to bee well tentered and streached well both in breadth and lentgh and cleane mild and well raised. Yorks.

Att Sheffild the have abundance of them low broad over fall watter wheels. The use them for to grind and finish all sortts of theire goods. Shefild mill rights are counted extroardnery workmen att makeing aney sort of engine. f. 205v

All frising milns to have theire plush fixed on with screws and if the have constant work to turn theire plush once every week and itt will both frise better and lastt longer. Your wooster shag to be worth 3s a yard for frising on.

Mill rights in Yorkshire always reckens thatt 5 pound will make a faleing stok wood and workmanship. To liftt the feet up the putt arms through shave and a rowler att end.

Fine head skin wooll sells verrey chap att Wakefild and Leeds. The best is six pound or 6 pound ten and is useed sell att 8 or 9 pound a pak. Augustt 26th 1757. (Itt sells £8:12:0 now in 1759.)[308] f. 206r

There is 3 sorts of Hondley planes 17 yards peice and 24 yards peices and 36 or 38 yards peices. These lastt are called long Hondleys the cheifly sold miled and in the baulk.

A reslution never to drink to exces nor ett to excess (nor call att James Scofilds)[309] butt always to bee good tempered when in drink yours JB. f. 207r

A reslution never to strk my wife nor mention shop brk[310] no more. June 25th 1757.

A fish skin will do verrey well for a frising board to frise peices the first time over you mustt fix your skin on to your frising board as the maner the fix them when the make books or letter cases.

307 Word interlineated.
308 Sentence interlineated below.
309 Phrase interlineated above.
310 These letters, 'brk', are quite distinct in the Ms, meaning unclear.

How to order millers dresers or frisers or dyers. Always make them to bring a note of the quantity of goods the liver begining with number one.

f. 207v For Leeds Markit. Peices caled Rushias the are made of wooll aboutt £3 10s or 4 pound a pack and are round spining. The bye them bye the cloath that is a couple of broods. Theire prise is cheif £3 10s for 3 pounds for a cloath. The length is to bee 24 or 23 yards. A brood these sorts of peices begins to go weell again the haveing lostt the Rushia trade for seven years bye past. July 4th 1757.

There is fullers earth to bee bought att Wakefild or Leeds of a white sortt thatt comes from the Ile of White. The sell itt att 14 pense a stroke. Itt is the bestt for whites milling with.

f. 208r Att Wakefild there is a sortt of cloath made for womans peticoats. The are blak and red stripe and 4 stripes outt bottom each yard ½ quarter long. When mild the are 6 quarters brood and as strong as a hatt. The are to be well rased of both sides.

The maner of piking goosberreys in Yorkshire. The putt them into a twild sack or poke so shakes and rubs them to and from and it does them verrey cleane.

All mearchants or country tradsmen to have a book filled with pattarns to gett orders by and the prise fixed to each patren.

f. 208v Raven greay is a gentel coalar for most sorts of old or midle aged men to ware.[311] This coalar is made of blak dyed wool with a little whit scribled with it.

Some coper browns to have 4 pound of blew wool (or 2 pound in two peices)[312] scribled in one peice and itt makes a prettey mixture in brown[313] cloath.

f. 209r The list of all white brood cloath to have 10 threads of double twined yarn and the outmost thread to bee thicker spining then the other. Itt makes a peice handle stronger and stouter.

f. 209v Ship named the Godolphin or the Liverpooll privateer comanded by Captain Wiliam Hutchison broughtt in a prise valued att 25,000 pound June 26th 1757 in this ship there is many Rochdale men aboard. (Another ship the 4th of August 1757.)[314]

f. 210v Itt is a verrey pleasant thing where the have conveniance for a boatt to swim in on the river and to have a companey of musitians on board to play as you swim long and itt sounds charming and sweet so take a bottle of good ale on board.

Itt is profitable to sow cowcumber[315] on a muck midin thatt has horse dung in. The will answer verrey well. The seed is the pipins in the inside of a ripe one.

It is profitt to bring up young pigs or to keep a breeding sow to breed on so sell young pigs to country farms or feed them fat is profit.

Meashonger and wholson makes good houshould bread or to mix them together does well.

311 Ms reads 'war'.
312 Phrase interlineated.
313 Ms reads 'br'.
314 Sentence in margin.
315 Ms reads 'cowcum'.

The list of some peices to bee two of red two of blak 4 of olive coalar threads. The red to bee midlemost. f. 211r

How to make the coarsest loafs. By a quantity of bran and dres itt thorough a verrey coarse cloath. Then grind itt over again twise or thrice. So to 10 pound of itt mix 3 pound of oatmeall so make your loafs of itt with yest in. f. 211v

Grind barley into meall so mix itt with oatmeal for cakes.[316]

How to make wheatt and rye loafs the best and cheapest way. You must grind wheat and rye and white oates nott shilled all down together so make your loaf of itt. f. 212r

How to make wheatt loafs the best way. Grind wheatt and white oates that are shilled both together so make your lofs on itt.

For makeing the finest bread you must have of the finest flower and a quantity of spanish white mixt together to 10 pound of flower mix 3 pound of Spanish whitte so make your bread with much yeast in.

Mr Yelar the wool man lives att Battla near Wakefeild and byes a deall of wool att Wakefild markett and seels itt again att Rochdale markitt in Lankeshire. 1758. f. 213r

John Taylor att Rochdale byes a deall of skin wooll of Robert Foster near the Bridge skiner att Wakefild Yorkshire. 1758.

How to make punch the beset and cheapestt way. Take a quantity of rum or gin in to your punch bowll. So putt to itt what shugar you plase so sett a quantity of milk over the fire and when itt boyls putt itt to your liquor. This is a verrey wholsom drinking. f. 214r

Elderberreys made in to wine and some putt into hott ale is good drinking.

Cowslop wine is good for weak people or for maney disorders.

Scotch blankets[317] bee made stript each ½ yard red and black of 2 inch strip before mild and to bee mild to 5½ qarters brood[318] and bee strong miled. f. 214v

Them thatt makes both white and coalared cloath to have their cards for either sortt one pare for white another pare for coalar and then the will be clean.

How to[320] have print rowles the cheapest way. For your midle rowll make a pattern of wood with figures cutt in so gett the same made of cast iron. Your wood rowles to bee well seasoned and make of softish wood your stove to bee near the rowles thatt you may change your eatters often. f. 21_r[319]

The right sortt of a rowl is made of brass then engraven att after all sort of figures.

Lead weights to have a hole in to hold oyll in and to bee made after this model.[321] The are to bee shaped like a wedge and the small end to hooken the shears bak. f. 21_v

316 Ms reads 'cak'.
317 One word faded, 'to'?
318 Ms reads 'broo'.
319 Folio number illegible, this folio located between folios 214 and 215.
320 Ms faded, meaning implicit.
321 Diagram showing a pyramid shape with a rounded top.

f. 215r Potaotes[322] will make bread with a litle flowr or you may make good puddings of pottatars if you chuse itt.

Att Holland is a good place to sell frises att allso in Ireland and Scotland and in Africa and Amerrica and att Lisbon is a plase for bokins and frises of all sorts.

f. 215v How to make striped[323] lincey thatt looks weell. Have two picks of red and two of white. So weave to the quantity of one inch then weave an have of inch all of blue. So weave forward for mens waiscoats.

Shalloons are used much for woman's quilted coates and is dyed clare yellows or pink coalar or scarlitt or crimpson and maney other coalars. Yellow damask looks weell for womans gowns.

Lincey looks well blew and white brood stripe 3 qarters of an inch[324] brood strip when . . .[325]

322 Ms reads 'pot. . .es'; sense clear from rest of entry.

323 Ms faded; meaning implicit.

324 Ms reads 'inc'.

325 Remainder of page and last two sheets too faded and torn to read clearly.

Volume Two

Inside of front cover

Archimedes screw for screwing up watter. To be worked by a horse when making locks or bridges when there is much watter and cannot be pumped. This is a double screw.[1] Single screw is this.[2] Made round a cylindar of 10 inches round with a nick cut round in form of a screw. Boards to bee putt round your cylinder has thus[3] so nailed and tard in a covered with boards . . .[4]

Norich pakhorses comes into Wakefild each Tuesday and waggons sets of 2 or 3 times f. 1r
a week for there. Likwise the go forward to Hallifax and the carryers lives about Halifax within 3 or 4 miles or 30. 1761.

The above waggons and horses brings a deall of wooll and coalard noyls from Norich to Wakefild Leeds and Halifax.

The Wakefild merchants buys abundance of fine Saddleworth planes at Hudersfild market. Likewise a deall of shalloons att Halifax markett. The are cheiff merchants at both markets for byeing great maney. 1761.

Some of the Wakefild merchants when they putt out a peice of broad cloth mixter the call itt and od dozen wich in some places broads are called dozens.

If you use swines dung let it be well drained through a seiff or itt is apt to mill the shudes in wich comes out in the dung and shews itt moatey.

For all breast wheells or under fall let the water strike on to fall streight down wich f. 1v
you see has above.[5] Number 5 is the watter number 4 is your clew to run in a nick cutt in stone or wood and to stand leaning has thus.[6] Wakefild friseing mill watter is laid excellent well on. 1760.

Some of the Wakefild merchants dyes red blew or green frises wich are basses has 38 weights milled up. Mr Norton in Wringate byes his from Manchester. Mr. Frank Maude byes his from Manchester and cottons frises from Hallifax. Now if the above peices was thickned up with soap the would look verry well butt the are allways thin and shews the threads wich makes frise never bee handsome.

Wakefild 1760. Observe that the weave all coalard broods with weet spows and when f. 2r
the weave 6 or 7 yards the pull it of beame and hancks itt up or else the heatt on the beame and if bloomey coalars the fade so itt is best to pull all coalars of has you weave each 6 or 7 yards and itt keeps them too theire coalars.

[1] Diagram in text showing a wheel to be turned by the horse and gearing and pulleys to attach to the Archimedes screw. Remainder of entries placed in margins around diagram; one too faded to read.

[2] Small diagram very blurred.

[3] Small diagram of a cup-shaped cross section.

[4] Two words illegible.

[5] Diagram in text placed above the entry shows a water wheel with water flowing towards it. A line drawn at about a 45 degree angle between the water and the wheel is numbered '4'.

[6] Diagram in text below, again showing wheel with a line at 45 degrees.

For country shop and country people the will not bye woollen cloath except itt bee stout and strong that makes Hudersfild cloath go of cheifly well and itt is only made strong with grease and earth and these sorts will frise handsomer then good sorts of peices such has is made in Saddleworth for them is oftens cleane and free from grease and earth and the do not frise so well.

The frise about Halifax a good deall of serges wich are made of black and white wool scribled together so mill up with soap and the look verry well.

f. 2v Att Leeds and Wakefild there is men kept called searchars wich some takes care of dressers shops and tenters others takes care of the cloath mills and there is for cloath mills searchars all over Yorkshire and the searchers for shops is to take care to see the do not work with cards or work fullers earth into cloath when rowing itt weett and the searchers for tenters are to see that cloath is not drawn in length or sett in breadth no more then what the ackt runs to and mill searchers are to stamp the right length and breadth on to every cloath has itt comes out in the mill when wett in watter and to see no cloath is made no narrower then 1 yard 13½ inches brood to liver out in the mill and if aney of these things bee found in faultt the penalty runs to 40s butt the are oftens catched and gets off as easy has the can. Searchers is paid out in the excise money.

f. 3r Observe that aney white thing that has a kind of a blewley cast with itt looks fairar and handsomer then then clear white and if all Lankeshire Basses had the lant coalard when wet[7] out att first with a little indigo they would look[8] well. Or if you mixt it in earth and water att after the grease is outt itt would do better.

The coalared brood cloathmakers wich keeps Leeds markit the allways observes what coalars goes of best has some times mixt broods or browns or drabs of divers kinds or blews has blew greays or dark full coalars dyed att dye house that is a full indigo blew wich one Walker att Leeds is cheiff for dyeing wool blew att present. 1761.

The best way for lifting up aney weight or for aney rope to ride or aney rubing is to have pulleys has thus so the weight lyes on the guttion ends wich has no power.[9]

f. 3v If a man was to boyl a few chips of logwood in liquor when you boyl itt itt makes itt a fine coalar and look has fine as aney wine.

Observe that aney thing wich lyes furthest of center gooes heavilys and hardest to turn except itt is a watter wheell and further a watter wheell arms is of the shaft and easyear itt goes that is larger wheell is and more strength and force.

Observe that except a millright is something of a meckanick hee can never bee a good hand of his bisness whilest hee lives for reasons 100.

Ther is some orders for the Leeds merchants has for mixt cloath has thus to bee dyed one coalar red the other blew. For red[10] first boyl the wool in (alom then)[11] peachwood and logwood so dash a little old lant in or some does without lant. For blew itt is boyled in allom then in logwood so saden with a little piss. Then boyled in another vesell with only lant called piss. Some uses no piss att all.[12]

[7] Ms reads 'wt'.
[8] Word interlineated.
[9] Two diagrams in text of pulley wheels with outside edges higher than centre.
[10] Phrase interlineated.
[11] Phrase interlineated.
[12] Sentence in margin.

A man may have aney cog wheell made provided hee makes a pattern of wood. First f. 4r
hee may have all cogs cast all solid in lett and whell not exceed a foot over has thus to bee in spur waye.[13]

The maner of Wakefild windmill wich grind rape oyl and rasps and chips logwood stands on a brick tower and is moved to wind by a large cog wheell wich goes round the top.[14] Number 3 & 4 two stones on the edge.[15]

Lett all calff hair bee carded over to loosen itt before you mix itt amongst the wooll f. 4v
and if you card the wooll once over itt will scrible evenar so pull them well together and scrible them even for making mixters.

For basses such has made in Lanckeshire if you dye your listing a logwood blew itt looks has well for listing if not better then if itt was and indigo blew. To dye logwood blew is boyl itt in allom then take itt out and put the logwood in and boyl itt up then putt a kitt full of old lant in so put the hancks of listing in and boyl itt slowely for ½ half and hour then cool itt. Then put some more logwood and piss in so boyl itt up again. So itt is done. Only sadden[16] with piss by itt self and not in same you dyed in.[17]

All crimpsons and pinks wich is dyed in grain is dyed has the do scarlits so made blewley with piss by some called lant.

There is men about Dewsberry and them parts that will make verry handsome f. 5r
coverlids of calf hair dyed blak so scribles itt amongst wooll and uses itt for blak weft in coverlids and some in and about Dewsberry makes low prised dark mixt broods of itt such has Mr. George Charnock merchant of Wakefild byes a deal of them wich some is frisd others prest wich he sends into Holland and of these mixt broods the make in and about Dewsbery and in and about Pudsey 5 miles of Leeds. Wakefild 1761.

Mr Steer of Wakefild sends a deall of 17 yards Hudersfild peices wich are frised and goes into Holland. Likewise hee sends a deall of fine Saddleworth planes and mixt brood frises wich goes into Ireland. Hee goes each year into Ireland himself in the month of May so brings great orders. 1761.

How to order calff hair best wich you intend to make into cloath is first lett itt bee f. 5v
well worked on a wooll teasar or by some called a devill to cleanse all the dirt and dust out then boyll it in allom so dye itt with logwood and old piss and if you have a mind you may sadden it with a little coperas. So drye itt then card itt over bye itt self likewise your wooll card itt bye itt self then pull them together then oyll them. So scrible them twise over and spin[18] weve itt into Hudersfild cloath and will answer well. You may use skin & fleece wooll mixt if you will or separate wich you see answers best. North Country calfs or young cows has hair that imitates wooll best for in good ground the cows has such a fine coat on theire bak that itt is to short. Black Scoth cattle has good hair.[19]

[13] Diagram of a cog wheel is placed in the text.

[14] Diagram in text of a 'Dutch'-style windmill and gearing connecting it to the two 'stones' numbered 3 and 4.

[15] Sentence in margin next to diagram.

[16] Ms reads 'sadde'.

[17] Phrase 'and not in same you dyed in' in margin.

[18] Word interlineated.

[19] Sentence in margin.

f. 6r The frise in Scotland by hand both bye turning of a mill and frise upon the shear board. Cheif places is at the frise most is in att Tiviotdale and Lauderdale and mills shears presses frises and all. 1760.

The carry a great woollen facktory att Newcastle begun of late and makes brood and narrow cloath. 1758.

There is some excellent fine wool grows on some of the Welch sheep wich theire cheif markit to sell it att for the Welchmen is att Srowsberry in Sropshire.

There is a deall of men is of and opinion that skin wool if made into blankits itt is apt to breed lice and flies and if into cloath itt soon mort eats or else itt makes the butifulls blankits and is wool that sells cheaphar then fleece but itt will not do for cloath.

f. 6v The Wakefild merchants if the think aney dyear uses aney logwood to blews they cutt a piece of the tayl end so boyls itt in allaker and itt quite discharges the logwood of leaving what indigo there is on.

How to make piles of planks wich is to joint att edges one in a nother is to have one thick edge and one thin edge thatt is make them like a wedge in the breadth way so always make a nick for the thin edge to go into the thick edge and this waye will turn watter and scarce let a drop go through.

Always observe to card wool on new cards wich is not very much worn I meane and itt maks handsomer cloath and it holds longar bye 2 or 3 yards then old card will.

For dyeing a clarritt boyl itt in allom then take redwood and saunders and a little logwood so sadden itt with old lant called piss.

For dyeing wool it is best to scowr it so dry itt then scrible itt over and so dye itt and it take dye beter.

f. 7r The proper way to make weft for makeing of rugs bye some called cadows to bee made of calff hair or hair wich comes of Scoth cows or north country beasts is to mix it amongst skin wooll and scrible itt well together so spin your cadow weft on itt.

The cloathmakers (coalard cloath)[20] in and about Leeds or Wakefild the prise the give for spining weft for cloath about 2s 8d or 2s 10d per yard in bawk is never above 10d a walltron that is 6 pound. Then itt is scribled to theire hands and needs little carding.

And blankitt weft is 9d for 6 pound spining in and about Dewsberry and att Wakefild itt is 10d pence for 6 pound. Spinning in and about Dewsberry and Wakefild itt is 10 pence for 6 pound. Lett blankits have a good plump soft thread and not to bee small spun or hard twined. Coverlids is cheifly made about Dewsberry and blankits to all that circuit and rugs are made in and about Ositt 3 miles of Wakefild. Waste will make good blankits.

f. 7v Observe to lett all mixt broads have a good plump thread and not to bee to small spun for if the bee small spun the will nott mill stout and strong and when you dye for a mixter do not pinch them of wares butt lett the coalar bee bright and full of a bodey and if a peice is good coalar and strong itt will sell lett wool bee never so coarse.

[20] Phrase interlineated.

Sopose blankits when milling had a little soap and some chawk shaved in (or spanish white)[21] so milled in itt would make them look fair and handle strong. So leave soap in. Dust flows on when near thick.[22]

In Yorkshire att after blankits is scowred and gone a while the give itt some white earth with a handfull or two of sallt in and sallt itt makes them rise loftey and soft and this is a good method for all Lanckeshire basses by some called shopwhites.

Observe that them people called Methodist are cheifly of a deceitfull bad meaneing people and theire teachers are given to secreet whorin. I knew a man att Wakefild wich was a Methodist pearson that lyed with a woman the verry same night shee buryed her husband and so forward for 3 or 4 nights afterwards whilest hee thought his courage would answer not well no longer so thought proper to retire a little. This is real fackt and truth. 1761. f. 8r

Observe that in a generall way there is no putting trust in no man for if you think you have a freind and hee does you perhaps a kindness now and then except hee has something to his advantage through you hee will not bee a freind long and so if a man can bee a freind to himself that is best freindship.

Places proper for a wind mill is if you can find a large open valley wich faces the west. The wind is strongar then upon a hill because itt is confined.

To dye brown boyl itt in redwood and saunders so sadden with a little coperas and some uses a little logwood in boyling. f. 8v

Some dyears uses a little fustick in dyeing reds and itt gives them a fine yellow cast. Wakefild 1760.

The best way of dyeing a logwood blew is thus first boyll itt in allom then put your logwood in and lett itt boyll up so putt the cloath in and lett itt boyll slowely so putt in a kittfull of old lant and boyl all up for ¼ of and hour so take itt out and cooll itt then putt some more logwood in and boyl your cloath ¼ of and hour then take itt outt and take all of the liquor outt you dyed with and putt nothing butt old lant in so boyll itt well up and itt strikes itt a full blew. Never pinch itt of logwood at first and if you mix some indigo in soap so mill itt in itt will look very weell.

The maner of a vesell for watter to come of great force onto and over fall wheel is has thus.[23] So make itt like a mill hoper and your watter to come out at Number 4. This method gives great force and has the power of the air. f. 9r

A thing to bee observed that is for a man to keep his mind and temper and not to lett his words slip. For some men will keep talking and caniving with others whilest the will learn other peoples bisness has well has themselves and att same time perhaps knowed nothing before the talked with you.

21 Phrase interlineated.

22 Phrase interlineated above entry.

23 Diagram of a large V with a little tail extending from the left hand stroke below the point where they meet extending to the right; this is labelled with the number '4'. Remaining sentences in margins around drawing.

A thing to bee observed is that except a man can live above the world hee stands a verry poor chance in itt for when people sees a man can live prettey well there is a maney will help him but if the see that hee is poor and can scarce live he will find few freinds if aney.

f. 9v The Leeds and Wakefild merchants in March and Aprill the bye abundance of stop lists wich before the are dyed has a cord sewed on the inside of the list has this way[24] and some is double corded has thus[25] and some has shapes of stars or hearts sewed here and there along the list about two yards distance of each other and on the inside of the head end the sew a cord on has this or this[26] and itt is called a running worm. All these sorts of goods goes over sea and are worn for womans peticoats and some is cloath of 6 or 7 shillings per yard and some is of 2s 6d. There is of all prises. The are dyed full scarlitts ½ scarlits crimpsons and a many of them dyed blew of coarse sorts.

f. 10r About Hudersfild the mill theire coarse low prised cloath has thus. The scowr butt little of the grease out so mills then up with blak earth whilest the are has thick has a board and bye giving them so much earth itt makes them handle has if not greasy alltho the was never scowred.

The way to make good and cheap starch (to sell in country shops)[27] is you may take a parcil of potatoes and pill them clean so gratter them into watter and wash them in two or three watters then putt them in a seiff to drain the watter out so drye itt leiserly a distance from the fire and this sort of starch is the whitest of aney and will stiffen well and if you have a mind to give itt a blewly cast you must putt a little stone blew in the watter when you wash itt last time over. This would do far to stiffen cloath in milling.

f. 10v The maner how some loadens or lifts stones out in a stone pitt is has thus.[28] So has only two poles wich stands on two sharp iron pins letten into two holes of wood or stone so has two ropes of either side the poles to draw them either way. Fix the ropes att top of the poles and to have them of a right length has the can not yeild to much neither way has this. Only only your rope to bee fixd cros the other ways on so you may yeild itt to wards stone pitt when you wind up and when you unloading yeild itt to wards the land. The rope to bee made fast att each end wich is number 3 and 4.[29] Some hooks a chain round theire stones so fastens the end has waggoners locks theire whels so hooks a blok to the chain to wind itt up bye. Some puts the two dufftayls on the stone pitt side to hold the end of your rope.

f. 11r The maner of two dufftayls and a plane even iron to putt into large stones to loaden into carts is has thus.[30] To bee made of iron about 6 inchs long and have holes for and iron pin to go through and when you have loadened you only need to give them a nock down and the dufftayls will bee loose to take out and putt into aney other stones. You must make the hole in the stone to bee widear att bottom than att top just like a dufftayll so put the irons wich is dufftayled in first so nock the midle most iron last and more weight the stone is and faster the dufftayls binds observe that you are to

24 Diagram of horizontal line.

25 Diagram of two horizontal lines parallel to one another.

26 Diagram of wave and then of a tighter wave and the words 'the go all prest' between them.

27 Phrase interlineated.

28 Diagram showing two poles in an inverted 'V' supported at the apex by ropes is placed in the text.

29 Diagram of the 'V' showing ropes coming off the apex of the triangle.

30 Diagram of triangular wedges with circles at the small end attached to a semi-circular 'pin'.

hang them att bloks. Wich blok you may fix to a three legs and have a rowler att side to wind up att has thus[31] and make use of two bloks and you may wind a great weight with a little ease so draw the cart under.

In France att a town called Oblivilla the make abundance of woollen cloath both f. 11v
broods and narrows and the narrows the call ratteens in France.

Some is cutt out in one solid piece or some will joint 4 boards together to make a square pump on and the suckar to bee has thus as after this pattern[32] and your leather to bee nayled onto two boards and to bee nayled cross over the middle so itt opens and shuts like two doors so lett the leather bee all in one piece and nayling itt cross over makes itt ride on itts hinges for both suckars.

You may work aney engine bye two large pulleys and rope has thus or thus[33] and lett all the puleys for this way bee wide att top and streight in the bottom has the rope will not slip.

How to make a ship sayl against the wind and strongar the wind is against you and f. 12r
faster itt goes. To work bye wind and sayl cloath has after this pattern.[34] Have 4 large pulleys att top to keep itt steadey. For shaft to ride or rub against or have a guttion is best. You must have 4 of these sayl cloaths to turn on the bottom guttion and top and when the face wind the will turn edgeways and turn flatways with the wind so fix itt on and upright shaft to go round on and guttion so fix itt in the ship and itt will drive against the wind.[35]

To dye a clear yellow boyl itt in allom and wowlds so give itt a little kimick to clear itt f. 12v
and these coalars looks well.

Peices called white greays goes best in March Aprill and May and are cloath wich is oftens bespoke of the cloathmakers the have about 14 or 16 ounces of blew wooll scribbled in to 4 or 5 pounds of white wooll then that 4 or 5 pound is scribbled into 120 pound of wooll to make a couple of broads on. The generaly use 40 pound of floks in. The have a broad list like Leeds broad cloath and a blew striped head end with a full name of the makers name in the garter to bee sett and above the head end att one corner near list sew some red yarn in like has red striped lincey is when itt is woven into square diamonds has thus.[36] This cloath is verry strong milled and mild with soap has coalard cloth is. The are all drest and prest for soldiers cloaths. The Dutch and Swiss soldiers wears this cloth. Not to be small spun but a plump thread.[37]

Mr Lumb dyer att Wakefild is a verry near his self man. Hee letts no butter scarce bee f. 13r
used in his own house butt sends the searvantt woman to markitt with itt and keeps only two cows and keeps all the money to himself letting wife have none butt what she gives accountt for and hee keeps 14 or 15 journemen att work besides prentises and has great bisness. 1748. For family hee only allows one pound of buter in a week.[38]

31 Diagram of tripod and a crank.

32 Diagram in text.

33 Diagram showing pulley wheel in cross section with central groove.

34 Diagram of large vertical pole with a frame holding 2 'wings' out to each side.

35 Diagram in margin labelled in several places with the number three similar to the pump on previous page with the words: 'A square pump and let all the four 3 bee joined together'.

36 Diagram in text of a rectangle divided into small squares inside.

37 Last two sentences in the margin.

38 Sentence interlineated below.

Where to bye silk noyls has att Stockport and Macksfild and Derby mills[39] and Sheffilld the are making a new silk mill. June 18th 1760.

Fustian flocks att Manchester and woosted ends called waste att Manchester.

Blak calf hair or young heifer hair or Irish cow hair is brought of the taners and stricker is bought of the hatters. The skim of theire kettles.

f. 13v A book called Geography Anatomy or the Geographical Gramer the ninth edition and a sett of new maps by Mr Senex. By Pat Gorgon MA FRS. His book gives account of all the countrys upon the face of the earth and theire liveing and theire trade maners and language. Gordons Geography.[40]

A book called Cambdens Britania late edition. The book gives a full decription of all the shires and theire ways of liveing and trade.[41]

Britania this exceeds aney geography book for England.[42]

A book caled Randals System of Geography 2 Voloms. New. Randal is a Wakefild man.

A book called Wheelers Travel.[43] This book gives acount of foregn[44] countrys and decription of thim.[45]

f. 14r Meronandums

To by a book Sir Samuell Moorland Vade Maeum or Goods Ready Cast Up.

Bible with cuts in.

A book Salmons Poligraphy. This is a good book for a painting.[46]

Two pots from Shefild at 4d and 6d each.

To bye a herball book.

Book History of England either Smolets or Rapins history.

Book Wisest New And Best Young Mans Campanion. New £0:2:6.

Book called Gulivers Travells.

To have a coatt a raven grear[47] or and oficers blew or a dark blew greay.

To buy a new pare of scribling cards from Leeds or Hallifax.

Book with all the fairs in England in.

The Instructor or Young Mans Best Companion a book.[48]

39 Word interlineated.
40 Phrase in margin.
41 Ms reads 'trad'.
42 Sentence in margin.
43 Ms reads 'trave'.
44 Ms reads 'foreg'.
45 Ms reads 'thi'.
46 Letters 'ting' interlineated above.
47 Presumably a misspelling of grey.
48 Entry crossed out with 'X's.

A book called Present State Of Greatt Britain of a new edition.

A book History of Buccaneers of America.

Merandoms f. 14v

To buy a book called Emersons Princaples of Mechanicks with cuts. 6 shil new old att 4 shill. Printed in 1758. 2 vollom best.[49]

A book called Persian Tales giveing a decription of many curious things but not very curious.[50]

Missions Voyage to Italy. Two volloms with cut. This is not very curious.[51]

A book intitled Britania and Hibernia Antiqua and Nova. This book I think is called in English Cambdens Britain late edition. This gives acount of all England and its produce.[52]

A Dictionary of the Whole Body of Arts and Sciences 2 Voll. These are brave books.

Humphreys Explanation of the Old and New Testament 3 voloms.

Observe them books with[53] red letters in the title page[54] are good ones.[55]

Either history or religion or any sort else the are most deverting. f. 15r

Observe there is 4 volloms of Attlas Geography one of Ureop one of Asia of Affrica and America with cuts.

Gordons Geography gives acount of all the world in one vollom with maps of each country in. Itt is about 3s in auction second hand.

Nises Newest Young Mans Companion with a map of the world gives acount of all the shires in England and Wales and their produce with fairs and maney things more. 2s 6d new.

Randalls Geography (2 voloms).[56] These books gives acount of all the world theire trade maners languge etc.

To bye a book thatt is a Dicktonary of the Whole Body[57] of Arts 2 Volloms. These are curious books. f. 15v

A book called Modern Curiosities of Art and Nature.

Just published the 23 of May 1759 wich exceeds all of this kind of books a New Geoagraphical History containing a full acount of the severall parts of the nown world as itt is devided into continents iselands oceans seas rivers lakes and the situations extent and boundary of all the empires kinghdoms states provinces in Europe Asia Africa and America theire constitutions revenues force climate soil produce

49 Sentence interlineated above.
50 Entry crossed out with 'X's.
51 Ms reads 'cur'; entry crossed out with 'X's.
52 Ms reads 'prod'.
53 Ms reads 'wi'.
54 Ms reads 'pa'.
55 Ms reads 'on'.
56 Phrase interlineated above.
57 Ms reads 'bo'.

manufacktures trade and comerce ciytys cheif towns universitys curious strucktures ruins antiquities mountains mines anamals vegetables minerals with the religions learning policy maners and customes of the inhabitants illustrated with new acurate sort of maps of all the parts of the nown[58] world makeing a compleat atlas the dreses of the inhabitants with a great[59] variety of plans and perspective views of the principal cytys towns harbors[60] strucktures ruins and other peices of antquities. Price ind . . .[61] 100 att sixpence is £2:10:0.

f. 16r Salmons Geography is a good book with maps of each country.

To bye a book with all the fairs in England and Wales.

Poetry bye John Brearley.

Interest sways all the little and the great
All seek theire ends and would each other cheat
Men only seem to hate and seem to love
Intrest is the point on wich the move

Now freinds are foes now foes are freinds agen
As intrest turn now knaves now honist men

Rabits are fatest in frostey weather.

Geese are best to wards Crismas when they feed on young spring brewert in old stubble old corn sprowted.

Mutton is worst in winter fed on turnips.

f. 16v Tim Oxley 2 remblands frised scarlit and green £0:0:6.[62]

Croper att allthrop rembland 3.

Croper in Kirgate left sixpence att floks £0:0:_.[63]

Ned Brevitt left 4 to pay att white rembland paid.[64]

1759 September 24 to 2 brood mixters Mr Steers for Tim Oxley to pay for. Paid.[65]

Going to Halifax for mill right £0:2:0.

3 yards of green frise to lap blew broad in to Chevitt Hall att 1s 4d per £0 4s 0d. Received.[66]

f. 17r 1759 Aprill 3th. To 3 pieces frised James Booths. Paid.[67]

Kirshaw in Westgate 1 blew brood frised. Jenuary 3th 1760. Paid.[68]

Mark Plows to 15 yards of drab plane drest and frised. Jenuary 12th 1760. Paid.[69]

58 Ms reads 'no'.
59 Ms reads 'gr'.
60 Ms reads 'harb'.
61 Remainder of word missing.
62 Entry crossed out with 'X'.
63 Last numeral missing.
64 Entry crossed out with 'X'.
65 Word in margin. Entry crossed out with 'X'.
66 Word in margin. Entry crossed out with 'X'.
67 Word in margin. Entry crossed out with 'X'.
68 Word in margin. Entry crossed out with 'X'.
69 Word in margin. Entry crossed out with 'X'.

John Plows 1 blew brood frised. January 10th 1760. £0:2:0.[70]

1760. Mr Emsly a scarlit cloak. January 14th frised. £0:0:6.[71]

Robert Lumb dreser in Westgate 4 yards of white brood frised. £0:0:6.[72]

Plushes making from 1756 and 8 plushes in a year at sixpence per plush.

Sopose a man was to dye a fine mokin blew and thicken itt with soap in a driveing stok so dress and frise itt att after itt would sell verey well for Josephs to shopkeepars. Raise itt well.

1758. Feberuary 1. Received of Mr Taylor f. 17v

	£	s	d[73]
to ¼ of pack of thirds	0	8	
ditto received	2	3	
March 2 received	2	8	
Aprill 1 received	2	14	
and 3s over paid	0	3	
May 1 recceived	2	10	
June 1 recived	2	11	
July 3 received	2	12	
Augustt 4 received	2	12	
Septemer 1 recived	2	14	

Jenury 1759. I am to receive each wages each 4 week begining with Jenuary first.

Febuary 12 Received £2 8s 0d

Itt being pay for 4 weeks in Jenuary

	£	s	d
March 7 recived	2	8	0
April 5 recived	2	8	0
May 2 recived	2	8	0[74]

First time shaveing begun the third of October 1757. f. 18r

Paid for the year 1758 £0:4:6
Paid for the year 1759 £0:4:6

New wigg May 26th 1759.[75]

Lent sixpence when paid for my wigg att 0:13:0.[76]

Mr Godly a peice of plush 0:0:4.[77]

Paid Godley October 25th 1760 for shaveing four and sixpence paid in our mill.

70 Entry crossed out with 'X'.
71 Entry crossed out with 'X'.
72 Entry crossed out with 'X'.
73 Column for pence illegible because of binding.
74 Addition of these three figures begun below but crossed out.
75 Entry crossed out with 'X'.
76 Entry crossed out with 'X'.
77 Entry crossed out with 'X'.

Some brood mixt cloath are made into shorn duffils. First the raise them twise over when drye then shers them lightley over then weets them and rows them. So gorts them and tenters them and brushes itt on tenter so when drye blows a little oyl on and striks itt down with a fine jak. The are only done on one side. Wakefild.

Some has a little tenter before the fire in bad wether for shapins.

f. 18v A cure for jaundice. Take some castiell soap and shave some into hott ale and beatt itt up and sweetten itt so drink itt when going to bed. Observe to take casteell soap and not comom casle soap. Learned of a French docktor. Wakefild 1760.

Mushroms are a thing that are stored much att Wakefild and are gotten each morning in August and September. Some uses them for to make cathcup[78] on and some fryes them others broyls them and puts sallt att top of them. 1760.

Some will put mushroms into the inside of a duck or a goose and it eats excellent well.

Some butchers will hold meat dear in markett and not sell itt reasonable and when itt does not sell of the will hawk itt cheap.

f. 19r Work done for Mr Daneill Made. 1756.[79]
August 12 to 10 peices drest £0:10:0.
August 19 to 10 peices drest £0:10:0.

Work done for Jonothan Thornhill. 1757.[80]

To 1 peice raised narrow cloath	0	0	4
August 6 to 8 yard of brood drestt and frised	0	1	4
Ditto to 10 yard of woosted plane drestt and frised	0	0	10
To 2½ leftt att raising a peice.[81]			
1758. May 4 to 2 pare blankits raised	0	3	0
	2	9	—[82]
Received of Johnathan Thornhill	2	3	—[83]

Mr. James Norton in Wringate Wakefild trades into Scotland and into Wales with frises and prest cloath in Wales the bye a deal of blew frises 1760 and with Mr. Compton of Hull merchant.

1762. Mr George Charnock Wakefild byes a deall of white brood cloath about 2s 4d or 2s 6d in bawk wich goes white to Holland.

f. 19v 1757. June 9 to 26 yards drestt for pressing for a man thatt mills with Robertt Rishford £0:2:2. Paid two pence for pressing £0:0:2.[84]

Joe Brigs 6 pare of Blankits helpt to raise £0:0:9.

Malt sells has cheap att Rochdale has att Wakefild for poor people that byes itt bye strokes for itt is ground att corn mills and mowter makes itt much less.

[78] Ms reads 'catchu'.
[79] Entry crossed out with 'X'.
[80] Entry crossed out with 'X'.
[81] Number scratched out.
[82] Numeral illegible.
[83] Numeral illegible. The number 0:0:6 is inserted above this figure but the referent is not clear.
[84] Entry crossed out with 'X'.

To 8 yard of brood drest and frisd for Jon Curtis living in Norgate £0:2:0

Wakefild 1758. Received of John Curtis £0:0:8.

Old Richard Whittly left sixpens to pay att floks. August 18th 1757.[85]

Some dyears att Wakefild will sett a new fatt att on a Satterday night and work itt on Monday following or Tuesday after.

Received 17 of August £2:8:0. Itt being pay to 12th of August f. 20r
September 10 recived £2:8:0
October 8 received £2:8:0
November 5 received £2:8:0
December 5 received £2:8:0

Recived in Full for 1759 £31 4s 0d per year wage

1760. Recived Jenuary 16th	1	4	0
Received Febuary first	1	4	0
14 Febuary	1	4	0

In maney towns people are confined to grind all theire mallt att one partickular mill and itt lyes verry hard of poor pople when the have a stroke a mallt to have a pint taken out besides going with itt and waiting till itt is done. Att Wakefild Leeds and Manchester the are confined to this ackt and maney more places.

Ben work to 4 peices Danell Modes £0:2:8.[86] f. 20v

A catolouge of book
Galans Method of Phisick
The History of Anmamals
The Compleat Angler
Culpepers London Dispensatay
A Posey of Godly Prayer
Three Prayer Books
A Cooking Book
A Testament

	£	s	d
Tom Browns Jester. Cost	0	1	0
History of the Rebelion In 1745. Cost	0	1	0
History of all the English Kings. Cost	0	0	7
Boyls Physicall Receipts Is	0	0	2
The Soldiers Monitor. Given itt to . . . Rish.[87]			

History of Our Savior a phamplitt f. 21r
The London Spy

[85] Entry crossed out with 'X'.
[86] Entry crossed out with 'X'.
[87] This entry crossed out with several lines; one word illegible.

	£	s	d
Mechanick Powers cost	0	1	10
Atlas Geography cost	0	2	0
The American Traveler	0	1	0
Streets Anthems	0	0	7

Them turners (dish turners are)[88] wich turns them large wood bowls or butter bassons or watter dishes and the like are the only men for turning aney sort of wheels or pulleys. The turn cheifly side ways and will take a peice of square wood and put itt in the throw and turn itt round verry quickly and for makeing cog wheels itt is best to turn them so then cut number 3 of (from number 2)[89] and you have a wheel to put in arms.[90]

f. 21v Received of Mr. William Denson[91]

To 2½ yards of cloath att 2s 6d per yard £0:6:_.

To ½ yard more received att £0:1:_.[92]

Book lentt to James att Fosters called The London Spy.[93]

Memorandoms to have a look a that machine wich weys carts or loadend wagons att Manchester. 1761.

Forged plates for presing in a stang press sells 2½ per pound. Castor forge near Leeds. 1761

Sold to John Horn 2½ yard of cloath att £0:6:_.[94]

Sold young Jon Horn ¼ of a yard of brood cloath att £0:0:6.

f. 22r Work done for Akworth hospital 1760.[95]

January 12 to 2 bases £0:1:4
January 28 to 2 bases £0:1:4

Meronadom that one Gregson liveing att Bury in Lanckeshire is thought to make the best and handsoms wheell shutles for Wakefild 1760 and weares longest of aney one makers else. Hee makes some with iron sides.

Observe if a man pays sixpence for a dinner when hee is from home that itt is has cheap or cheaphar then hee can furnish himself with a diner att home and considered the goodness of dishes.

f. 22v June 1760. A curious way of getting money is to gett some long blak calf hair or long blak that comes of Irish cows of a long sort so scribble some long wooll in and comb itt and gett itt spun so weave itt into hair shagg and lett your warp bee woosted. So dye itt blak so when dyed and dry dres itt of and engine that is cast over with coarse sand like a friseing board so do itt on to a barrill like a perching mill is sett with taisills so itt will gloss itt and shine.

88 Phrase interlineated.

89 Phrase interlineated.

90 Diagram in text of two concentric circles, the outer labelled '3' and the inner '2'.

91 Entry crossed out with 'X'.

92 Last numerals in these two lines illegible.

93 Entry crossed out with 'X'.

94 Last numeral illegible. Entry crossed out with 'X'.

95 Entry crossed out with 'X'.

Came to Wakefild on Jenuary first being Thorsday and begun on work on Friday f. 23r
Jenuary 2nd 1761 and to receive 24 shilling each two weeks for friseing att Sir Lyonells mill Wakefild.

The mill above is sessed att 60 pound per year and payes three pound per year taxes and itt is a mill wich oftens in back watter some times in winter for 3 days together (and scarce of watter in sumer because of corn mills).[96]

Jenuary 1761. The money has I am informed my father had of Mr Entwisle was 40 pound and hee lett itt run to 8 years and paid no intrest wich makes itt bee 56 pounds besides the use of that 8 years. The first year 2 shill the second 4 the third 6 the 4th 8 shill the 5th 10s the 6th 12s the 7th 14 shil the 8th year 16 shill so in all now to pay yearly is £2:16:0.

How a man may sett a tenter in a house wich hee maye dry cloath 2 or 3 times of a f. 23v
day or night is make itt of crooked wood has this maner.[97] So you may tenter from one end to the other so have a fire under a large iron pot like has a stove is for drying fusitans. This would bee conveniant for them that keeps Hudersfild markit with cloath. Itt is some times verry empty in bad dryeing weather and a man might sell to his advantage att them times. 1760.

How to graft the best way take a pruneing nife and cut top of the stok of sloaping then clip itt and put the graft in and lett itt bee cut sloaping so put itt in with bark to bark so tye itt round and cover itt with clay (and horse dung mixed).[98] Never to saw no stoks of.[99]

There is some cow (or calf)[100] hair has a finear shortar staple then some buttock skin f. 24r
wooll and scrible itt amongst wool would do to make low prised Hudersfild cloath

Some dyars att Wakefild are begun of presing shalloons with such plates has is oftens used for presing kearsey. The heat them in a stove so puts two att ech end of each peice and so screws them down and the are finished. This is and easey and quick way of presing. 1761.

Att Wakefild on the 30 of Jenury the musell the bels only of one side the clapar and when the ring itt sounds like treble and base and is pleasant to the year.

There goes a deall of stop lists from Wakefild wich are blews and reds with a cord run out list. The are worn for peticoats.

Observe to make all puleys that are to turn aney engins to have the chanell brood att f. 24v
top and narrow in the bottom so the rope fastens and will not slip butt puleys for to lift aney weight to bee has brood in the bottom has top

1760. Coffee in a generall way sells att Liverpool att 1s 8d per pound unburned and may bye it bye single pounds so and burn itt yourself is great profitt.

Observe that aney man that has been a soldier and is a pentioner hee may sett up aney bisness in aney town in all England.

96 Phrase in margin.
97 Diagram of a spiral with five turns.
98 Phrase in margin.
99 Sentence interlineated above.
100 Phrase interlineated.

Aney man that has to gett a liveing bye working or keeping of publick house the must rise att 5 in morn and wife stay up att nights till 10. Money maney has gotten this way both publick and private houses.[101]

f. 25r This engine works bye two cranks and will turn a great weight with a little ease. Itt is mechanical.[102] This upright spindles to work in bushes both of them.

This low engine[103] is worked bye two pulleys and I think itt is full has good has the engine above in mechanicks. These spindles to work in bushes.

f. 25v Both these friseing mills may stand in chambers and works bye pulley and rope.[104] This crank to work the pumps to return water bak. This works bye a worm round the upright shaft and moves easaly.

f. 26r Sir Lyonell mill att Wakefild. June 1754 made att London.[105] Card beam whell to have 30 cogs in wich is turned by thatt wheell with cogs 20 in number 18.

f. 26v How to order shear floks to make them to spin. Gett a wire riddle made of a fine pitch so dress all the shortest through and the long ones you may scrible amongst wooll for to spin. The shortest will sell to London carryears and the would rather have them in longish shear floks. Shear floks makes a peice have a close bottom and the lye lowar then long floks and looks finear. Some cloathiers would rather have them in long floks. 1761.

Sopose a man had and engine made like print rowls but the middle rowl to bee cut full of holes has full has could be made only leaving has much distance has holes about ½ and ½ this engine would set a nap on cloath wich would stay well on.

f. 27r The prise of a mixt brood made of ½ cow hair and ½ wooll your fleece wooll costing 7 pounds per pak. Now we will say

	£	s	d
30 pound of wool at 7d per	0	17	6
30 pound of cow hair 1 per	0	2	6
grease 5 quarts of rape oil	0	3	0
spining weft 36 pound at 2d per	0	6	0
spining warp 24 pound at 2½d per	0	5	0
scribling hair and wool together	0	2	6
weaving and siseing	0	6	6
milling with meall and soap	0	2	0
	£2	5	0

Now this peice will hold 30 yards and sell at 2s 2d per yard in bawk

so it comes to	£3	5	0	
	2	5	0	
	£1	0	0	profitt and

sold cheap

To gett a strong pare of scribbling cards called breakars will open waste verry well.

[101] Sentence in margin.

[102] Large diagram of mill wheel and gearing placed in the text. Next sentence placed in the diagram.

[103] Second diagram of mill wheel and gearing placed in the text. Next sentence placed in the diagram.

[104] Two diagrams of mill wheels and different gearing arrangements. Remainder of entries in margins around drawing.

[105] Two diagrams of the mill wheel and gearing with the number of cogs on each wheel. Last sentence in margin.

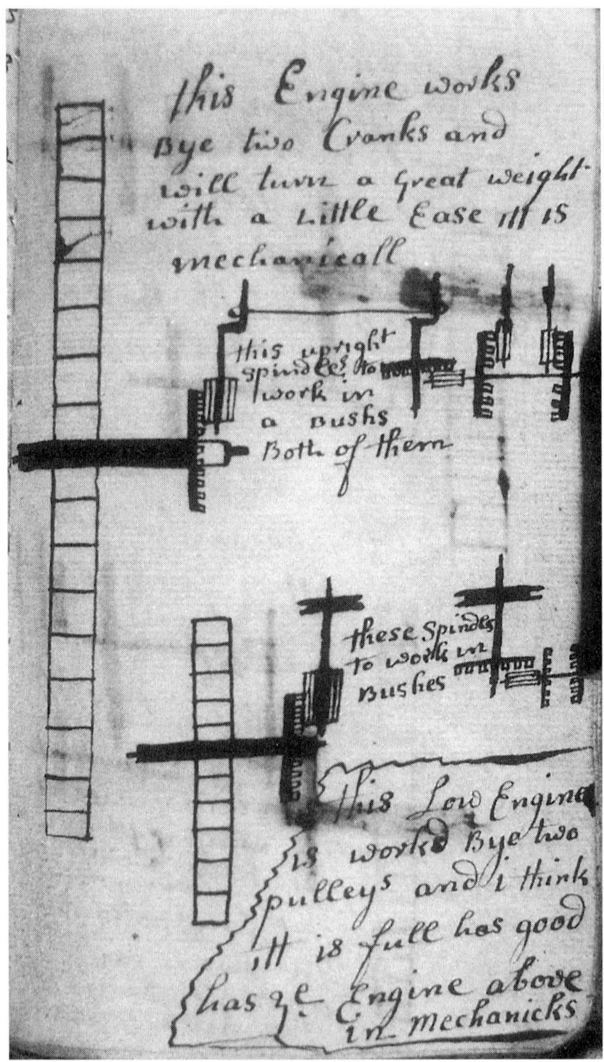

'This engine works bye two cranks' (f. 25r)

Mr. Gawtress pork shopkeeper. 1761.[106] f. 27v
January 16 to 1 brood drest £0:5:0
to 1 brood dufild £0:2:6

In a genearall way things sells has dear att place where itt is facktored has itt does att 20 miles of. For instance ale is less measure att Wakefild then itt is in Lankeshire and mallt goes from there a great deall. Likewise cheese is sold att Wakefild has cheap has in most towns in Lanckeshire. Likewise each other things in proportion. Likewise down

[106] Entry crossed out with 'X'.

towards Hull and York the farmers eats the worst of corn for bread and so does the inhabitants. The send theire best corn to markits to make money on to pay rents.

All Lankeshire 42 weights are to hard spun and to small for to make stout even cloath. The make theire Hondley planes of broken wooll and 7 or 8 pd of floks in a piece so spins theire weft soft and to a plump thread so the mill stout and scribbling floks and wool makes even cloath provided spinning bee all of a thickness and even.

f. 28r 1760. Thos Kirshaw debtor.[107]
July 5th to 1 brood frised mixt £0:2:6. Received.

William Burill debtor.[108]
1769 October 18 to 1 brood frised mixt £0:2:6. Received.

1761

Mr Gawtress shopkeepar.[109]

March 5 to 1 brood drest for frise 30 yards	£0	5	0
Ditto to 1 brood duffild	0	2	6
Recived.			

Mr Gawtress debtor.[110]
1761

August 20 to 3 peices frised over again. Frised at Hudersfild	£0	1	6
September 6 two halff broods dufil	0	2	6
Ditto to two halff frises 18½ and 20 yards att 2d per	0	6	5
15 to 20½ yards frises drest	0	3	5
ditto to ½ brood duffill	0	1	3
Received	0	15	1

f. 28v Mr. Preistly work 1761[111]
January 16 to 7 peices drest

5 short ones two 24 yards peice	0	9	0
ditto 6 peice oyld and raised	0	1	0
30 to 1 peice 24 yards clarritt nop taken of and shorn	0	1	6
Febuary 17 to 1 peice drest 17 yards	0	1	0
	0	12	6
Aprill 23 to 1 peice drest blew 38 yards	0	3	6

How to order peice for scarlits lett them bee small spun and not to strong milled and rase them weet and shear them drye butt give them no oyl att all for if you do the will show spottey when the are frisd. So when dyed and tentered strike them on the tenter so turn the wool att prk[112] pole when dry and frise itt 3 times over blow a little oyl on before you strike. 1761.

Barnsley fair and Wakefild fair and Lee fair near Wakefild and Adderton fair are all great fairs for horses.[113]

107 Entry crossed out with 'X'.
108 Entry crossed out with 'X'.
109 Entry crossed out with 'X'.
110 Entry crossed out with 'X'.
111 Entry crossed out with 'X'.
112 Sic, presumably refers to a perching or perking pole.
113 'For cattle' interlineated above.

Sir Lyonells estate lyes att Ekester near York and at York and Tadcaster and . . .[114] f. 29r

Att Akworth Hospitall the make basses and 42 weights for dyeing into blew frises and coalard planes like Saddleworth planes and blankitts. But none is done right seldome one yard together but what is cockled. They are to hard spun and some spining thick some small and some hard twined some soft and all sorts woven together. If there spining was sorted the would do better.[115] Richard Hargreaves is governer there 1760. Hee is a Rosandale man.

In Yorkshire the cheifly frise with coarse wild board and for mixters wich is inclined to be greasey and chawked the do middleing well butt when the come to dyed peice has drabs or greens or scarlits espesaly scarlits the seldome can frise one and if the strike them the coarse board does them worse. Dewsberry mill 1761. f. 30r[116]

For the watter wheell going 1½ times about will turn number 8 eight times about. This mill will work verrey easey and return watter bak bye a crank wich is your number 9.[118] Lett your crank number 10 bee made with two screws has thus[119] so bye baking itt up to wards number 8th you may make itt biger or lesser. f. 31r[117]

Observe that makeing mixt broods is good profitt when a man can vent them of. Sometimes att Leeds and Wakefild the go verry sharp of and some times the are att a full stop that cloathmakers keeps them 8 or 10 months and in that time the oftens mort eat except the put them in the stok each 6 or 8 weeks so freshens them up again. The merchants seldome byes aney of them except haveing orders for them. 1761. f. 31v

Mr Rickaby Mr F Maude Mr Steer Mr Daniell Maude does most fine Saddleworth planes of aney att Wakefild. 1761. The bye all in bawk att Hudersfild market.

To have a brushing mill sett with brushes to brush planes on is a verry good thing. Itt is great profitt to make Saddleworth planes fine sorts.

Mr Jeremy Naylor Wakefild merchant byes abundance of white brood cloath about 2s 6d and 2s 4d or aney prise betwixt and three shillings per yard in bawk wich are dyed blews reds and greens and cheifly all prest. Only now and then and order for frises wich hee sends a deall of saxon greens frises. Hee trades all to London to the merchants there. Wakefild 1761. f. 32r

Mr Denison of Leeds Mr Blades Mr Markaram Mr Oatses Mr Peacok all above Leeds merchants byes a deall of brood cloth and frises a great deal. 1761.

Some thick spun thinish Saddleworth planes when the do not cover well the dresers att Wakefild the dust them short shear floks wich came of itt so wisks them easily over and leave all the short grimill floks in the bottom so preses itt without aney more brushing and itt helps to cover the threads better.

Att Leeds and Wakefild all broods dyed blak are cornered in both corners. The one corner blew the other white. First the dye one corner blew in the fatt so tyes itt up f. 32v

114 Entry continued in margin; illegible except the words: 'estate is his near Healand'.

115 Sentence in margin.

116 Previous leaf blank.

117 Previous folio too faded to read, perhaps accounts.

118 Diagram of mill wheel and gearing with numbers of cogs given. Next entry refers to part of this engine.

119 Diagram in text.

then tyes the other corner in the white. Itt is the reason of them doing itt is first to make them beleive that all the whole peice was dyed blew before blak and is what is called a blew blak and is better liked amongst shopkeepars and for tyeing the white corner is to lett them see that itt is a fresh peice dyed out in the white because it oftens hapens that if the have aney fowl bad coalar wich has lyed bye them the generaly turn itt into blak so the shopkeepers has got a notion of itt and the will have a white starr in each peice. 1761.

Woosted trade goes excellent well at Leeds itt being a ½ per hank spining and a peney per pound allowed for reeling. November 1761.

f. 33r Let all friseing mills stand in a chamber and the are not so apt to softens boards and to make thing mowld and damp so has a low room cheifly does.

How to cure a light motall or a bloomey motall wich has layed whilest itt changes itts coalar and faded is weet itt over with pis butt first lett itt all bee wetted out in gort so lett itt go in the stok with a nother mottall att after itt is scowrd so itt will bring natture into itt and dye itt all even coalar. Some puts them in a peice before itt is scowrd so gorts itt easily att after lett itt go in a driveing stok for 1½ hours and itt will bee even coalar.

A man may brighten aney coalar if you coalar soap the coalar you intend so mill itt in with a driving stok and leave itt in so dress your cloath in the coalar. This is a curious method.

f. 33v To make mixt broods is good profitt to sell to the Leeds or Wakefild merchants wich if made of shear floks and wool will make them look fine and close bottom because of floks haveing a fine staple. Now say that

40 pound of wool at 6d per	£1	0	0
20 pound of shear floks	0	5	0
grease and making	0	10	0
milling and soap and flowr	0	3	0
	£2	18	0

Now this peice sold in bawk to bee milled to 30 yards long and one yard 13 inches brood. But if you sell them finished frised or duffiled the must hold 6 quarts or within one one inch and will sell in bawk att 3s 2d or 3s 3d wich 30 yards is att 3s 2d is £4:15:_.[120] £1 17s 0d profitt is one peice. The allways sell a couple of broods together wich is called a cloath.[121]

f. 34r All Hondley planes of good sorts are milled to 30 inches brood and 24 yards or 25 or 26 yards long low prisd ones to 28 inches brood and 17 yards (long)[122] brood and low prisd 24 yards. Some is only 28 inchs brood . . .[123] sold in bawk.

Woosted bisness is verry good 1761 that wooll is combed now of £4 10s 0d per pak and made into woosted stuffs. Leeds.

If a man has money hee may get money if hee has but a good head and whether hee has a good head or not no bisness is carryed on without money for without itt there is nothing to bee done.

[120] Numeral illegible.
[121] Sentence in margin.
[122] Word interlineated.
[123] Word illegible.

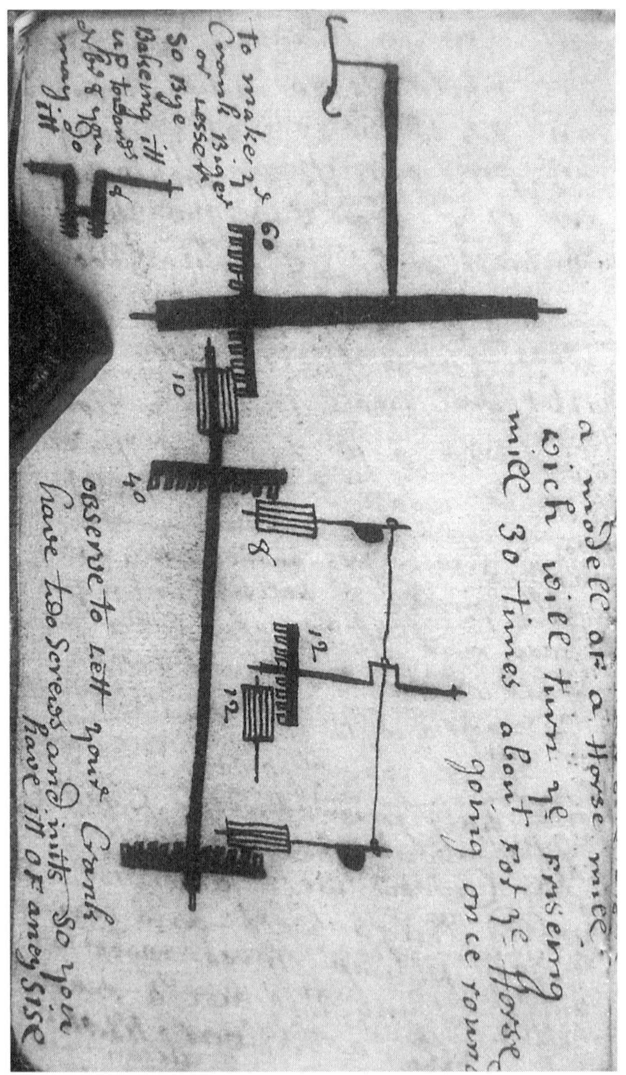

'A modell of a horse mill' (f. 34v)

All low prisd Hudersfild cloath is spun about the same thickness has caddow weft otherwise called rugs weft and having a good plump thread makes them mill strong the use a deall a deall of shear floks scribled in wool.

A modell of a horse mill wich will turn the friseing mill 30 times about for the horse f. 34v
going once round.[124] Observe to lett your crank have two screws and nutts so you have itt of aney sise. To make the crank biger or lesser so bye bakeing itt up towards number 8 you may do itt.

124 Diagram of horse mill with gearing and numbers of cogs shown. Other entries in margins around drawing.

f. 35r 1761 Joseph Hirst milling[125]

May 29 to 1 base scowrd	0	0	9
June 21 to 2 basses flanells	0	1	6
July 20 to 2 basses for womens ware	0	2	0

Mr. Willis of Wakefild byes now and then some white brood cloath from Rochdale the letter in the head end are only two CH or CM butt these broods are made of skin wool and allways mills to a coarse wild staple. Willis mills them over again 1½ yards att a peice and gives them a pound of soap and the look much better. Willis is a bad chap.[126]

If a man was to make a fleece wool and such like spinning has Jon Openshaw of Burey makes such has is sort wich hee puts in the head end J+O B wich stands for Jon Openshaw best and make itt into brood cloath the would sell to great profitt to the Leeds or Wakefild merchants 1761. Lett all broods bee milled with soap and itt is better.

f. 35v There is some merchants att Wakefild wich will not lett the men give theire Hudersfild frises no oyl so the men will blow them over with the watter instead of oyll before the raise itt so the are dampey and difficult to shear because of being dampey. They are apt to shear uneven and when the come to bee frisd the are verrey bad to nop making a soft twisling nap but to order these peice is blow them over with oyl first thing you do so then wisk itt over to wisk the oyl even on then frise itt twise over so chawk it then wisk itt over again to wisk the chawk evenly in so frise itt again but the will never look handsom to bee blown with watter. The reason is the think oyl makes them mort eat soonar because the Hudersfild cloath aney of itt will mort eat in 12 months and this is much in question now 1761. But itt will not answer for frise.

f. 36r 1761 Mr Zouch
September 5 to 1 peice shorn 45 yards £0:2:6.[127]

Jon Openshaw of Burey
These patterns [128] are of John Openshaw of Bury making and sold to Mr. Samuel Zouch merchant of Wakefild these come drest so hee gets them dyed and frisd att Wakefild and the are as small spun has aney white brood cloath of 3s 6d yard in bawk only the are made of fine skin wool and broods in Yorkshire are all made of fleece wool. Hee sells them into the country to shopkeepars for lads wayscoats and for womens Josephs. Wakefild October 19th 1761. Soft spinning is best.

Let all frises wich are dyed bee stricken on tenter has soon has tentered so when dry turn the wool on the end and the look much better bottom and frise handsomer.

Mr Norton of Wakefild buys 5 or 6 pak of frises in a year from Manchester wich are to rap fine peice in prest cloath.

f. 36v The friseing mill will go 16 times about for the watter wheell going 3 times.[129] Friser att Dewsberry in 1760 is names is Joshua Perking. Now in 1762 with John Hunt att Wakefild horse mill.

125 Entry crossed out with 'X'.
126 Sentence in margin.
127 Entry crossed out with 'X'.
128 It is clear from the arrangement of the text that swatches of cloth were orginally pasted on the outside edge of this sheet.
129 Diagram of mill wheel and gearing with numbers of cogs. Other entry in the margin.

There is a fondling hospitall att Ackworth near to Pomferatt in Yorkshire. One Richard Hargreaves is teachar and governor of the children to spin and weave woolen 1761. f. 37r

Likewise a fondling hospitall att Srewsbury in Sropshire wich one Thomas Booth a Bury man is governer to teach the woolen manufackture. Both hospitalls are under London Hospital and kept in the country for cheapest. The are all for bastard children and are verry good things. The prevent a deall of murder. All children comes from London Hospital. 1761.[130]

To make that sort of cloath called fearnoughts and sell itt to country farmers to drive theire carts in would bee great profit so sell itt down behind Wakefild amongst farmers.

Thomas Kirshaw debtor.[131] f. 37v
1761

July 15 to ½ brood frisd white	0	1	0
23 to ½ brood green	0	1	0
Received of Dane Scot	0		

How to fitt top bushes in a friseing board the trust way is fill your low bushes with a large cork so have a hole through the middle of the cork with a sharp bodkin or priker in. So lay your top bord on then putt up your cork with priker in so where itt priks bore your hole for your top bushes so the will work true. Butt before you bore the hole center and score itt out from the prik the compass of your bushes so then bore the hole after.

1762 The Wakefild merchants them wich trade with woollen cloath the all have tenters and keeps dressers and preses att home.

The easyest way for card beam wheels to goe is lett them have guttions driven in att end and to run on two guttions. The easyest way of lifting the card beam out is to have a leaver under itt thus so lift itt up and put a pin into the post to bear itt up so itt will run bak with ease. Likewise have your low rowlar to run on guttions and itt makes itt go easyar 1761 John Hunt mill of Wakefild.[132] f. 38r

This pattern is att 3s 1d per yards and sold to Mr Steer Wakefild 1761. It is a mixt brood.

Matthew Wolton pressing.[133] f. 38v
1761
July 23 to 4 half basses prest £0:3:0.

The best way to put steps the truest way of friseing mill spindle for spindle foot to run in is gett a cork and put itt in the low bush and let your cork fill the hole so have a hole through the middle of the cork through wich put a band so hang a small bitt of lead shaped like a pyramid has thus.[134] So have a pin driven in att end with its head cut of so drive both ends down so hang the band to itt. Or there is another way first measure the hole of the low brush with compass so half the compass has thus is[135] so

[130] Date interlineated.
[131] Entry crossed out with 'X'.
[132] Diagram showing a man working a lever.
[133] Entry crossed out with 'X'.
[134] Diagram in text.
[135] Diagram in text.

strike a round circle in pres paper to fitt the low bush hole so put a hole through middle of the press paper so hang the plumb to and the mill go truest.

f. 39r The Wakefild merchants byes cheifly all drabs browns snufs points and cheifly all mixters att Leeds cloath hall and all low prised cloath is ready money only keeping 15 or 20 shillings in theire hand to see if itt is lentgh when itt is wetted and if itt is not the maker hee bates for short length and when the hapen so the cheifly call itt more then itt is but if itt is length the maker goes for his money in 8 or 10 weeks and this is called watter length. One Mr Markaram and Mr Blades Leeds merchants byes a deall of browns otherwise called copers bye some wich are low prised ones about 2s 8d per yard in bawk or 2s 6d made of wool about £5 per pak. Leeds 1761.

There is a maney makers about Wakefild wich will carry cloath to the Wakefild merchants houses butt att Leeds hall the get better prises.

f. 39v Itt is a greatt advantage to cloathmakers wich makes coalared to mind what sorts of cloath and coalars goes of best has browns blak and light browns drabs or mixt broods called shephards these last are cheifly frised. For except a merchant has orders for cloath hee will not bye aney or except hee expects orders soon and nows such and such sorts will go of in the next order. Leeds Wakefild 176_.[136]

Mr Daniell Maude Wakefild merchant send thousands in a year of them low prised Hudersfild 17 yeards peices wich are all drabs and some goes of frised others prest to Mr Samuel and Thomas Floodshire London merchant. Hee sends to Boston in Lincolnshire and hee likes a good round nap not to low.[137]

Aderton fairs in winter season before Crismass itt is each fortnight or six weeks[138] and itt holds 3 or 4 days each.[139]

f. 40r Let all low bushes and top bushes bee made taperish with holes shaped round and taper like has a cork is shaped and lett your bushes bee put in with holes that is the wide side of the hole to hang downwards has the low board is and when top bord is on the wide side of bush will hang down or otherwise when you put itt in put top wide side upward and fitt your spindles to the bushes to a hairs breadth so the spindle necks and low shoulder will bee taper and so bye raiseing or lowering them you have more or less throw. Wakefild 1761.

Lett all spindles fitt bushes to have butt a little room but to fitt so close has to the thickness of a sixpence and thus the will move the board exacktley round without aney false strokes or jerking and make a complete round nap.

f. 40v When you frise peices wich has oyl blown on att after shorn lett the board bee fine and close greett and the other board to bee not to close butt a little willd and open. The reason for itt is thus when a board frises oyld peices itt works sharphar with working and chawked peice will soon make a bord sliperey if itt is to fine a close greet. 1761.

The make no sort of wool wich is skin wool into cloath in no part of Yorkshire. All the skin wool is sold out in Yorkshire to Rochdale markitt except some little now and then used for combing.

136 Number illegible.
137 Sentence in margin.
138 Ms reads 'we'.
139 Ms reads 'ea'.

Mr. Mills and Mr. Jeremagh or Jerrey Naylor Wakefild merchants does most dyed broad frizes at Wakefild.

Aney man wich is in a trade and can vent his goods itt is much better then working att f. 41r
aney bisness and 10 times better then working servant lett his wages bee never so good.

To scrible shear floks and wool together itt makes the wool look excellent fine. The prise of a 42 weight made of white shear floks and wool costing after £7 per pak now say

30 pound of wool	0	17	6
shear floks 12 pound at 3d per	0	3	0
3 quarts of rape oyl	0	1	9
makeing at Rochdale	0	12	0
milling	0	1	0
	£1	15	3

Now this peice will seell att £2:4:0 and look much better then made of all wool.

Wakefild streets are verrey bad that there is holes that oftens breaks cart axelltress and f. 41v
in winter for dirt itt will take you over shoes top. November 18th 1761.

There is a deall of taylors that keeps a woollen drapers shop and furnishes gentlemen with all sorts of cloath and finds them triming. This is and excellent bisness when a man gets into the way of itt. Wakefild 1761.

Observe that let all scarlits bee striken or tenter so when dry and of tenter blow them over with the sweet oyl so turn the wool bak with a brush and frise them with a board wich has frisd no coalar besides since itt was washed or if itt is clean washed either will do and thus frise all scarlits and the will keep the coalar and frise handsomer and look better. Lett all spindle necks stand up streight and fitt close in bushes and make round nap.

There is a deal of lin yarn comes to Wakefild keay wich comes in great casks so goes f. 42r
forward to Manchester. 1761.

Hudersfild trade allways goes best from betwixt Mickelmas to Crismass espesaley coarse goods. 1761.

Att Leeds and Wakefild the oyll all theire white cloath and the oyl itt with theire hands wich is a way the cannot lay itt even on and if apeice is dyed dark blew there is spots shows where the oyl was not even layed on except the are well stok washed after dyed.

Making blankits is a good bisness and sell them to country houses and gentlemen houses and lett them bee well raised and cornered and a cleane coalar and not to small spining tho never so fine.

Mr Tenant of Wakefild bespeaks Hudersfild cloth to bee made and milled to a yard f. 42v
wide wich are light drabs so frised and goes to Hull for womens cloaks to one Mr Nowell or Newsley. Mr Frank Maude trades much with him. Wakefild 1761.

On Fridays att Wakefild there is swine to sell through out the year and cows with calf att foot. Flesh meat is oftens cheap att Wakefild and flowr butt for aney thing else itt has dear has aney place. 1761.

Chawk and calley sand sells cheap and Spanish white at Leeds and Wakefild.

At Wakefild fair in November there is abundance of fatt oxen and large bullocks to sell.

f. 43r Shear flocks scribbled amongst wool makes apeice look fine and have a close bottom. Some of the low prisd peice made att the Hudersfild are made of shear flocks and wool and when about ½ scowrd so milled up with earth the are right strong and will make very handsome frises. These sorts is coalard cloath and are verry thick spun or else the would not mill stout and country farmers will not look att a peice of thin cloath alltho itt is never so fine and the could have itt as cheap has course thick.

For all light coalars a rule to bee observed is that the allways oyl Hudersfild frises and oyls them with theire hands wich the cannot laye itt even on so when a peice is chawked and lyes in a shop them places where oyl was most will turn quite another coalar and fades.

f. 43v When Hudersfild trade goes well the cloathmakers gets a deall of money bye low prised peices. The have such advantages of makeing them has of noyls floks waste calf hair dyed blak for mixtures indeed the will make cloath of aney thing. Itt goes well just now does Hudersfild trade. November the 18th 1761.

To gett money is has thus. Sopose a man was to bye one of them 38 weights or 40 weights such has is sold in Rochdale markitt so gett itt milled to 28 inches brood so gett itt dyed blew on bawk so wash itt and put itt in a driveing stok for 8 or 10 minuts to wring watter out then give itt a pound of soap and a pound of flowr and mill itt well in Itt makes itt strong so coalar your soap with indigo. Give the soap att three times not all at once.[140]

f. 44r Itt is much better weather about Wakefild Pomferat Leeds and that circuit then itt is in Lanckeshire itt being 10 times more rain in Lanckeshire.

A rule to bee observed is that lett a man be in never such good caracter if hee bee a servant and lett him do 19 good turns if hee mis the 20th all is good services are void for there is few men if servants can allways please butt some or other has a splen towards them to do them a mischeiff.

There is a deall of light mottals and blew close bodeyed top coats worn in Yorkshire wich are much in fashion 1761. Mixt broods are for top coats.

There is some few broods made att Wakefild for cloaks wich are dyed scarlits and are 2 yards brood and some 9 quarts wich are to brood to frise.

f. 44v 1760. Mr. Lumb dyear att Wakefild hee allways boyls his scarlits att night so when boyld he washes them and lets them lye cool all night so finishes them in the morning and kills his spirits 12 hours before used and to his spirits he puts one third of watter in when he kills them and thus the will frise has well has aney blew when spirits is lightley killed. Hee dyes most att Wakefild.

140 Sentence in margin.

The maner of makeing a good blood puding such has is made in Yorkshire. First the boyl up some milk so pours itt on to a peney manchitt so letts the manchit suck up all the milk then mixes blood and ½ pound of shuitt and 3 or 4 onions with some time sweet marjoram and sallt so stirs all up togehter and bakes itt under goose.

Some of the Leeds dressers the turn the wool of frises before the white cloath goes to f. 45r
the dyeing so tenters itt when dyed and sends itt to the friseing butt this is not a good way att all. 1761. The raise mixt broods weett frises this is right.[141]

Most of the Wakefild merchants wich drive a greatt trade keeps a man cheifly for drawing woolen cloath has Frank Maude Daniell Maude Mr Charles Steer Mr Mills. Theire wage is cheifly about 20 pounds per year and other benefits. The reason is of so much draweing all peices are burled if for presing and maney frises are burled wich some fine planes has 5000 burls plucked out and some of the large burls makes holes in the cloath so the are all drawn before prest att after drest and burled. Some will have frises all burled lett them bee never so coarse.

Sir Samuell Fludyer the greatt London merchant wich trades so much with all kinds of f. 45v
woolen goods was chosen Lord Mayor of London for the present year September 19th 1761. His name is Fludyer and not Floodshire has is commonly called. Hee has a son born September 1761.[142]

1762. Mr Daniell Maude is cheiff man att Wakefild for doing the most narrow Hudersfild fines. Hee sends a deall to London and into Scotland. Likewise Mr William Naylor does the most mixt broods frises and duffils of aney att Wakefild. Hee trades into Scotland and to London. Mr Jeremy Naylor and Mr Mills does most dyed frises. Mr Naylor sends to London. Mr Mills trades over sea. 1762.

How to order scarlits to frise best and cover the threads and to keep theire coalar and f. 46r
not frise white in the bottom is lett them bee well drest in the white so when dyed strike them on the tenter with a fine jak card the right way of the wool so when dry blow itt evenly over with a little sweet oyl so turn the wool with a fine card or a brush and frise itt with a board cleane washed or one wich has done scarlit before and has done no other coalar since itt was washed but scarlits. All peices for scarlits or aney thing for Josephs ought to bee milled in a faleing stok. A driveing stok crimps them att heart wich when drest and frised shows crimpy. 1761.

Good method.[143] To blow a dark mixter over with oyl att after shorn so turn the wool bak and frise itt twise over so chawk itt and wisk chawk even in so frise itt again.

The coalard cloathmakers the sise all theire warps and weaves with weet spows both f. 46v
coalard and white. Wakefild 1761.

Mr Mills Richard and John and Pemberton byes a deall of Lanckshire 42 weights sayls and cottons. Some comes frised but cheiff most comes in the white and dyed and frised att Wakefild. Hee trades with Mr Walmsly Thomas Hold George Low Jonathan Clegg att Heights. The are only 12d pence per peice friseing and 3d tentering. 1761. Dyers tenters none.

141 Sentence in margin.

142 Sentence in margin.

143 Phrase interlineated.

The prise of a 42 weight made of shear floks and wool wich shear floks is the finest staple and exceeds all others not to short. First saye

30 pd of wool att 6d per	0	15	0
14 pd of floks 3d per	0	3	6
Scribbling for weft floks and wool	0	1	6
grease and makeing	0	14	0
	1	14	0

Now this will sell at £2:4:0.

f. 47r A thing to bee observed that when you see the sun rise whether in winter or sumer there the day breaks forth in that quarter for itt is the sun wich gives light to the whole world. 1761.

When aney white cloath linceys or blankits mises scowring and lett in grease hang them to dry so when drye weet them over with earth and watter so work them in stok till you see the will scowr. If the are verrey greasey the use earth and lant. Wakefild mill 1761.

The cheifley put 14 or 16 pound of floks in to a couple of mixt broads. The make mixt broads all about Leeds and Wakefild. Breadth in bawk 1 yard 12 inches. 1761.

Shear floks looks verrey well scribled in wool and make apeice look close and fine bottomed.

f. 47v The maner of roasting a rabitt the Yorkshire way. Put some onions sage peper and sallt so sewe up his belley with a little catchup in. So roast his liver and hack itt and mellt some butter and mixt itt all together in the dripings wich comes from the rabit.

The cropers and master dresers has the liberty of cutting the corner of a tayl end wich the hook on a slant on tenter so cuts 8 or 9 inches of one corner to make it streight and the head ends the letters of wich are all sett in the garter and these are sold for to make aprons on. Leeds and Wakefild 1761.

The master dresers has to theire post is cheifly to take in work and when finished to buckerom itt up if for over sea and if for the country trade to make itt up in parcils and sopose hee has 10 men hee has ½ of profitt the all get.

f. 48r How to dress and frise all Hudersfild 17 yards coarse frises. First lett them bee well oyld then well raised and and shorn about the midle of the wool. Do not shear them to low. So frise them once over or twise has you think proper then to chawk them evenly over and wisk the peice well over to wisk chawk evenly in. So frise itt once more or twise again. Mr. Daniell Maude[144] att Wakefild byes abundance of them 17 yards and hee likes a good round nap and hard and not to very low for coarse goods if a peice is low itt seldome is hard to abide paking. Wakefild 1761.

To frise mixters or Hudersfild drabs frise them single one att once the first time so two att once the last times in another mill.

f. 48v How to manage a stoved white to make itt handle soft and scymit is att after stoved put itt in the stok and work a pound of soap in so dress and frise itt att after for in a generall way stoved peices handles ask and hard and but few will frise handsome. 1762.

144 Word interlineated in two places, above and below.

Some cloathmakers when milling a couple of mixt broads will use 3 pound of flowr (or 4 pound)[145] and 4 threepeney balls of soap (or 6 balls of soap some uses).[146] The way the do itt is the shave theire soap into a kitt so pours hott watter on and beats itt a lather so mixes flowr in cold watter sad has watter poridge allmost so mixes all up together and leeks itt over then the open att first time so att after milled in the keep lecking each hour or so has itt turns round in the stok some boyls soap to make it toughar and the stiffen better. Wakefild mill 1762. Some boyls soap and flowr alltogether and some not.[147]

Some country people will tye yarn and so dye itt blew red or green and itt makes f. 49r
prettey lincey for wayscoats. Wakefild 1761.

Light mixtrs broods sells the high prise then dark ones in a general way. Mr. William Naylor Wakefild Merchant byes a many mixt broads for frises and duffils wich hee send to Mr. Flodshire of London merchant 1761.

A sort of hair cloath called pompilion in Yorkshire itt is made of that cow hair wich comes of salted hides. Itt is a sort of strong stapled hair and free from lime or dirt but calf hair has the finest staple to make cloath. Cloath on pompilion is made like wadding and is used for to lay shear boards with all in Yorkshire.

For 20 miles round from Leeds or Wakefild itt is judged to bee the best liveing and good meat in plentey of aney where in England. 1761.

Wakefild is cheiff blankit markitt of aney town in Yorkshire and a man may bye 1000 f. 49v
pair aney Friday in winter time. Some att afters blankits is scowrd and watter well wrung out will give them some soap and Spanish white or flowr so mills itt in and some scowrs itt out again and some leaves itt in. Spanish white is 4½d per stone at Wakefild 1761.

Mr. Daniell Maude Wakefild byes a deall of low prisd 17 yards Hudersfild frises from 14s 6d to 19 shill bawk wich goes to Mr. Fluider London merchant. 1761.

A rule to clothiers. Them men wich trades with duffils and frises mixt broods the do not mind if the have a little greas in but if the are for presing the must bee cleane or else the will not face when out in press and the cropers oftens send them to the mill to cleane and maker pays charges.

Att Bradford fair on St Andrews day old stile itt is cheif fair in all Yorkshire for fat f. 50r
swine. Fair holds 3 or 4 days and Ambry is a fair for swine.

Some is of and opinion oatmeall and or bean meal and grains will feed a swine has well as aney thing and is the cheapest feed. Oatmeal sells much chephar att Manchester then in aney part of Yorkshire. Flowr is has cheap has oatmeall att Wakefiled if not of a fine sorts.

If a man goes to hawk or sell woolen cloath into the country hee must bee of a mild temper and please his words with much dexterity and if a man bids you a low prise for your goods put itt of with a smile and saye praye Sir if you understood these goods you would not talk after that maner for there is few men can judge of a fine plane to 6d per yard and a man gets 10 shill oftens with talking.

[145] Phrase interlineated.

[146] Phrase interlineated.

[147] Sentence in margin.

f. 50v To mill white cloath with soap ball or castle soap makes itt have a fine kindley handle with itt and to handle solid att heart and not spungey and scowr itt out never so cleane itt makes itt handle well and thus all white cloath is milled at Wakefild if of good sorts the allways scowr soap out just att last before the finish so cuttles up and puts itt in the stok in the cuttles and lets itt go 10 minuits or so to take all the crimps and scrumples out. The mill all in driveing stoks.[148]

For Scarlits mill in falling stoks and no soap att all and the dye much better and does not cutt white when soft and scimit.

The make some excellent good fine broods in saddleworth both white and coalard and best spinning of aney in all Yorkshire.

f. 51v Manchester carryer comes into Wakefild each Tuesday night and sets of on Wednsday about noon. 1761.

Hallifax carryears comes to Wakefiled Mundays Wednesdays and Fridays three times a week pakhorses and wagons. Theire time is not just certain to one day. Wakefild November 18th 1761.

Rochdale carryers wich goes through Healand seldome comes to Wakefiled going to Leeds 10 times for Wakefild once. If a man sends parcils itt is best to send to Hallifax so they go forward to Wakefild direcktly and are verry carefull are Hallifax caryears both waggons and pakhorses for there is a deall of them wich makes carrige scarce some times of the year. 1761.

All men of trade should now carryers stages well so goods goe forward.

f. 52r There is one Sugdin and Glasebye shopkeeprs att Pomferat byes a good many Hudersfild and blew frises. July 18th 1761.

f. 52v In Glostershire att Bridgewater and betwixt Bath and Bristol the are verry good mecanicks for mills of all kinds has coper logwood wire paper corn mills. A man invented and engine there to make bricks another to weave diaper to work itt selff. Att Bristoll there is 18 churches and the cathederall besides 7 or 8 meeting houses. There is has fine a seaport has aney in all England and great trade there. 1760.

The brokers in London byes a deall of frises some for mens coats both mixters and blew and maney for josephs wich is brood cloath fine spun and good wool wich the sell at extravagent prise.

f. 53r In bad dryeing weather peices are oftens scarce at Hudersfild markit and if a man could have a tenter in a house has verrey well hee might hee might sell cloath to great profitt. Badest dryeing is December and Jenuary peices sells best in October and November.

f. 55r The drye all theire oats att Wakefild mill on tin wich is layed on made like a chamber floor and the tin is of a strong sort and punched full of little holes so has corn cannot gett through and this is best way of aney. The drye with cyenders. Hops are dryed has above and the have a tin cover compass of the floor wich the can raise bye pulleys or lower and the lett the cover down with in one foot of the hops and itt reflects and dryes the top side has well as bottom and makes the hops smell much better. 1761.

148 Sentence in margin.

From Skiption in Craven and Guisburn and Settle there is 1000 and ten thousands of f. 56r
Scoth cattle driven into the south of England down towards London and Norich and Norfolk each year. The go down in Aprill May and June and a deall of sheep. The go through Leeds and Wakefild and towns about. 1761.

It is a great folley to put to much confidence in aney man for if you think you have f. 56v
never such a good freind hee will not bee a freind long if hee can gett nothing to his advantage bye you.

The are verrey cuning sort of people in Yorkshire doing theire bisness excellent well. Lett goods bee never so coarse the dye and press them or frise them verrey well doing them with great care and exacktness and are verrey covetous seldome giveing aney thing and but few cares who sinks so the swim. Wakefild November 18th 1761.

Itt is and old sayeing that the are cheifley sharp witted people in the North and given to bee knaveish but Yorkshire is has bad has aney in England.

A proud man is allways a simple minded man.

The make att Hallifax shagg wich is a mixter that is blak and white wool scribled f. 57r
together before itt is combed and sort of plush made of tyed yarn like has thunder and lightning is made and some is tyed in the yarn for the weft wich is to cutt the shagg on. First itt is dyed a fine yellow so tyed when yellow then dyed a full dark green and the yarn is tyed so has the spots will shew allmost round and this looks verry prettey for wayscoats.

The prise of 30 yards of woosted shagg the wool costing 6 pounds per pak f. 57v

	£	s	d
30 pound of wool at 6d per	0	15	0
combing your wool	0	5	0
spining and twineing	0	17	0
weaving att 6d per yard	0	15	0
	2	12	0
Now this will sell at 2s 6d per yard and 30 yards is	3	15	0
	2	12	0
your profitt	1	3	0

In Scotland theire wool is verry coarse and all in the North part of England wich makes them bye a deal of woolen cloath out in Yorkshire both mixt broods and Hudersfild cloath and the Yorkshire men can aford cloath has cheap has aney shire in England espesaly coalard the use so maney floks in. 1762.

Itt is worst thing in England to hawk woolen cloath for reasons to maney to shew. f. 58v
Butt if a man getts orders for itt hee may gett money and trades with good chaps and the woolen facktory is has good has most facktorys in England to gett money bye if hee understands his bisness right.

The Wakefild merchants all keeps dresers att theire own houses and gets frises done has cheap has aney where in all England. For a Hudersfild 24 yard peice a master gives his men one shilling for raiseing and shearing one cutt and bakshearing 5 or 6 boards in head end and one shilling a peice friseing. For a 17 yard peice 8d dresing shilling friseing. So the garge of a 24 yard peice is only 2 shillings dresing and friseing and a 17 yard peice is 1s 8d. Then a master finds shears and oyl and cards then hee has floks and the will pay verey well for tools.

f. 59r If a man observes that wind is strongar in a pasage then on and open plaine in a passage betwixt two houses or in entrys. If you mind the wind blowes verrey strong and a wind mill such has is described in this book would answer well.

Mr Daniell Maude and Frank his brother are the cheiff men att Hudersfild markitt byeing more cloath then aney one merchant in Yorkshire of narrow goods has all kinds of Hudersfild frises both coarse and fine and all kinds of Saddleworth plane att Hudersfild markitt in bawk wich hee keeps 10 or 12 men dresing at[149] his own shop in Wakefild and hee byes white broods for dyeing and mixt broods of all kinds and blankets[150] and some few Rochdale goods and Hondley white planes. Hee trades to London and Scotland and into the country. Dan and Frank Maude partners. March 28th 1762.

f. 59v Some of the Wakefild merchants will have Hudersfild frises dufild on bak others will bak 5 bords end.[151]

f. 60r The Wakefild merchants wich trades into the country byes a deall of kersey coalard cloath att Hudersfild markit wich is[152] dark drabs and middle drabs wich the send into the country att about 3s per yard when finished so down to 1s 6d and the country people towards Hull and York Tadcaster and Thorn and Snathe the like them does country farmers best for except a cloath is strong the farmers with working out the pull itt into peices and tears like paper so strong cloath is fittest all over England for farmers.

Observations on windes for North and East winds are both cold and further you go north and coldar and likewise eastward futher you go and coldar and further you go south and wamar and likewis further west and warmar and warmar a country is and finear the sheeps wool is. March 1762.

Country people all down towards Rotherham and Barnsley Pomfrat Doncaster and the like the make a deal of striped lincey for wayscoats and striped and plaine serge for their own wareing and sends itt mostly to Wakefild to mill dye and press or to Selby or York dyear.

f. 60v Sir Lyonell belongs Wakefild mills wich hee bought in 1750 and Mr Mills of Wakefild bad 15 thousand for them and hee gave 15 thousand[153] £500 for them with the ground belonging them. So Mr Mills (Wakefild merchant)[154] was vext att itt wich makes Sir Lyonell and him att varriance. Then Mr Mills encouraged pensioners to grind mallt on steell mills wich is a thing the can do verrey well but Lyonell overpowered them bye law with money. The was forced to liver up and now the town of Wakefild is confined to grind all theire mallt att his mill wich hee moowters verry deep oftens and hee cast a man for bringing flour to sell in the town of Wakefild wich is and out of way thing. That in short hee is such and opreser of

149 Ms reads 'a'.

150 Ms reads 'blank'.

151 Meaning not entirely clear here; appears to refer to how much of or in what fashion the back of a piece is finished.

152 Word interlineated.

153 Ms reads 'ths'.

154 Phrase interlineated.

poor that every one does not like him and some judges hee will go to the deivill when ever hee dyes. 1762.

Sir Lyonell now has power to mowter and grind both flower and maltt and beans or pease wich is to bee used in the town of Wakefild bye and Ackt pased in 1761.

In some parts of Scotland the are verrey poor and verry ill sett to get cloaths wich f. 61v
makes a deal of low prised coarse frises go into Scotland.

Mr Whitlock frisear near Leeds att Shipscar when a dresser carryes a peice hee gives f. 62r
them a pint of good ale wich gains him a deall of love amongst dresers. Leeds March 1762.

Some merchants marks theire peices over 10 shilling more or 15 or 20 according to f. 62v
goodness more then the cost them. The do itt to blind dresers.

The comon prise for a journiman woolen cloathmaker about Wakefild is 6 pound a year meat drink and lodging and that is the highest and some 5 pound a year. March 1762.

Mr Frank Maude Wakefild cheifly goes to London in Jenuary or Febury and gets order for brood cloath has blews saxons greens and mixt broods. 1762.

Looms made of deall will answer to weave woolen very well and will stand and is f. 63r
good to make and comes in cheap.

Mr Frank Maude Wakefild send each year to Mr James Smith of Norich 8 or 10 f. 63v
Hondley planes dyed blew and prest for Norich Hospitall. The go a week before Crismas cheifley. 1762.

Mr Daniell Maude sends green to the above order for Hospital.

One Mr Fuidyer comonly called Floodshire and one Mr Jones merchant are two of f. 64r
cheiff London merchants in all London for byeing mixt brood frises wich the have from Wakefild of Mr William Naylor and Mr Dan Maude sends them all sorts of Hudersfild goods both frises and prest cloath a great maney of 17 yard frises and 17 yard prest cloath. 1762.

The maner of a wind mill to go round has a watter wheel does and to work in full sayll all ways and to receive wind by a slide wich is to go up and down to that sayl and to have 4 or 6 sayles to itt.[155]

Mr George Charnock Wakefild merchant sends a deal of frises to Lisbon and in to f. 64v
Holland. 1762 and a deal goes in white only drest frises.

The make a deal of files att Shefild and Liverpool.

There is a deal of windmills att York and Liverpool.

In all light Hudersfild mixters and into light mixt broods the allways put a deall of f. 65r
floks in. The prise of a mixt brood made of fine base floks and wool wich costs 7 pound per pack

[155] Diagram in text shows an axle with sails perpendicular to it; the number '8' is next to one of the sails.

	£	s	d
Now say 45 pound of wool at 7d per	1	6	2
15 pound of floks at 4½ per pound	0	5	7½
grease and scribling	0	3	0
spining	0	13	0
weaving and milling	0	8	0
dyeing the 20 pound of wool	0	2	0
	£2	17	9½

Now this peice will sell for 3s 4d per yard in bawk and hold 33 yards and one yard 13 inches brood. At 3s 4d per yard it comes to

	£	s	d
	£5	10	0
	2	17	9
the profitt att one peice	2	12	3

f. 65v There goes a deall of Hudersfild frises from Wakefild all into the West of England and south part for where the make such fine cloath itt is not fitt to weare for everey days close or indeed poor people cannot bye high prised cloath so the sell theire fine cloath and byes lowe prised for theire own wearing and sends theire fine sort all over England for gentlemans ware. 1762.

Att Aberforth the make a deall of pins and some sorts are hawked in Wakefild att 10 rows a peney. But theire slender ones and fitt for nothing butt fine linen or rag men to change for rags. Aberforth is 8 miles of Leeds. 1762.

There is some Hudersfild peices of drabs inclineing to a sandey drab and is comonly called a Floodshire drab will make verry handsome frises. This sort of drab took its name from[156] one Mr Floodshire London merchant now living. Hee is used to bye so maney of this coalar brood cloathirs calls them Floodshire drabs. 1762.[157]

f. 66r The maner how Jon Hunt man (one of Atkison men fomerley was)[158] now frisear att Wakefild does his board. Hee casts itt each time itt needs washing or wore sliperey first hee shoots his low board with a plaine has even and true has he can likewise his top board. So then casts itt about thicknes of and old worn shilling so dryes itt and rubs itt and readey for working and when itt is worn sliperey hee washes most of the old of and so has glew and allakar and sand boyled up together and layes itt over again about the thickness of a sixpence. Hee has been a frisear at Dewsberry 11 year so now is turned of and lives with John Hunt Wakefild. Hee allways used to cast them thick ¾ of inch so keep washing down whilest all was of till comeing to Wakefild and hearing that I did not wash mye boards down but had some other method of doing them so he judged itt to bee has above and so tryeing that waye liked itt better then old waye for this way they do not crak or blister or weare into holes or bee uneven (has washing down does).[159] 1762. But hee does verry poor work at present.[160]

f. 67r The dress frises att Hudersfild verey well likewise att Rochdale and Burey and them parts. The dress Lanckeshire goods verrey well att Wakefild for a Lanckeshire peice of 40 yards the think 4 shillings to little for itt. The do not understand dresing frises att Leeds or Wakefild has in the above parts. 1762.

156 '1762' interlineated above.

157 Phrase 'brood cloathirs calls them Floodshire drabs. 1762.' in margin.

158 Phrase interlineated above.

159 Phrase in margin.

160 Sentence in margin.

In war time there goes a dell of reds brood cloath wich are none drest only prest for f. 67v
soldiers breeches to London.

1762. Mr Gorge Charnock trade into Holland cheifly to Rotterdam to one Mr f. 68r
Youngsman is has follows mixt broods both frises and prest ones of low prised sorts some he trades to Lisbon.

The cloath makers above Wakefild the do not like to mill strong cloath in frostey f. 68v
weather itt does not mill so well or look so nise has att other times butt some are so poor the cannot wait butt must go forward frost or not frost.

In the West of England att Cheddar near Axbridge in Somersetshire there is a spring f. 69v
that rises and drives twelfe mills in a quarter of a mile compass wich are corn mills and cloath mills and friseing mills and logwood mills with divers others. The frize much att Devises and Bradforth in the Countey of Wiltshire in the West of England. Good fine cloath is much better to frise then a deall of Yorkshire coarse cloath. If a man can peform to frise the coarse Yorkshire cloath hee neeeds not fear butt hee may frise well in other countys.

The prise of a mixt brood made of wool costing 5d pence per pound f. 70r

	£	s	d[161]
60 pound of wooll at 5d per is	£1	5	0
dyeing 40 pound of wool	0	2	0
scribling	0	1	6
makeing	0	16	0
milling and flowr and soap	0	3	0
	£2	7	6
grease to bee	0	2	0
Now this peice will hold 30 yards and will sell att 3 shillings per yard			
and is cheap at	£4	10	0
	2	9	6
so the profit is	£2	0	6

The merchants cheifly byes two of these broods togehter wich is comonly called a cloath. If the bye and od peice the call itt and od dozen. If you use fine base floks at 5d per pound in your peice about 16 pound itt looks much finear.

Att Dewsberey Mill when the work att friseing att nights the have 4 lamps fixed att f. 72r
each corner of the mill and one to run about with that if the frise att nights the lamps casts as good light has att noontide. The have and oyl mill so oyl is plentifull. 1762.

The maner of a wind mill to stand in a house and shutt up att nights and to give wind bye slides going up and down.[162] To stand in a chamber and the mill to frise on belowe. This mill will answer well.[163]

In Wiltshire in the West of England the make brood cloath in the serge way and frises f. 73r
itt and milled has above[164] and is used in and about London and in country for gentlemans banians and looks verry well and exceeds aney brood cloth for that use. Itt

[161] £ s d headings are implicit.

[162] Diagram below: central pole with square 'sails' to each side attached to mill gearing.

[163] Two sentences in margin.

[164] Refers to previous entry describing how to mill using soap after the cloth is dyed.

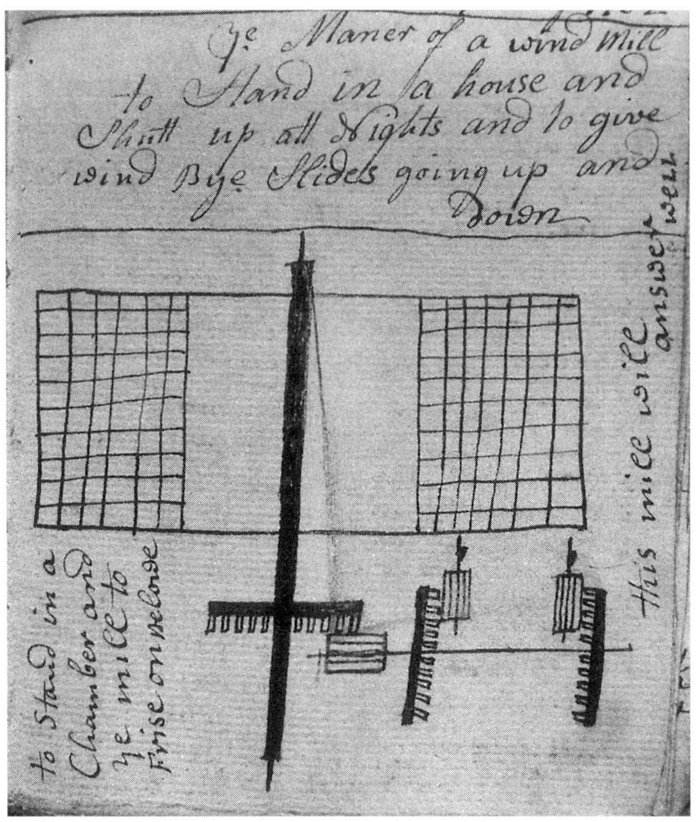

'The maner of a wind mill to stand in a house' (f. 72r)

is fine thin ware and looks close and is not open like one that is woven plaine and slender milled. 1762.

At Wigan in Lanckeshire the make has good screws for hott preses has aney where in all England.

f. 74r A verse on a man wich had spent all his money att alehouse and resolved to have one merry glass before hee reformed himself so got a glass of good napey ale and holding itt out att arms length and said
Gett thee from mee
Thou hast undone mee
Yett come to mee for I love thee
Thou hast made my freinds my foes
Thou has made me go with tread[165] bare cloaths
But if I gett thee to my nose
Then of thou goes.
1762

[165] Word interlineated.

So drinks itt up and resolves not to flinch a cup of good Napey ale. This is a true verse for ale has ruined maney thousands of men and familys.[166]

In some places a man may bye crooked wood inclineing for bends and may light of itt cheap so cutt itt up and saw itt into felix for watter wheels or cog wheels and keep them drye by you. The are things that sells verry dear about Leeds or Wakefild and in some country towns the are bought in cheapest of aney wood is crooked wood.

Wiltshire and Glostershire are cheiff places wich stands both wholley by the woolen f. 74v
manufacktory. Att Stround in Glostershire the dye a deall of scarlits that on a fair day you may see 2 or 3 hundred peices all on the tenters att once. Scarlits blews and greens but scarlitt cheifley. The make mixt cloath and drabs dyed in the wool in some parts of Glostershire. Stroud watter is verry good for scarlits.[167]

In Sropshire att Oswestrey the make cloath called Srowsberry cottons and frises. Att Oswestrey and att Srowsberry the have a hall for Srowsbery cottons and Welch flanills that 5 or 6 hundred pound is worn each markitt day. The frise at Srowsberry. 1762.

Att Whitby[168] in Oxfordshire the make a deall of blankits verry large ones and rugs and coverlids and tilts for wagons wich in this branch the exeed all other shires in England.

Att Kendall the have a great facktory of Kendall cottons called wich is dyed blews and reds and a maney frised white and att Kirby Stephen and att Kirby Lonsdale the make the above cottons for Kendal merchants.

In Yorkshire where the follow the woolen manufacktory is att Leeds in and round f. 75r
about and Wakefild and Peniston Hudersfild Hallifax Dewsbery Bradford Saddleworth and in a maney country villages in the West Rideing of Yorkshire.

In Lanckeshire where the follow the woolen manufaktory is att Rochdale Bury Rosondale Haslingdin Radcliffe Bridge a little att Wigin for rugs and coverlids and att Prescott and att Bolton the stand bye making of fustians and has a good markitt on Monday for cheese. 1762.

Att Lisbon and Oporto the weare cheifly bases and a maney is dyed blak itt being cheif coalar the use wareing wich the purchase from the English merchants.

In Esex the make a deall of all kinds of bases wich the sell att Leaden Hall in London being a weekly markitt for Coldchester bases for them there.

In Lanckeshire the make all kinds of basses and has a great factory of them. Rochdale is the markitt for them. March 1762.

The Wakefild merchants has all shops att Hudersfild to take theire cloath in when the f. 75v
have bought itt and to pay theire money. Every merchant has a seperate shop to himself.[169]

[166] Sentence in margin.

[167] Sentence in margin.

[168] Presumably means Witney.

[169] The following list was in a single vertical column.

Wakefild Merchants	Charles Steer +	Luck Anison
Mr Samuel Zouch +	Daniell Maude +	Richard Carr
Richard Buxton	Frank Maude +	James Norton +
Mr Mills +	Mr Rickaby	George Charnock +
Mr Tenant	Wiliam Nevison	Jeremy Naylor +

These merchants above trades with narrow cloth cheifly and where you see this mark '+' the trade with broods and narrows to besides there is more in the brood way.

f. 76r There is men wich trades with wool att Wakefiled att sends a good deal of brood cloath to them wich the have wool from and some few Saddlworth planes. The can vent them.

f. 76v The Leeds merchants has oftens orders for Hudersfild cloath some wich is double peices. The are cheifle drabs and the purchase them of the Wakefild merchants. Mr Ward of Leeds byes his of Mr Daniell Maude in Wakefild and Mr Dixon in Leeds byes his of Mr Nevison of Wakefild. The are some frised some is prest. March 1762.

There is one Mr Fountain att Leeds does Saddleworth planes and Hudersfild cloath att his own shop in Leeds and no one else does in that way there. 1762.

One Mr Walker of Walter Clough att or near Hallfax byes a deal of Saddleworth planes and sends a deall into Ireland and his going to sett up four friseing boards near Hallifax. April 18th 1762.

The prise of a white brood made of wool broken out in the fleece worth £12 1s per pak

	£	s	d	
48 pound at 12d per is	2	8	0	
spining 30 pound of weft spinning 4d per pound	0	10	0	
18 pound of warp at 5d per	0	7	6	
weaving	0	6	6	
grease	0	2	0	
milling and soa	0	2	0	
	£3	16	0	
This peice will hold 26 yards at 3s 10d per	1	3	2	profit

f. 77r Most of the cropers at Leeds and Wakefild are drunken kind of men and 12 or 13 men oftens works together and perhaps some 1 or 2 of them would bee saveing of theire money and when the other men finds the are so the allways piking att them and soon flings them outt in place for a verry little fault when perhaps the are 5 times more faulty theire selfs. The must bee all of a sort att a shop or else the never agree one with another. March 18th 1762.

Observastions of a perching mill is first lett your barrill bee butt a small way round and your handles to bee putt has near one another has you can to have 12 handles in going round and fasten them on with sprad nayles each end one. So have a nick att each end of your iron gates so spring them in and lett your barrill go of a slow mottion not to quick and to wind up not to fast but easily and thus you may raise better and much easier.

The Wakefild merchants pays ready money for low prised cloath under 44 shillings f. 77v
per peice att Hudersfild markett and some pays for fine cloath redy money. Some of them will wear 100 pound of one markitt day att Hudersfild Markitt. 1762.

There goes a deall of 17 yard Hudersfild frises into Holland has browns and light drabs and blewely coalard drabs inclineing to a lead coalars. The are oftens made of verry coarse wool. Mr Charles Steer Mr George Charnock Mr Tenant Mr Nevison all Wakefild merchants sends of them into Holland. The Leeds merchants has orders for them sometimes wich comes with brood cloath orders so the purchase them of the Wakefild merchants does the Leeds men. 1762. The are all for cheap and low prised goods in Holland.[170]

The cloath makers about Dewsberrey formerly was verrey poor sort of cloath makers f. 78r
and made poor sort of trashey cloath and used to sett theire name in the head end in full length and place where the live and theire cloath was so noated for bad that the changed Dewsbery and now sets Row in to decive people because the are obliged to set name in. Now makes good cloath. 1762.[171]

In the West of England the can frise 9 quarters brood wich is for womens scarlitt f. 79v
cloaks made with out aney peiceing or seam att all. 1762.

Leather wich is oyld leather is the best thing for lineing of breches and comes in has f. 80v
cheap has flanell.

How to make a chymney draw well lett itt smoak never so bad is to fill all your sides of bak of fire fire with brick and your to leave a vent hole for draft about 18 inches square. This hole to bee ½ yards highar then your fire iron so you have room to lay your coals. Some has slides to the draft hole to make itt biger or lesser.[172]

Mr Mills Wakefild merchants byes 4 or 5 hunderd scarlitt shalloons and crimpson in f. 81v
one order cheifly in March and Aprill and is dyed ½ scarlits and ¾ some is but not maney. Mr Lumb dyear near Wakefild Bridge is his dyear and keeps 15 or 16 men att all the sumer round and 9 or 10 in winter. March 28th 1762.

The above dyear keeps tentering and teeming on a Sunday all the day long and gives his men ½ per shalloon for tentering and teeming and the will on a fine day gett 60 or 70 peices drye so 60 peices att ½ per is two shillings and six pence. His tenter hooks are all tined and the will not rustey and are done for one peney a hundrd and itt makes them sliperey and keep theire sharpness and good to tenter on. 1762. In a throng time hee dyes blaks in the night boyls and saddens and all so hee is readey for drabs or other coalars in the day afterwards.

Saddleworth planes and the West of England coalard brood cloath are the cheif ware for gentlemen and better sort of people all over England both for Holidays and everey days wareing. 1762.

The make a deal of blew planes in Saddleworth wich are good tough ware and much in fashion now. 1762.

Yorkshire brood cloath never wears well att all.

170 Sentence in margin.

171 Sentence in margin at top of entry.

172 Sentence in margin. Phrase 'For a smoke jak or' interlineated above.

f. 82r To gett a calff skin milled up with oyl and drest by the skiners itt makes has good breeches has aney in England little inferior to buck skin.

For butchers froks in some places the scrible dark brown or blak into white wooll so weaves itt into lin warp and is used in maney towns and looks well.

f. 83r The merchants all keep dresers att theire own houses att Leeds and Wakefild. Then there is maney of them can employ 3 or 4 master dresers and some master dresers keeps 8 men and 10 or 12 and 16 in sumertime and a master dreser has just ½ of benefitt clear of whatt the men gets and some times the gett 10s per week 12 and 14 some times butt take itt the year about the reeken itt 8 shill per week. So if a dreser can employ 5 men the recken his profitt a £100 per year. Then hee is obliged to find shears taizels preses and tenters in short the all gett money fast when trades goes well. Master dreser his post his to look bisness in and help to buckeram itt and bayl itt att merchants houses when itt is finished. This is brood cloath trade. 1762.

1762. Mr. Daniell Maude and Frank his brother partners sends a deall of low prised mixt broods duffills into Scotland and some dyed drab duffills and mixt brood frises. The make them paye well for cloath in Scotland butt the have long credditt with itt. The London merchants payes down money direcktley att the receiving of the goods and a maney of them trades with Wakefild merchants and alows them so much pound for wareing there money.

f. 84r Att a town called Rasen 12 miles of the cyty of Lincoln there is a country dyear wich has a cloath mill and a friseing mill wich goes bye watter. But hee does not understand friseing att all makes nothing of itt butt itt is all country work hee does.

f. 85r To pik and dress wool and have itt of a good country cloathmaker will find itt much to his advantage in the way of cloath makein.

Where trade is money is allways in moveing cheifly.

f. 85v Most of Wakefild merchants if a peice is a good frise the make themselfs shure itt will please theire chaps alltho the wool bee but coarse and iff the wool is fine and the can aford itt cheap if itt is not a good nap itt will not answer. A coalar and nap is what sells the cloath.

f. 86r Some makes two head ends of one peice so the merchants cutts these in the middle and calls them short cloaths when the send them of. Mr Dan Maude cuts a deall of his mixters and sews ½ of the head end on to the middle part but to weave them with two ends is much handsomer. 1760.

Some makes Rushias for Leeds merchants all of noyls and thus the answer best being free from moats and looks finear. The sell at 2s per yards when the go well and 1s 10d sometimes. The are 10d a waltron spining weft. Mr Bishop Leeds merchant byes. 1762. There is a deal of money gotten bye them when the go well.

f. 86v Low prised mixt broods made in the West of England are cheifly seven quarters brood and is milled to that breadth and not done has mixt broods in Yorkshire is for the are milled to 5½ quarters brood and when the merchants byes them the weet them and draws them 2 yards att a peice and sets them in breath to six quarters. That if the are low prised sorts itt makes them thin and takes the bottom away and makes them verry bad to frise and the West of England broods are made all of wool and none strained and the will frise better and Yorkshire brood has floks in and looks has fine has theirs and sold cheap.

In most of houses in Yorkshire wich is better sort of houses the have a deal of beef and f. 87v
bacon hanged up and in March and April the find a great profitt bye itt in the way of house keeping and cheifly has some leftt whilest the time of year comes again for hanging.

The way how a man may swear and lye take advantage and sin not is. First he may take a safe oath. Secondly hee may lye down to rest himself. Thirdly hee make take advantage on getting onto his horse by getting on to a set stope.[173]

Mr Charles Steer Wakefild merchant sends a deal of mixt brood frises and duffils into f. 88r
Ireland cheifly to Dublin amongs shopkeepars and merchant taylors and the bye into Ireland a deall out in the West of England but Yorkshire cloath if of low prised sorts has a maney floks in and itt makes a peice look fine and close hair and the can aford itt cheap that there is no shire in England can aford such cloath att prise the have such and a deceitfull way of makeing and finishing itt up that the would cheat the devill with itt. 1762.

Mr Mills Wakefild merchant trades into all parts has into Germaney Spain Lisbon Italy Holland and all parts of Rushia besides country trade has to London Bristoll and to a deal of seaports besides. Sometimes hee has letters from abroad with patterns in that one letter will cost 16 or 17 shillings postage. 1762.

1760. Mr Samuel Pearsons millright in London is the cheif man there for makeing f. 88v
friseing mills. Hee made Sir Lyonells mill in London now standing near Wakefiled bridge upon the River Calder. The above millright understands casting a board sound verry well.

Mr Lumb byes a deall of ackofortis from Edinborugh in Scotland and the sell cheaphar and better spirits in them wich comes from London 1762.

The are reckend to bee excellent dyears in Holland and dyes verry good scarlits and has dyeing wares cheap and byes a deal of brood cloath in white from Leeds and Wakefild.

All the cloath makers about Leeds and Wakefild or Dewsberry the all understand f. 90r
milling theire cloath allways going and stayes whilest itt is mild so the have itt milled to theire own likeing and just has the think will best suit the market. The miller att mill wich is kept there constantly hee onlys is has a helping hand for the cloathiers are all of diferent opinions some one way some another.

In Yorkshire about Hudersfild for narrow cloath and about Leeds for brood cloth the can imitate fine cloath to a greatt advantage for sopose you was to make a peice of wool worth 8 pound per pak the will make a peice of floks and wool thatt will look has close and fine a staple has that made of good wool and perhaps will be better liked in maney places.

[173] Ms reads ‘stop’ with the ‘e’ interlineated above. ‘Stope’ could be a misspelling of stoop; possibly the ‘e’ was to replace the ‘o’ to leave ‘step’.

f. 90v A frise is but bad ware only itt is good for coarse goods. Itt makes them sell haveing a nap on and is a good method to deceive people is friseing.

Itt is a verry bad method for a man to bee a soldier for if the make but a fault there shure to be whiped severely. I saw a man whiped att Wakefild wich had 300 lashes before and 700 then that when hee had the 700 the flesh was cutt of his bak that it flew in peoples faces that stood watching him. His crime was because hee recived with 3 more 16 ginuis of French prisoners and lett them loose out in Winchester goal. He was whipt on Setterday Arpil 22nd. He was a militia man. 1762.

f. 91r A pattern of a shearing mill to work bye watter and to draw the cloath under shears bye Nbr 8 a screw and rowler with cards fixed on like to a friseing mill.

f. 91v The prise of a 42 weight the wool costing 6 pound per pack.

	£	s	d
Now say 42 pound of wool at 6d per is	1	1	0
grease	0	1	6
making att Rochdale	0	11	0
	£1	13	6

Now this peice will sell for £2 4s 0d att Rochdale markitt wich is 10s 6d profit att one peice and if a man can vent 4 pecies in a week through out the year itt is £100 pound profitt clear money and 6 pound per pak is good wool better then is comonly made and sold att prise now in 1762. There is good wool to bee bought att £5 per pak wich is comonly called combers cast or broken wool.

Att Norich the make a deal of cloath called fearnoughts of coarse wool and jersey ends called waste and att Notthingham the make a deal of stokings of all kinds and makes a kind of cloath for paper mills of woolen warp cow hair weft.

f. 92v In and about Wakefild or Leeds the recken a corn mill (one wheel)[174] to bee worth £100 pound per year wich most of them clears that money weather country mill or towns mills and grinding of mallt is extroadnery bisness where people are confined to a mill to grind itt has they are att Wakefild. The have a pek for grinding 16 strok wich is one quarter and the cand grind 4 quarters in one hour wich is 4 pecks mowter wich is 3 shillings per hour when mallt sells att the cheapest. 1762.

When the line a driveing stok the allways pins theire bords on with owler pins so the pins wears has fast has the boards or else the pins would stik up and cutt the cloath when boards was worn down.

f. 93r About Wakefild the fish much with a nett called a cast nett and another called a cleek nett wich is fixed on a pole and is used in floods when fish creeps to side in high watter time.

f. 93v On May first the cropers at Leeds and Wakefild the have a generall meeting and has a great diner provided att some alehouse and each man pays one shilling and bye diner is well over some is has drunk as Davids sowe. 1762.

[174] Phrase interlineated.

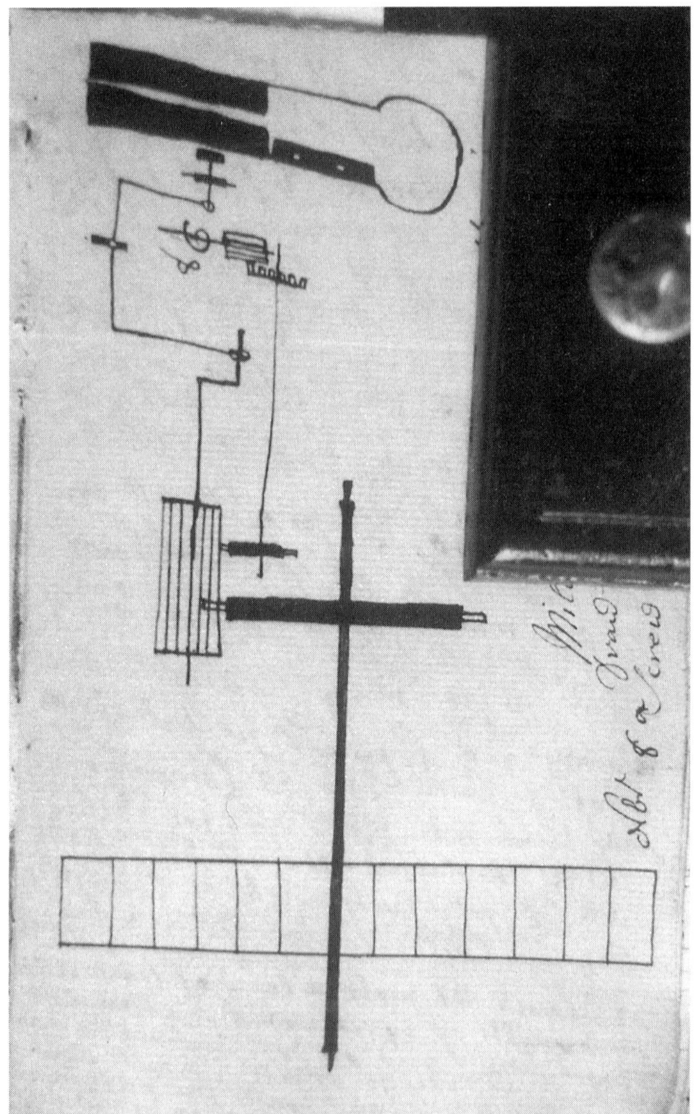

'A pattern of a shearing mill' (f. 91r)

Cheif place in France where woolen cloath and plush and other stuffs is made is att Obliville itt is all the place in cheiff where the woolen facktorye is carryed on. f. 95r

At Wakefild att after the first of Aprill the do not allow aney swine to bee in streets or aney where out in some yard or swine coat for the keep a man called pinder wich looks after them and sheep or aney cattle going wrong in peoples ground.

All them blak mokins dyed att Leeds and Wakefild wich is comonly called brood basses the go into Portugall has to Lisbon and them parts and is worn bye friars and

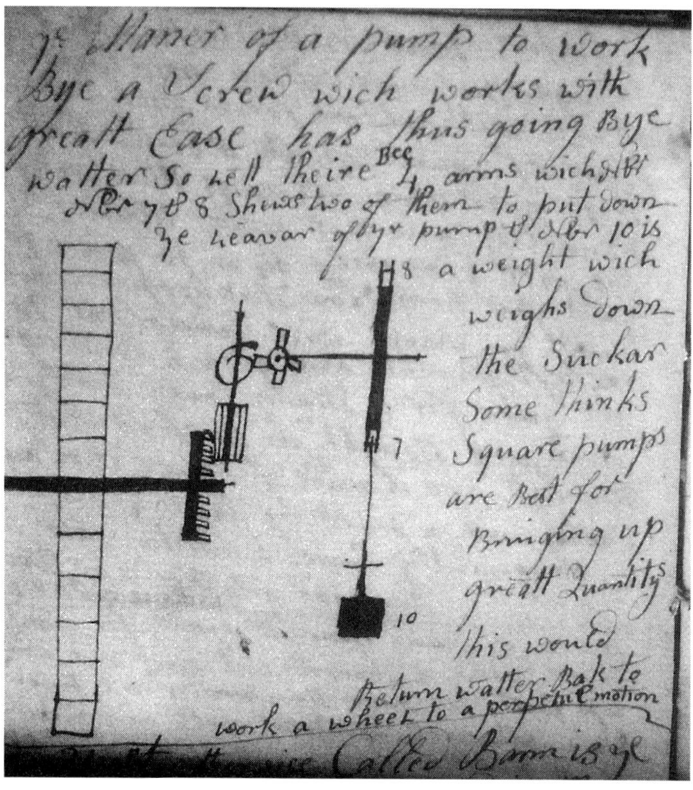

'The maner of a pump' (f. 100v)

Jesuits preists and old nuns wich the like these sorts of base better then brood cloath becaus itt being slender the can lap itt about them and comes in cheap.

f. 96v The Leeds and Wakefild merchants are all in generall way verry wealthey substantiall rich men and pays well acording to bargain if peoples goods proves right and no ways faultey.

f. 100r There is maney brokers and merchant taylors in greatt towns wich byes a deal of mixt broods to make up into new cloaths to sell made up.[175]

f. 100v The maner of a pump to work bye a screw wich works with greatt ease has thus going bye watter. So lett theire bee 4 arms wich number number 7 and 8 shews two of them to put down the leavar of your pump and number 10 is a weight wich weighs down the suckar. Some thinks square pumps are best for bringing up greatt quantitys. This would return watter back to work a wheel to a perpetual motion.[176]

[175] Emphasis in the original.

[176] Diagram in text, entry arranged around it. Diagram shows a waterwheel and gear train attached to a horizontal line from which the two arms numbered 7 and 8 extend perpendicularly. One of these arms is attached to the square object (number 10).

Croping trade goes best att Leeds and Wakefild from March till October and Saddleworth plaines goes best in the spring of the year. The shear with a monstrous weight on theire shears never less than 60 or 70 pound weight on wich is bad for frises and hard work to carry such a weight 14 hours for one shilling has the do att Leeds. 1762. f. 101r

Spining the best white cloath weftt is 3d per pound warp 4d highest prise.

When England att peace with Rushia the have a verry great trade[177] of coarse brood cloath into them parts wich is about 2 shillings per yard in bawk. The all go reds and blews drest and prest. Leeds 1762. f. 101v

The above cloath is milled has thus. When you see it scowrs well lett the watter on and take itt of before itt is quite cleane. So give itt earth and work itt in and leave itt in not scowr itt outt.

In May and June the farmers brings fleece wool to Wakefild and sell itt in the open street likewise att Pomferatt. The sell good wool in cliping time and Saddleworth men oftens comes and lights of good peneworths for some of itt is excelent good wool. f. 102r

In all bisneses lett a man observe soberiety for if a man is given to drunkenes there is no one cares to encourage him in a way of trade and if a man is poor there is a maney people care not to have aney concern with him for the way of the world is catching money and gett itt out in poor people. A rich ones thinks if hee trades with one hee is shure to gett little bye itt and so them that has money will gett money with a little trouble. 1762. f. 102v

Pigeons sells cheifly cheap att Wakefild in May and June 15d a dozen or 18 pence is the highest. The are all young ones taken out in nest just when ready to flye awaye. 1762. f. 103v

Mr Lumb dyear att Wakefild will dye verry good blews 42 weight for 7 shill per peice. May 8th 1762.

Mr Samuell Zouch Wakefild merchant byes a deall of fleece wool out Norfolk and Suffolk. Hee trades much with one R. Bird and J. May both of Ipswich. Hee breaks itt into 5 or 6 differnt sorts so sells itt to cloath makers and some to Rochdale to Robert Woolfindin and Mr Vavison. Hee bye a maney thin broods of Robert Woolfindin wich hee dyes reds for millita lineings. Hee finds cloath and getts them made up for millita of Wakefild att so much a suitt. Hee trades largely with wool and byes Hudersfild and brood cloath. 1762. f. 104r

Mr Vavison was prentice att Wakefild to bee a grocer and served 4 year so his unckle att Rochdale took him and putt him in wool stapleing way.

1762. Att London att Mr Lintails friseing mill in Sudderick and one friseing mill in Gravill Lane the dres a deal of Mr Walmslys 42 weights and rough dicks and lamswools and a deall of Welch and Srowsberry cottons. Some is shorn in coalar some white and is all frised. The above mills goes bye horses and maney peices the freshen over again att is frised in the country 2 or 300 att onece just before the go of. Att Lambeth there is a friseing mill goes bye watter.[178]

[177] Word interlined.

[178] Sentence in margin.

f. 105r Some of the Wakefild merchants puts out wool to make into brood cloth has mixt broods and browns or drabs and white broods. Mr Jeremiah Naylor puts out whites and Mr Zouch mixt broods Mr Willis mixt and coalard and white besides. A maney master dressers puts out wool has Robert Lumb William Burrill and maney more. All the merchants wich puts out wool to make trades and sells wool besides. The are verry dificultt of haveing them right milled that is not to handle greasey or to smell badley or to thin or not cover well or shewing bare. If the have aney of these faults has above the maker takes itt to the mill and makes itt right. 1762.

Liquorish is sold at Pomferatt cheifly bye weight and some is att 4d and best 5d per pound. Then on the small tag ends the grind them down and mixes something in wich is blak so makes round cakes about largeness of a crown peice with a stamp on Pomferat Castle and is good for colds.

f. 106r A rule to be observed that when you pay money beshure to have a receipt and keep all receipts bye you on a file for there is so maney roughs and people that brings bills in twise over that the make a common pracktice of makeing people pay twise over if the know the was paid the first and did not give a recipt or if the think a man was not carfull and does not file his notes or papers the will come over him again so if a man has a note or receipt bye him on a file hee may shew itt them and soon find out those villans that cheifly contrives cheattery.

Dark blew and white scribbled in makes a prettey grave mixter for old mens ware or marryed men. So make itt like unto a Saddleworth plane and dres itt and pres itt easily not to glos itt to much.

f. 106v Att Leeds the dresers raises all mixt broods for frises in the weet so tenters them and gives them a little oyl when dry and strikes them well down and shears them one cut. 1762. Att Wakefild the weet them to sett them to the breadth and draws them 1½ yards att a peice so raises them and gives them a little oyl and one cutt. Butt I aprove of the Leeds dresing to bee much easyar and better way to raise a peice to a good bottom and not to hurt cloath or make itt thin.

f. 107r There is a deall of men wich byes fleece wool att Wakefild from all parts of England and breaks or sorts itt into 5 or 6 diferent sorts so sell itt again to cloathiers or to other people and a man may suitt himselff with aney sort either coarse or fine and has little quantitys or has much has hee thinks proper so hee butt pays for itt. There is now in 1762 Mr Samuell Zouch Robert Lumb Mr Hargraves Mr Hardey John Clark Mr Norton[179] and a maney more att Wakefild and Hallifax there is a deal. Skin wool is bought up in Blak Bull yard for Wakefild men seldome trades with itt. Itt goes to Rochdale.[180]

f. 107v A draft of shears going bye watter. So draw your cloath[181] under them has a friseing mill draws cloath under the board.[182] Observe your nog is to have a hole through so put a spindle neck and your spindle to work in a bush has itt does in a friseing mill. This is turned bye puleys. Lett your low blad of shears have a scrow att point and another to go through your billett.

f. 108r The press all shalloons att Wakefild with loose plates and finds itt a greatt deall easyar way. The was used to do 12 shalloons of a day for a days work a journiman and very ill

[179] These names entered in list format.
[180] Two sentences in margin.
[181] Word interlineated.
[182] Diagram in text, other entries placed in margin around drawing.

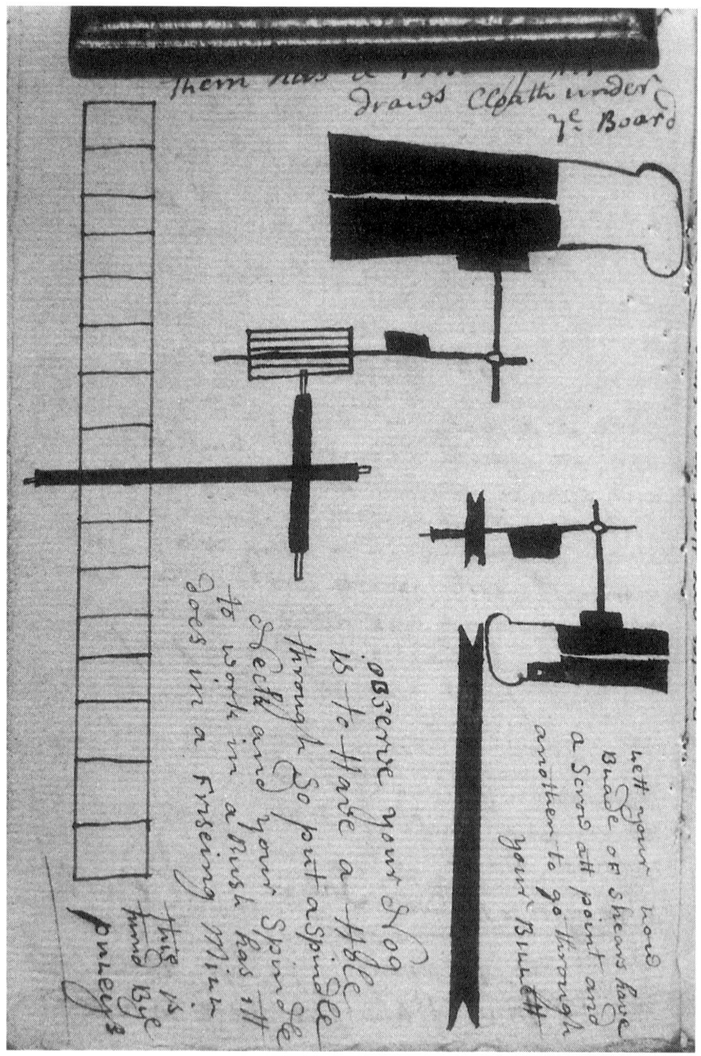

'A draft of shears going' (f. 107v)

killed with shifting and turning so oftens and hard screwing each time. But now the can put 8 peices in a time into press so screw itt down and the need no more trouble. When the press with loose plates and one man can press 24 of a day or 16 is comonly reckend a days work at 1½d per peice that is 2 shillings a day and when the used to press with sett plates the had 2d per peice had journimen and did 12 peices of a day was 2 shillings wages. Then when a man works bye the peice hee has broken days sometimes for 5 or 6 together in winter time but when a man does bye the year and is hired itt is a common prise is 8 shillings per week and some is 7. The preser does not make them up only livers them out in papers. The dyears all keep preses. 1762.

f. 108v To make a floatt to stand on to work in deep watter has driving piles and other bisneses is first dewill and tar each joint and make itt 8 yards square of boards then nayl ribs on like joyce wich is under a chamber floor then cover itt again with boards and leave a whole to lade itt now and then betwickt the joyce. So lett the bottom side to the watter bee well pitched and tarred over. This has flatt bottomed boats is made only itt has no sides (on Wakefild Navigation).[183]

A tide mill might easey bee sett on one of these floats so itt would lower and rise with the watter so wheell itt about att the return of each tide. 1762.

The maner of burying and old wife in Yorkshire wen a lad is loose of his prentiship. The make and old woman of paper so carryes itt on a pole and att last fiddles over itt and burns itt so puts in river.

f. 109r Cloath[184] dyed in the wool makes the hadsomst ware and looks genteelest on the bak. For mens ware lett itt bee brood cloath or Saddleworth planes.

f. 109v Att Hamborough or Hamburgh in Holland there is a deal of merchants meets there and dayly resorts and the bye a deall of all kinds of woolen cloath espeally Lanckeshire 42 weights cottons and sayls. Mr Mills of Wakefild sends a deal there and John Taylor of Crankeshaw near Rochdale sends of his own bottom goods to there. Wakefild May 1762.

All broods for Scarlits if for cloaks are wanted to bee 2 yards one inch brood then one yard will bee a cloak with out aney peiceing and hollowing out of neck will make the head. Cloaks comes made ready from London into the country and the merchant taylors byes the cloath out in West of England so fitts them up and sells them by wolesale to all country shops and the get a deall of money bye itt.

f. 111v A blew dyed in the wool and made brood cloath way so milled up slender for womans josephs and banians and mill itt with soap so dress itt and frise itt afterwards. These are the best blews for standing the coalar and is cleane and does not direty or daub or coalar peoples close has all dye house blews does dyed in the cloath for lett a man stok a dyed blew in cloath never so well the will dirty peoples linen when worn and a blew dyed in wool does not. Wakefild May 1763.

f. 112r All Lanckeshie 42 weights the are cheifly to hard spun and made of skin wool wich if the was of flece woold and fine base floks and fine soft wefft the would answer much better for dyeing into frises. 1762.

Frises begins of going best in August for country trde and so continues till Crismass.

f. 113r Mr Jeremey Naylor sends a deal of broad cloath dyed reds greens and blews wich are for soldiers cloaths to Mr Floodshire London merchant wich Mr Floodshire sells to the king and Parliment. Naylor Wakefild merchant sends bye comision Floodshire finding money and allowing so much the pound for wareing his money and Mr Naylor has benefitt of dresing and in spring of year and all summer hee keeps 26 or 27 men agate croping them for soldiers breeches are only sett up hard and close bak shorn so prest. The are all red breeches and all brood cloath is strained on tenter and to make it handle strong the weet itt 3 or 4 inches of list so dryes itt agaim and thus itt turns up

[183] Phrase interlined below.

[184] Ms reads 'cloah'.

to itt former compass and the list is not strained when the rest of cloath is hard strained so itt handles stout and strong this is a Yorkshire bite. Wakefild 1762.

Mr Floodshire London merchant suplyes the English armey with cloath for cloaths f. 113v
and lineings for them and has a great trade this way has aney one merchant in London. Hee purchases brood cloath of all sorts from Leeds and Wakefild for soldiers coats and Rochdale 42 weights and Srowsberry cottons and peices called rough dicks and thin broods from Rochdale for lineings. Some is dyed and frised some dyed and raised others worn white has hee byes them. Samuel and Thomas Flooshire London 1762. Draggoons wears brood cloath.[185]

Observations on the suns coarse that in June itt rises north east and sets north west that in the north of Scotland dayes are longest in sumer shortest in winter.

Except a man can gett orders for woolen cloath hee had better sell itt att his own f. 114r
markitt. Itt is a bad way hawk itt from town to town. A corospondance abroad is best tradeing. Mind to trade with safe chaps.[186]

A tradesman should mind to trade with good merchants for some will give 2d or 3d f. 114v
per yard more for a peice and perhaps think itt cheap has them wich gives less. There is a great advantage in observing this.

There is a maney logwood blews sold att Hudersfild markitt wich is drest and frised f. 116v
and country shopkeepars can sell them because the are strongar then in a common way then dyehouse blews dyed out in the white and comes in cheap alltho with wearing the weare to a drab. 1760.

Att Leeds and Wakefild the cropers when the tenter brood cloath the sett the tayl end on and sets itt a slant that is one corner longar then the other. So when prest or frised the cutt the tayl end streight so perhaps att one corner itt is 4 inches brood so these the sell for to make aprons on wich is much worn in all the West Riding of Yorkshire both bye cropers and servant women. Some people is so fancyfull to bye a great quantity and sew them together uniform and make a top side of bed quilt. 1762.

French men are a kind of sober civill good behaved men and verry good mecanicks f. 117r
and extroardnerry full of maners and genteel in theire dress verry much given to pride and walks verry much with and air alltho the bee never so poor. Butt can abide no hard working att all rather to gett theire riches bye polocy then hardship or labour.

Croping att Leeds and Hallifax is verry hard gotten money to work from 5 to 7 at night for one shilling has is the common prise att both the above towns. 1762.

The scowr a deal of blankits quilts and rugs att Wakefild mill and cheifly against fairs or races.

The cloathiers about Wakefild the mix swine turd and piss caled lant together so squeses itt out with theire hand then drains itt through a wire seiff thatt no moats gets in. So lecks itt over on the cloath att first when itt comes out in loom and itt makes itt scowr better. But itt is apt to gett some moats into the cloath. A penorth[187] of sweet soap in piss would do much better.

[185] Sentence in margin.

[186] Sentence in margin.

[187] Presumably 'peneworth'.

f. 117v Att Wakefild church 8 bells and chymes a different tune each day Sunday a psalm tune. 1762.

f. 118r Most of Yorkshire cloath is much adicted to mortt eatt for reasons to tedious to mention that makes the merchants will not bye except the have orders for itt.

To keep a rider to ride about seeking in orders is a greatt charge for a tradesman. Hee is obliged to charge his goods hardar that some of them cannot aford a cheap peneworth because theire att such charges. Betimes a corospondance is best to send bye orders and stay att home.

Drapers formerly in June or July was used to come to Wakefild and furnish themselfs with goods of all kinds butt now in these late years none comes but Mr Smith of Norich. The can have aney sorts for sending for and riders is on theire journieys each week some or another is cheifly in the country. 1762.

f. 118v In the West of England the will not allow aney one to make woolen cloath except hee has aprentice to the trade and a native of the same county wich is a good method or else the would bee over run with cloath makers from most parts of England. 1762.

f. 119r If a man has a thing of his own itt is a double advantage to him for to want a thing and has to borrow itt or seek itt and pay for itt. Itt comes in verry chargably and has the old saying is a thing of ones own has and iron haft and is allways ready when wanted. 1762.

f. 119v Att Wakefild old corn mills the are obliged to have the watter to keep grindin for publick use lett cloath mills or the friseing mill stand in scarce watter time the must have the property of itt or else the publick insits of grinding elswhere if in case corn is not ground within 48 hourse after the deliverey of itt so the corn mills must have watter lett all other bisness stand in scarce watter time. All belonging Sir Lyonell Pilkinton. June 1762.

f. 120r Mr Atkison sons trades both north and south and makes a deall of brood cloath att home and byes his narrows att Hudersfild markitt. Cloath sells cheap now. In 1762 that a 17 yards peice of drab stout milled is sold at 17s 6d and some 24 yard sorts at 25 shilling wich is 7 or 8 shill cheapar att one peice then the was in the year of 1761. Butt observe these are verry coarse ones and thick spun and oftens makes prettey good frises.

f. 120v There is sallets pease and beans and pottatoas att Manchester soonar bye 2 or 3 weeks then aney where about Wakefild Pomferatt or Leeds and in short haye time is has soon or soonar about Rochdale Bury Bolton or Manchester. But Cheshire is the soonest crops in a generall way. Hard corn grows best in Yorkshire itt being a dry country nott much rain cheifly.

1762. A description of Wakefild mills 4 corn mills for publick use and 2 cloaths mills one friseing mill one wheell for 7. Grinding upon French stones wich Sir Lyonel badges all the flowr belonging French stones.

f. 121v Ground sets att very high prise in and about Wakefild that for a cowgate is 40 shillings and for a horse is 45 shill and not very good pastures. 1762.

f. 122v The man whom God doth with contentment bless
Tho hee has little doth the world posess.
Content is all wee aim att with our store

And haveing that with little needs no more.
Cast of all needless and distrustfull care
A little is enough to much a snare.
Know when to speak and silent went to sitt
Fools silent oftens pass for men of witt.
Immodest words admit of no defence
For want of decency is want of sense.

Itt is a fine thing for a man if hee goes abroad to do bisness to keep himselff sober and f. 123r
not bee concerned in liquor. But lett him if hee loves drink gett his belley full att home then hee both has itt cheap and does not lett people see his weakness of temper not to refain but bee drunk.

Dyears att Wakefild seldome letts theire wifes bye aney stone blew. Allways the make f. 124r
use of indigo and finds it much cheaphar and better then byeing stone blew.

To stak hay the best way is to fix a high pole in the middle of the stak and itt gives air and vent to itt and makes it stand better.

To brush aney wood over with linseed oyl and a little oker preserves itt well from the weather and keep itt from roting.

Tenters or watter wheels done with oyl is a good method.

In a generall way in most part of engines and mills att after made and worked a while a f. 124v
man may find out a faullt or two that if the said engine was to make again itt might bee in a better method and this is a thing that oftens hapens and att first is sett out to the best advantage thinkingly.

A cloathmaker that once gets into a good name of makeing cloath and his goods f. 125r
answers a merchant will bye of him and not take so much notice of a fault has of other makers wich hee but seldome byes on and itt is so in most bisnesses a good name of doing well things pases if perhaps another person did better his goods pleases.

Some merchants wich drives country trade will go to gett orders and look has grand has posoble and will wear a gold laced hatt that is to shew theire worth money and gentlemen like and can bye goods in att best hand and can give credditt. This is performed by Mr Steer and maney others at Wakefild. 1762.

There is frises wich are mixt broods goes out in Yorkshire to the London merchants f. 125v
and a maney of them is sent into Yorkshire bak again and all over England amongst shopkeepars and merchant taylors and to brokers shops wich makes coats out in new cloth ready for wareing and the above cloath pases for West of England brood cloaths. 1762.

A fine low wrank sharp nop is the thing much admired in these days. Now in 1762 there is some men can have goods upon creditt whilest such times has the have sold them and drawn money for them and doing thus if a man has butt a little stok hee may drive a great trade by tradeing with other peoples money.

A man may imitate fine brood cloath bye makeing cloath on floks and wool mixt or a f. 126r
fine mok imitates itt and lett warp bee of woosted made of fine fleece wool and the weftt of fine fleece wool small spun.

f. 126v Att Wakefild them wich sells cheese the lett itt lye damp in some cellar all wich the have not in the shop so itt keeps moist and will wheigh heavier then kept dry to loose weight and to harden the put a deal of tallow into cheese in some places to taste itt. 1762.

A cloath millers post att Leeds and Wakefild only to help the cloathmaker to mill itt for the maker brings itt wett with piss and helps to mill itt and takes itt home and tenters itt and pays 3 shillings for a couple of broods milling comonly caled a cloath. The are 12 hours or 14 in doing a fine cloath. August 18th 1762.

f. 127r Some merchants when the gett orders for maney kinds of goods the can bye them and pak them of and have no more trouble then paking them only and in these kinds of goods how easey itt is to gett money for such like men that has money itt is poor working people wich keeps up common wealth and trade. 1762.

There is mixt broods to bee bought att Leeds markitt in bawk wich comes in at 3s 4d per yard bawk and 3d per yard dresing and friseing wich the merchants charges 6d per yard profitt wich is 4s 1d in all. Now I have seen one of these broods come bak from London and pased for a West of England frise and charged att 6 shillings per yard or 5s 9d in comon way to merchant taylors and shopkeepers att Wakefild. March 18th 1762.

f. 127v Sheep feet att Leeds and Wakefild sells 14 or 15 pence a 100. The are layed of a heap whilest the stink so the bone is broken so boyled. All the flesh goes into siseing and a deall of good fatt and oyll is scumed of. The siseing is used bye cloathmakers cheifley. To gett the hair of the lime them has skins is done. Leeds 1762.

f. 128r There is one Mrs Foster att Aluthorp or Alverthorp near Wakefild byes some fine moks of George Low of Rochdale wich goes to her brother att Lisbon. Edmund Smith is cheiff man for doing most moks blak att Wakefild wich are dyed and bayled for Lisbon. 1762.

There is some cloath makers will send mixt brood frises into the country to wool staplers and change for woll and gets money by doing thus.

f. 128v Itt is a fine thing to bee beholden to no one if a man can help himselff itt is a great comfort and few freinds will be freinds long except itt is something to his advantage. 1762.

Down towards London the want cloath to handle soft and silkey and not to verrey thick milled butt in the north the want them stout thick and strong. Mixt broods are cleanear scowred then formerly now in 1762.

A man wich must have a country trade hee must seek in to the country and give credditt with goods and hee may gett money and trade with honist men.

f. 129r To put a little shugar into ink makes itt gloss better and not so apt to synk into the paper and makes itt write better then thin weak ink does. A teaspoonfull to a gill or a pint is eneough. 1762.

f. 130r There is one Mr Robinson living att Ositt near Wakefild puts out wool to make into mixt brood frises and trades much to London with them. 1762.

Likewise one Joseph Benitt near Dewsberry makes himselff and gets made a great maney and trades much to Norich and into the country and can aford goods better and cheaphar then a merchant can because hee has two profits. 1762.

Mr Zouch Wakefild merchant puts out wool to make into mixt broods and trades to Ipswich and into Norfolk. Mr Steer Wakefild merchant trades into Ireland and gives 3 pence per yard for mixt broods more then some merchants will do then hee has six months creddit with them.

Att Rochdale itt is a little drunken town for I heard a gauger say that itt pays in a year f. 130v
has much excise has Leeds does for in Yorkshire att markits when people has done theire bisness the go home directly and not stay. Drinking after bisness is done has is verry comon att Rochdale and some drinks all night over. 1762.

There is butt two different men has print rowls and wattering rowls in Yorkshire one f. 132r
. . . [188] Plowes att Wakefild a dyear and a dyear att York has. The both go bye horses and has a peney per yard for printing or wattering and will gett 3 or 4 pound a day and the cheifly work each fortnight a days work. 1762.

The maner of print rowls made has hott callenders is att Manchester only. The middle f. 132v
rowll is is of cast iron so cutt full of figueres and is cased round with bras to work the figure on so puts 3 or 4 hott heaters in made with a hole in the end to stick a large poker in to liftt them in and out has thus.[189] So heats them in stove so shoots heaters in att number 8. This pattern shows the middle rowl with hetters in.[190] To have two rowls one above this one below itt.[191]

In a generall way Hudersfild cloath is verry bad ware espesaly that wich is mostly f. 133v
frised for itt looks well and handles strong and much deceives the country people that few that has bought of itt once will have itt twise because itt does not wear acording to expectation. That was itt not for a foreighn trade there would not bee halff so much friseing has theire is. Leeds low prised brood cloath is has bad ware or worse butt theire is excellent cloath both att Hudersfild and Leeds markit to bee bought. 1762. Hunters and shorn duffils. . . .[192]

Mixt brood trade into Yorkshire was stolen out in the West of England about the year 1726. Likewise blankitt trade was stolen into Yorkshire from Witnay in Oxfordshire and now the work so cheap in Yorkshire that the have great trade.

In[193] a generall way att Leeds Wakefild York or Manchester Hallifax the will not allow f. 134v
poor people to begg. For if the offer to begg if the do not belong town the bang begar sees them out in town and if the return the are shure to bee whiped for there is no ocasion to begg the will say and good workhouses all over England if people will go into them and may live well. 1762.

Itt is a fine thing when a man can do a thing himselff for if a peice of work goes f. 135v
through 3 or 4 different hands itt oftens gets mistt in some point and if a man can do itt himselff hee is shure itt is right.

188 Word – presumably the first name – illegible.
189 Diagram showing a solid cylinder with a hole in one end.
190 Diagram showing a hollow cylinder–the interior space presumably being used for the heaters described earlier in the entry–attached to a gear train.
191 Sentence interlined below.
192 Entry in margin; remainder illegible.
193 Ms reads 'n'.

f. 136r In and about Hallifax itt is butt a cold barren soyll and little fruitt is grown about itt. Only the have a good trade and has money. The purchase corn and fruitt from Wakefild potatoas and oatmeall from Rochdale and still for all that things that are bought in bye little deals are has cheap has att Wakefild or Rochdale. The are sharp industrous people att Hallifax. 1762.

Serge is woven twilled like a kersey and druggitt is woven with four treadles and is plain with woosted warp woolen wefft.

f. 136v How to make cloath turn rain for 20 hours is mill your cloth dyed in wool and dress itt then give itt lant and oyll to weet itt all over so work itt in stok ½ and hour give itt some blak earth and mill itt in and leave itt in. So strike itt down weet and brush itt drye and press it easily. The do a a deall of brood cloath blews thus at London wich is used for top coates for coachmen and gentlemens servants and is worn all over the country.

The above cloath handles sharp in hand cheifley and stifish but itt is liked well.

f. 138r Observation on raising seed of aney herbs or plants is mind to gather them dry and keep them in the husk for 8 or 9 weeks in a dry place. So rub your seed out and mind to lett all your seed bee ripe when you cutt itt. Cabage seed is raised of a good cabage taken up and sett in a sunshineing place so itt seeds.

Bury and old catt or dog near the roots of trees makes them flourish well and synk dirt.

f. 138v In a droughty time or in bad dryeing weather the Leeds and Hudersfild markitt is oftens scarce of cloath espeasly of that sort wich hapens to go att the same season weather itt is in winter or sumer.

A man in good bisness and haveing 2 or 3 good prentises hee is in a good safe way of thriveing for there is no wages to pay only meatt and cloathing and some lads will do has much work has a man if good lads.

Printing lin or chynce or calicoas or cottons to stand washing is verry curious and beautifull bisness and are things much worn now. 1762.

f. 140r A man in bisness must keep sober or else few people will concern them selfs with him butt what rayly cannot help itt.

f. 140v How to graft. Saw your stok top of then cutt two gashes with a sharp nife. Then with small wedges sharpened to the bigness of your graft being thrust in raise the bark of the stock and put the graft exacktly shaped has the wedge. Then close itt hard with your hand and bind itt about with clay and horse dung mixed. Aples are oftens grafted into crab tree stoks. Gather grafts in the middle of Febuary is best.

Mixt broods are much worn for top and close bodyed coats in and about London. Both in frises and duffills.

f. 141r Att Sturbridge fair in Worchestershire the fair is holden on a common and is a great fair for all kinds of goods and there is to bee bought a deal of skin wool there brought in bye country skiners to sell att att that fair. The fair began has thus. Att first a Scotchman haveing got a sup a drink and lyeing down to rest a little people came about him and hee haveing a bitch with him hee thought att first the was come to do him and injury and hee oftens cryeing out stur bitch and hee sold a deal of his goods to people so itt is continued and is a noteable fair now in 1762.

White cloath broods are layed 32 yards or 31 in loom so miled to 25 or 26 yards long in a generall way. The sell all bye the yard att Leeds markitt. Brood cloath att Hudersfild markitt all coarse goods is sold bye the peice. f. 141v

All kinds of narrow frises begins of going in August so continues all whilest Crismas and over sea trade is best all summer season. Leeds and Wakefild 1762.

Dyears att Wakefild does goods excellent coalars has in aney town in England and are verry industrous sorts of men all of them getting money verry fast and is a comon sayeing amongst people that a dyear may spend with a squire. f. 142r

The Hollanders in a generall way the purchase from England a deal of low prised woolen cloath wich the bye in att low prises so sayls and traficks itt into most parts of the world. The bye a deal from Leeds and Wakefild and are a cuning crafty people is the Hollanders. 1762. f. 142v

The French in generall are a kind of people verry craftey and scameing and has a perlight way with them and behaves well and verry full of maners and compliments.

The think in the West[194] that cloath of 5 shillings per yard is of a coarse sort and is much worn by the inhabitants of them parts. Theire fine broods the sell to London and all over England.

Mr Lumb dyes all of them blak moks wich Edmund Smith of Rochdale sends to Lisbon and Mr Lumb brother in Wakefild tanters them and strikes them over and bales them for 12 pence per peice and hee gives his men 5d per then hee has 7d for himselff. Edmund Smith finds rapers and band and ropes. 1762. f. 143r

There is a maney broods cloath made white att Wakefild wich are doulbe mild ones and made of wool about _[195] pound per pak. These are dyed blew and prest and goes to London for gentlemens servants top coats and coachmen and all kinds of liverys butt blews dyed in wool answers best and will not weare white in bottom and will come in has cheap has the above white considering the wool and makeing for coalard cloath is never so well made has white acording to the prise and will look handsomer and better will coalared. Mill all with soap.

And some of the above cloath is dyed red whatt is called cold madder reds and is used for to make dragoons cloaks on to put on in rainey wether[196] Likewise the above blew some is used for oficers cloaks. There goes a deal of brood cloath from Wakefild wich is for cloathing comon soldiers.

Att most of cloath mills in and about Leeds or Wakefild the cloath makers takes theire turns has the do att coalpits and there is no respeckting of pearsons wether poor or rich provided a man pays well has far has hee goes. Wakefild 1762. f. 143v

194 Refers to the West of England.

195 Numeral illegible, possibly '8' or '6'.

196 Ms reads 'weth'.

A cloathmakers post about Wakefild is wich is a master is to bye in wool and to fetch yarn from the spining wich is a great distance from his house and go to Leeds markit and sells his cloath and to go to mill to see itt rightly miled and he seldome concerns himself with aney other branch of itt keeping prentises or journimen to weave itt if hee is a wealthy cloathier.

f. 144r A Scoth trade for woolen cloath the Wakefild merchants sends a deal and the pay well for itt butt only wants long creddit 12 or 15 months. The London trade is mostly ready money. 1762.

Att Coventry the have a way of guming shalloons (and isenglas)[197] and about Coln and Burnley the do all so and itt makes them gloss and press hard.

f. 144v Strong Hudersfild kersys and coalared planes are much worn by farmers and lads coats. Mixt frises for top and close bodyed coats.

f. 145r The maner of and horse mill with a wind mill to work in the chamber to help the horse when wind blows and when not to put it out in geer so you never need to stand but the horse may work wind or no wind so when itt blows brisk wind will do itt selff and when slow put horse to help itt forwards. To have 4 sayls wich number 7 and 8 shews two.[198] So have 4 slides att each corner of your room to slide up and down to receive wind and your mill will work with aney quarter of the wind and in full sayll. The wind mills advantage is some times the wind blows when watter is scarce and when a watter mill is in bakwatter so wind mill may go. The have one of these att Paris in Frances and does well.

f. 145v Mr Atkinson of Hudersfild has prettey well of watter in a droughty time to frise with that hee can lett one cloath mill wheel stand in that season wich makes him verry throng att that season haveing a deal of brood cloath from Hallifax for Hallifax watter is butt a weak watter and the can do verry little in a dry sumer. Likewise att Leeds and Wakefild the are has ill pinched for watter alltho the are both strong rivers. The reason is that the towns mills wich is kept agate for publick use to grind corn takes most of the watter and are obliged to bee kept agate lett friseing mills stand and in winter Wakefild friseing mill is troubled much with the bak watter and in sumer lack watter. June 1762.

f. 146r There goes and old sayeing that Yorkshire and Whipshire are two of sharpest shires in England. That is the mean except a man is sharp and minds his post hee brings a whip on is own bak and so for that reason the judge Whipshire to be has sharp has Yorkshire alltho theire is none such a shire. 1762.

f. 147r To have a good cellar and butterey is a great advantage to housekeeping in way of keeping meatt and drink wich maney one bears losses for want of keeping espesaly in hott sumers.

f. 148r If a man must have a trade hee must look after itt and mind to keep in with good chaps for in these dayes there is so maney traders and riders about for orders that goods is has cheap in the country has att the markitt where the are made. Att Wakefild there

197 Phrase interlineated above.

198 Diagram in text: two large rectangular sails shown in vertical orientation around a central pole which is attached to a gearwheel. Remainder of entries are scattered in margins around the drawing.

was a merchant kept a rider in 1762 and was out in the country 5 weeks and brought orders. All hee brought was for one ½ peice of plane wich being att such charge of rideing about the cannot aford a cheap peice or else hee might have had more orders a deall butt could not do with prises.

If a man is a master dreser hee is obliged to have tenters and preses of his own and itt f. 148v
takes a deall of money to sett a master up for dresing. 1762.

Att Wakefild in sumer time the duck a maney children. Some it does good some itt does hurt.

Formerly in 1727 and them days the cloathmakers att Leeds markitt has gotten bye a f. 150r
cloath and sold itt for ready money has much has the have gotten a cow and calff bye itt and now in 1762 itt is a common saying if the gett a calf prise the think itt well.

There has been has much money gotten out in the woolen facktory has aney branch in England and is yett.

To by and History of England wich is of a new setting out wich comes out monthly f. 150v
with the magazines Gentlemans Magazine with maps of each county and the maps and cuts sett out bye Ben Martin. Itt gives a particular acount of each shire with its produce manufacktorys and each partickular with and history of Wales not yett finished in June 1762.

A man some times spends 30 or 40 years seeking after worldly riches and att same time f. 151r
little regards either body or soull and has for worldly afairs there is nothing for mans use butt meat and cloathing and if hee gets never so much riches when a man is dead whatt better is hee for haveing riches upon earth. Hee had better bee rich in heavenly works then to go to a bad place concerning his mispent life for riches in heaven is best riches and a good life gains them.

There is excellent wool all in the south part of England towards London out in Susex f. 151v
Surey Hampshire and Bedford and Buckinghamshire and them parts and a verry great deall comes to Wakefild Leeds and Hallifax and a deal is used in the West of England amongst the fine brood cloathmakers. Itt comes to Wakefild bye waggons wich in some waggons has 40 paks in and drawn bye 8 horsess. Waggons are used now into the most principle towns in England both East West North and South.

1762. Mr Jones Mr Grime Mr Flooshire are 3 of cheiff London Merchants that byes f. 153r
mixt broods duffils and frises. Mr Daniell Maud trades with all 3 of them and so does Mr Naylor Wakefild merchants. The prise the are in bawk is from 3s 6d to 2s 8d in a comon way.

Att Otley 6 miles of Bradford the make a deall of all kinds of press papers att the mill f. 153v
near Otley Bridge.

From Wakefild there goes a deall of peices called hunters. The are Hudersfild and f. 154r
Saddleworth planes drest has if for press and raised a little on the bak. Now these peices when drest the cuttle them up streight and lays a plank on them and a weight on them. But if these peices was brushed on a brushing mill and left all night on the rowler itt would bee the best way and sadden itt and gloss itt well. These goes instead of frises and is liked better.

The higest prise of mixt broods frised att Wakefild is 4 shilling in bawk so down to 2s 4d or 2 shillings is the lowest price.

f. 155r Some cloath makers can sell cloath to a deall more profitt then others. Some and perhaps is has well liked has others that sells cheaphar for the mind good chaps and keeps in with them and cane give creiditt and thus the seldome come bye aney loses has many a cloathier does. Leeds and Wakefild 1762.

f. 156r Most shops in Leeds and Wakefild has scarlitt cloaks to sell made up readey wich the purchase from London. Cheifly these are called cardinels and a deall of money is gotten by them in 4 or 5 different branches. 1762.

f. 157v In Somersetshire att Taunton there is 1100 loom employed in makeing of serges sagathies shalloons duroys and att Bruton the make serges and a great trade in stokings and att a town called Frome Selwood the make abundance of brood cloath and the make a deall of wool cards there. 1760.

In Wiltshire att Bradford the make excellent fine brood cloath and att Malmsbury has a good trade for brood cloath and att Chippenham the woolen trade is carryed on and att Devises the have a great trade for cloath and serges made brood cloath way. The have excellent wool att Devises and att Westbury and Trowbridge and Bradford the make superfine cloath.

f. 158r Likewise in Wiltshire att Salsbury the make a deall of druggits and flanels and brood called Salisbury whites for the Turkey trade and Salisbury plain and excellent place feeding 5 or 6 thousand sheep and has good wool.

Blakwell Hall wich joins to Guildhall London is the cheif markitt for the West of England cloathiers to sell their cloath att in bawk and is the largest cloath hall in England.

f. 159r A man of trade if hee can aford to give now and then 6 pence or a shilling to journimen or to a merchants son itt pleases each side much and keeps together corospondance much better.

f. 160v The prise for a journiman weaver that weaves plush of woosted is from 5d to 6 and 7 and 8d per yards if a master finds him his loom. Leeds and Halifax factoryes.

Observe if a man wants a thing lett itt itt bee of what kind itt will hee may bye itt has cheap out in the shops has bespeak it made and perhaps cheaphar and there is few meterials of aney branch in England butt what is sold most markitt towns in England excepting the proper sort of shagg for friseing on.

f. 161r In most towns in Yorkshire the Quakers wears light drab or stoved whites brood cloath frises for womens cloaks wich looks verry well. 1762.

About Leeds and Wakefild some calls mixt broods shephards. The reason is that the was used in a maney places formerly for shephards to tent their sheep in and was milled strong and made of coarse wool but now the are made fine and nise and used for coats and top coats. 1762.

f. 162r Mr Richard Buxton and Mr Daniell Maude Wakefild merchants has oftens orders in March and Aprill and some times in November and December for Hudersfild cloath wich are drabs strong milled and coarse wool to bee 34 or 36 and 38 yards long and these are called double peices and pays double prise for dresing and friseing. These goes into Scotland cheifly so the Scoth merchants traficks them over sea into some parts where dutey is layed on them to pay so much a peice for woolen cloath perhaps into Ireland for all cloath payes duty that goes there from England. There are bespoke made. March 18th 1762.

Mr Jeremiah Naylor Wakefild mercant sends a deal of dyed goods broods to Mr f. 163r
Floodshire London merchant wich are reds blews and greens and prest and ½ scarlits ¾ and full scarlits and the are all for soldiers cloaths and them wich is for breeches are only bak shorn on that side wich is usealy drest so dyed and prest and hee sends a deall of dyed frises to Mr Floodshire greens and blews scarlits and crimpsons. Hee byes bye comision. Mr Floodshire sends down money and allows him so much pound for wareing his money and hee keeps 10 or 12 men dresing does Mr Naylor besides what hee puts out to Mr Dresars.[199] All the Wakefild merchants when the send goods of the cutt the makers name of for fraid whom the send them to should see where the bye them but Mr Jeremiah Naylor sends letters on so them cloaths wich the like best the send again for writeing for such a mans cloath because hee bye for them bye commison. 1762.

Mr Mills Wakefild merchant has cheifly orders for 15 or 16 hundred shalloons wich f. 163v
are low prised ones and is all dyed ½ scarlits. The order is in March Aprill and May and perhaps 2 or 3 small orders besides in a year for ½ scarlits shalloons has 2 or 300 att a time. Mr Lumb dyear att Wakefild his dyer of the above orders. April 18th. 1762.

A shilling mill for oats and a friseing mill both requres a steady motion wich makes f. 164v
them shill bye horses att wind mills where oats is ground.

A horse mill is steadyar then wind and watter is stedyer then either. Itt is truest mottion is watter.

At Wakefild mills the allways reken 12 hours in milling a cloath that is a couple of f. 165r
broods. Then two stoks mills 4 broods on a day and 4 att night and 3 shillings a cloath is 6 shill a day and 6 att night. That is £4 4s 0d per week wich is £200 and 10 pound per year a cloath mill is capeable of getting and one will lett att Wakefild for 30 pound per year. There is two above bridge and one below Wakefild bridge. 1762.

1762 Lyonll Pilkington has 7 watter whels att Wakefild 5 for corn mills one fuling mill one att friseing mill and 4 att Horberey 2 cloath mills 2 corn mills three att New Mill a dam for corn mills. One att Park mill and one att Park Mill for corn wich is 15 in all. 1762. The 14 wheels clears above 1000.[200]

There has been abundance of money gotten bye byeing wool out in Lincolnshire f. 166r
formerley but things are more sought into in these days that all profits are less in most bisneses and and caleings. March 1762.

Salmons Poligraphic is and excellent book for coulerin and painting and teaching to f. 168r
mix coalars with oyll and other ingrediants and for to know how to make the buatifull

[199] Sentence describing a piece-dyed grey cloth omitted; not obviously relevant to remainder of entry.

[200] Sentence in margin.

coalars and mix itt in soap and mill itt into cloath when milling itt or att after dyed work itt in the stok itt would brighten coalars and and make them look verry well. This last is my fancey and methods.

f. 169r If a man can gett one yard of fall of watter itt will answer to turn a watter wheel verrey well and not less will do but bee oftens in bak watter.

f. 169v Mr Lumb dyear att Wakefild in the spring dyes everey day a cart load of cloath besides other goods has shalloons bokins and the like. Cloath is has greens scarlits blews reds blaks crimpsons buffs straws clear yellows and the like. March 1762.

f. 171v The pleasantness of a country house to stand is to have itt in the brow of a hill faceing the sourth with the gardins under itt the front of itt.

f. 173r Sopose a man was to bye of them green sweet pease and order them has mallt is made so grind a stroke down to a load of malt. Itt would make excelent drink in Jenuary Febuary and March. There coms to Wakefild a deal of all sorts of pease beans barley and all sorts of hard corn. Pease sells much cheaphar than malt and would make far more drink. Wakefild 1761.

Some men will bye hams in the markitt and give 3d per pound for them and att that prise the are best part and cheapest in swine flesh. Some men will bye 6 or 8 hams and no pork else. Wakefild markitt 1762.

How to build houses a cheap way and to have itt moavable so if you have a mind to flitt you may take your house along with you is to make itt all of wood and where ever there is a joint lett itt be screwed.

f. 173v To make syloop. Burn barley into coffee so mix a little brandey in and milk and sweeten with treackle. (Best to sweeten with coarse sugar.)[201] The charge of a gallon and profitt when[202] sold out bye penyworths

	£	s	d[203]
First a pek of barley		0	6
Burning trouble and butter		0	4
6 peneworth of brandy in		0	6
one pound of treackle or half pound of shugar		0	2
one pint of milk		0	0
		1	7
Gallon at 2d a gill is	0	2	8
		1	7
profit		1	1

Some sels 3 or 4 galon a day. It may bee made much chephar then this and good to itt will bee.[204]

f. 174r A good cure for chincough is att after you see a child has gott itt take some brandey or rum and air itt bye the fire so rub the childs bak bone with itt whilest you see itt will take aney in and this is a perfeckt cure with 2 or 3 times rubing some thinks brandy is best to rub in.

201 Sentence interlineated below.
202 Ms reads 'whe'.
203 £ s d headings implicit.
204 Sentence in margin.

How to make coffee verry little inferior to the right Turkey coffee is get some barley of about 6 week after shearing when itt has sweat in mowth a little. So burn itt in a coffee raster has you do coffee and grind itt in a mill and mix some of the right sort along with itt. Not one in ten thousand can destinguish itt from the true coffee so sell it ground to the country people would bee great profits. Or some burn malt.[205]

A thing to bee observed is if you sell a thing to a man that keeps journimen under him allways observe to sell to profitt that you can aford to give something to his journimen and itt keeps together corospondance much better for if a thing does not answer so well a sup of drink hides fawlt.[206] f. 174v

To bye coffee att Liverpool att 1s 8d per pound unburned itt is cheap wolsome liquor in a family so burn itt your selff and itt exceeds aney tea for healthyfull. March 1762. f. 175r

Coffee att Wakefild sells at 6 pence per ounce out in the shop and that is 8 shill per pound wich is extravagent prises.

The Wakefild merchants wich sends mixt broods into the country would have them to handle strong and stout milled. Them that sends goods over sea would have them soft and scimitt for the former you may give them flowr in amongst soap the latter only with soap.

The millers dressers and dyears att Wakefild does work verry expeditious never leting work lye in theire hands butt allways getting forward with itt directly.

The Wakefild merchants when the intend to bring up a son in the woolen trade the make him learn to shear and to understand how to dress a peice so when hee comes to do for himself hee may understand when[207] work is well done. The all keeps dresers att theire own houses and when the dresers finds the have and easey ignorant master the will slight theire work and lett the master bee never so carefull and byes his goods cheap in the will break him with theire[208] bad management for except goods be well done there no ones money. f. 175v

Saddleworth planes of a fine sort there is most money gotten bye makeing them of aney kind of woolen cloath and a merchant gets most profit bye these goods and the shopkeeper gets a deall bye them for in fine cloath there is few can judge to the vallue of itt to 12d per yard and if the have a coalar wich is in fashion your shure to gett money bye itt. f. 176r

The maner of a 4 squared frame to sett a mill in and to bee posted and rayled. This represents one side of itt so screw all your joints together and not pined.[209] You may make this frame has firm has aney house and may work aney engine bye a horse and bye un screwing your joints you may move itt and sett itt up elsewhere where you think proper. 56 cogs in large wheel is better then 100 in and goes much easier so put your other mottions quicker.[210] f. 177r

[205] Sentence in margin.
[206] Ms reads 'faw'.
[207] Ms reads 'whe'.
[208] Ms reads 'thei'.
[209] Diagram in text showing two posts with long bar connecting them with mill gears and a horse hitch in the centre under this frame. The rectangular frame is braced with two long diagonals drawn from the top across the posts and to the ground.
[210] Sentence in margin.

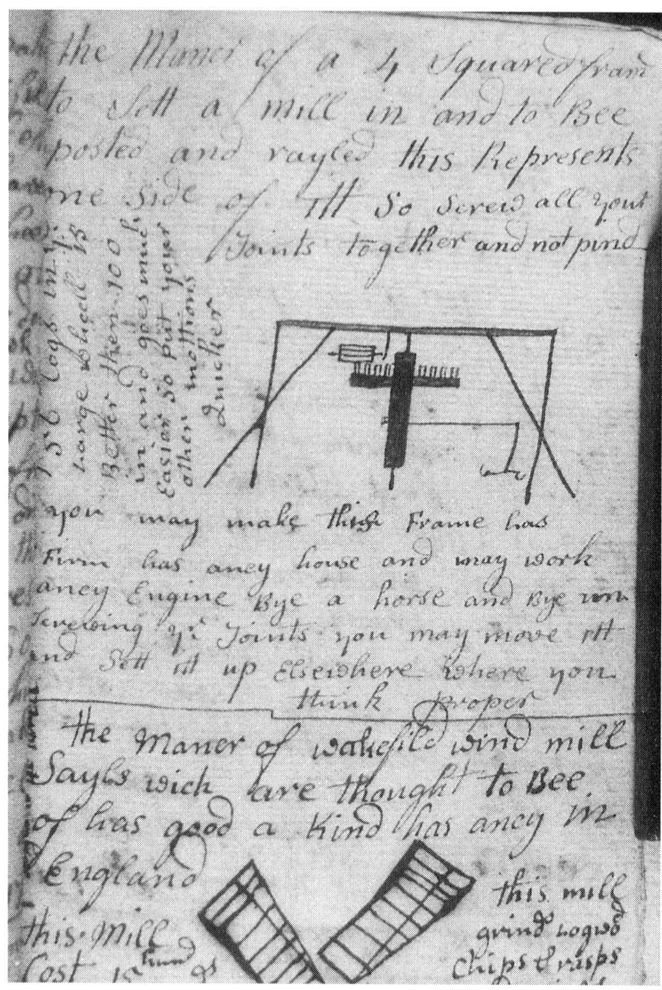
the Maner of a 4 Squared fram
to Sett a mill in and to Bee
posted and rayled this Represents
one side of itt So Screw all your
Joints together and not pind

you may make this Frame has
Firm has aney house and may work
aney Engine Bye a horse and Bye un
screwing yr Joints you may move itt
and Sett it up Elsewhere where you
think proper

the maner of wakefild wind mill
Sayls wich are thought to Bee
of has good a Kind has aney in
England

this mill
grind logwod
chips & rasps

this Mill
Cost 15

'The maner of a 4 squared frame . . .' (f. 177r)

The maner of Wakefild wind mill sayls wich are thought to bee of has good a kind has aney in England.[211] This mill cost is 15 hundred[212] pounds with all its meterials for working on. This mill grinds logwod chips and rasps and grinds rape seed for oyl. 1762.

f. 177v A wind mills propertey is that itt is not quite of a steadey mottion and some times the wind does not blow. Then a wind mills advantage of a watter mill is first itt is every one property that can sett up a wind mill. The wind is free to everyone and £50 will make a good one and watters mills can butt bee sett att proper places and sometimes to keep a horse or two to carry and recarry and some time a mill is in bak watter when perhaps the wind mill might go. Other sometimes a watter mill[213] is of great rents

[211] Diagram in text of windmill with four sails arranged radially around a central point.

[212] 'Hund' also superscripted above.

[213] Ms reads 'm'.

when you have wind for nothing and watter is scarce in sumer when perhaps the wind may blow and mill may go when watter mills stands. So that[214] wind mill is conveniant in some cases.

The maner of a wind mill to pump up watter bye square pumps to work a watter wheell in countrys that lyes upon a flatt where there is not conveniance of a fall of watter. So have a verry large dam that when the wind does not blow you may work 4 or 5 days before itt is drawn of. This is for mills wich requires a a steadey mottion for a wind mill of itt selff cannot bee steadey. So fix your mill near a river and pump itt up into a valley of a riseing ground so there make your dam.[215] Observe this mill will sett to wind of itt selff bye the help of its weather cok tayle being number 8. Work your pump bye cranks thus.[216] f. 178r

There is maney men about Hudersfild will carry a peice or tw[o][217] of cloath on theirs bak and haw[k] itt down towards Burton Snath and Thorn amongst farmers and there is some will driv[e] 3 or 4 paks before them and go dow[n] to Hull and in most parts of Lincoln[shire]. f. 179v

A rule to bee observed is if a man his in a waye of getting of money to keep itt to himself and not let no one now his bisness whether itt is in trade or working part for in these days there is no trusting aney person lett him seem to bee never such a freind for no trade or bisness is of little vallue when everey one knows itt. 1762. f. 180r

Any flesh meat wich swels in the pot itt shews that itt is well fed and denotes good eating espesally swines flesh. 1762. f. 180v

All mill rights now in these days work theire wheels in a fine pitch and the geer goes easyest and not so apt to break and things goes swetley and quitley in a fine pitch. A coarse pitch goes roughley and when cogs are old the fight and breaks oftens. London 1762. f. 181v

Butter sells at Wakefild in Febuary and Mar[ch][218] 7½ and 8 pence per pound and att that time a maney people will mix swines grease amongst itt and about Micklemas and betwi[xt] and Crismass the keep cows with turnips wich makes theire butter verrey bad.

Feather fowl rabbits mutton and beeff is has cheap has most parts of Yorkshire att Wakefild. Likewise flowr but oatmeal is not so cheap. You may bye midling flowr has cheap has oatmeal.

All Lancashire goods has George Charnock byes of George Low of Rochdale hee sends them into Holland has hee buyes them in the white. So makes them up in bayls has bokins thin broods fine 38 weights and lamswools. Some of his 42 weights George Low purchases of William Holt and son of town mill of Rochdale. Wakefild Febuary 18th 1762. The lamswools has Smyrna in heading set.[219] f. 182r

The maner how to stove white brood cloath is thus. First the weet them over well in warm watter so lets them go a while in a driveing or falleing stok to wring the watter f. 182v

214 Ms reads 'th'.

215 Diagram in text of a radial arm windmill on a tripod arrangement with gears and a tail fin which is labelled with the number 8. Other entries placed in margins around drawing.

216 Small diagram in text.

217 Ms illegible on right margin; additions in brackets.

218 Ms illegible on right margin; additions in brackets.

219 Sentence in margin.

out for a little. So then gives them a little castle soap and leaves itt in. So the hangs them up in a stove wich is made close without aney window in and a little door wich fits close. So has and iron pot with fire under with mouth downwards. So then heat[220] itt red hott and lyes brimstone att top in a hole made on porposes. Itt takes fire and so shut your door and make it close up with clay at sides so lett them bee all night hanged up on hooks att the joyce wich drive full of hooks like a tenter. Then when stoved take them and blew them with indigo and cold watter. So tenter itt. Att Leeds the have 2s 6d per shalloons and 5 shillings for a woolen brood.

f. 183v Att Whitby the church stands on a hill and the go up 75 steps to itt and from top of the steeple on a clear day may see into Hollond through a prospeckt glass. Itt stands all bye saylors and ship carpenters and keels to carry coals.

Blew frises would sell well att all seaports either to woolen drapers or brokers or merchant taylors. Itt is and excellent bisness to keep goods made ready into close.

f. 184v Att Wakefild the have a kind of fine bran wich the grind down like oatmeall wich is used cheiff[ly][221] to mix in oatmeall dough in morning about 2 hours before yo[u] bake itt with a little yeast in. Itt rises and is light and make a deall more bread and this called wholson or bye some itt called pollard. Wakefild New Mill.

Att Wakefild spiritous liquors s[ell] dear for a pint of gin itt [is] 10 pence and so all other li[quor] in proportion att the public houses. December 18th 17[6_].

f. 185v In most towns in England butchers wears blew lince[y][222] froks for theire evereday wearing wich makes a deal of linceys bee worn all over th[e] kingdome.

When a merchant puts out wool to make a mixt brood on the cloathi[er] for oyl scribling dyeing making milling the comon prise for a p[eice] about 3s 6d or 3s 4d per yard in ba[wk] the maker has 1s 8d per yard [for] makeing and is paid has maney [word illegible] has itt will measure when itt com[es] out in the mill and is wett an[d] this is good wage for the makers.

f. 186r [17]38[223] for poor lads [A]tt Wakefild one Mr Bromley left [a]nd estate of 50 pound per year [to] continue for ever and this use [is] for to put out 5 prentice lads [w]ich are put out each year the day before Crismas daye and every master of such a lad has 5 pounds with him and each lad [has] soon has loose has 10 pound to set up [w]ith and 10 pound more when marryed. This is for woolen fackt.

f. 187r Prest cloath allways shews spotey if[224] itt getts aney rain on and is never handsom till wetted over.

[220] Ms reads 'hea'.

[221] Ms illegible on right margin; additions in brackets.

[222] Ms illegible on right margin; additions in brackets.

[223] Ms illegible on left margin; additions in brackets.

[224] Ms illegible; meaning implicit.

Index

THE YORKSHIRE
ARCHAEOLOGICAL SOCIETY

Enquiries about subscriptions to the YAS Record Series should be addressed to:
The Yorkshire Archaeological Society, Claremont, 23 Clarendon Road, Leeds LS2 9NZ

The Editor welcomes suggestions for possible future publications, which should be addressed to:
YASRS Editor, Borthwick Institute of Historical Research, University of York, St Anthony's Hall, Peasholme Green, York YO1 7PW

Record Series volumes can be purchased from the publisher:
Boydell & Brewer Ltd, PO Box 9, Woodbridge, Suffolk IP12 3DF
or via the Boydell & Brewer website:
http://www.boydell.co.uk